The Steppe and Beyond: Studies on Central Asia

Series Editor
Jean-François Caron, Department of Political Science and International Relations, Nazarbayev University, Astana, Kazakhstan

Surrounded between Europe and Asia, Central Asia has been neglected by many experts for a very long time. Many reasons may explain this situation, such as the language barrier and the fact that the region remained inaccessible for the most part of the 20th Century. However, this situation is clearly about to change in light of the growing interest of the academic interest for this region and the purpose of this series is to enhance the understanding of this region which is has always been at the crossroad of various civilizations. From a multidisciplinary perspective, this series examines the history of the region, its past struggles with colonialism and communism as well as the political and sociological challenges Central Asian countries are currently facing with the emergence of the new Silk Road and the strategic power shift in the region. It also proposes to render accessible to English-speaking readers the important oral literary tradition of Central Asia, which is one of the largest in the world.

More information about this series at
https://link.springer.com/bookseries/16223

Jean-François Caron · Hélène Thibault
Editors

Central Asia and the Covid-19 Pandemic

Editors
Jean-François Caron
Department of Political Science
and International Relations
Nazarbayev University
Nur-Sultan, Kazakhstan

Hélène Thibault
Department of Political Science
and International Relations
Nazarbayev University
Nur-Sultan, Kazakhstan

ISSN 2524-8359   ISSN 2524-8367 (electronic)
The Steppe and Beyond: Studies on Central Asia
ISBN 978-981-16-7585-0   ISBN 978-981-16-7586-7 (eBook)
https://doi.org/10.1007/978-981-16-7586-7

© The Editor(s) (if applicable) and The Author(s), under exclusive license to Springer Nature Singapore Pte Ltd. 2022
This work is subject to copyright. All rights are solely and exclusively licensed by the Publisher, whether the whole or part of the material is concerned, specifically the rights of translation, reprinting, reuse of illustrations, recitation, broadcasting, reproduction on microfilms or in any other physical way, and transmission or information storage and retrieval, electronic adaptation, computer software, or by similar or dissimilar methodology now known or hereafter developed.
The use of general descriptive names, registered names, trademarks, service marks, etc. in this publication does not imply, even in the absence of a specific statement, that such names are exempt from the relevant protective laws and regulations and therefore free for general use.
The publisher, the authors and the editors are safe to assume that the advice and information in this book are believed to be true and accurate at the date of publication. Neither the publisher nor the authors or the editors give a warranty, expressed or implied, with respect to the material contained herein or for any errors or omissions that may have been made. The publisher remains neutral with regard to jurisdictional claims in published maps and institutional affiliations.

This Palgrave Macmillan imprint is published by the registered company Springer Nature Singapore Pte Ltd.
The registered company address is: 152 Beach Road, #21-01/04 Gateway East, Singapore 189721, Singapore

Contents

1 Introduction   1
Jean-François Caron and Hélène Thibault

2 *Uyat* or the Culture of Shame as a Vector of Covid-19 Contamination in Kazakhstan   7
Jean-François Caron and David Orlov

3 Understanding the Impact of Misinformation on Psychological State of Uzbekistani Citizens During the COVID-19 Outbreak   35
Deniza Alieva and Asal Dadakhonova

4 The "Sick Man of Asia": Exploring Popular Perceptions of China in Kyrgyzstan   53
Dana Rice

5 Anti-Chinese Sentiment, the BRI, and COVID-19: Kazakhstani Perceptions of China in Central Asia   75
Jessica Neafie

6 Contamination, Cohesion and Coercion: Essay on the COVID-19 Pandemic and the Revolution in Kyrgyzstan (2020–2021)   97
Julien Bruley and Iliias Mamadiiarov

7 A Frontier Market in the COVID-19 Era: Kazakhstan's
   Economic Diversification in the 2020s   139
   Wilder Alejandro Sánchez

Index   171

Notes on Contributors

Deniza Alieva is Ph.D. in Human Research Psychology and D.Sc. in Economics. Currently she is a leading lecturer at the School of Business and Management at Management Development Institute of Singapore in Tashkent (Uzbekistan). She collaborates as a lecturer in undergraduate and postgraduate programs at Bangor University (UK), Sunderland University (UK), Binary University (Malaysia), and Webster University (USA). She is a member of the Laboratory of Personal Networks and Communities at the University of Seville (Spain). In addition to her scientific and academic career, she has published works on personal and organizational networks in tourism, on community-based tourism, education, and health sector. In addition, her research areas include semantic network analysis and human resources management and development strategies. She coordinates various research works on topics such as community-based tourism, innovation and investments in Uzbekistan's economy, market research, and management of organizational networks.

Julien Bruley holds a Ph.D. in social anthropology from the University of Lille (Clerse/Sesam). His doctoral dissertation focused on the Kyrgyz epic of Manas and its recent evolutions on the edge of politics, tradition, and spectacle (2009–2019). Research associate at French Institute for Central Asian Studies (IFEAC), Bishkek, Kyrgyzstan, he is engaged in an epistemological analysis of Kyrgyz discourses and representations of ethnos, language, and the *Manas* epic and their practical uses and developments in the sphere of cultural and political relations with other countries, such as Turkey and China. In parallel, he is starting a study in the realm of Kyrgyz traditional and contemporary arts and performance as a new space for public debate and a tool for social and ideological criticism.

Jean-François Caron is Associate Professor at the Department of Political Science and International Relations at Nazarbayev University. He holds a Ph.D. from the *Université Laval* (2010) and has published more than a dozen monographs. He is the editor of "The Steppe and Beyond: Studies on Central Asian" series with Palgrave Macmillan.

Asal Dadakhonova is a holder of Bachelor of arts in Business Administration from the University of Westminster (UK) in 2015 and Master of Business Administration major in Marketing with Merit from the University of Sunderland (UK) in 2018. Currently she is conducting her professional and research activities within the premises of Management Development Institute of Singapore in Tashkent (Uzbekistan). Her research interests are centered on management, psychology, marketing, and organizational behavior.

Iliias Mamadiiarov is a Ph.D. student at the Europe-Eurasia Research Center (CREE), INALCO, in Paris, France, and a research associate at French Institute for Central Asian Studies (IFEAC) in Bishkek, Kyrgyzstan. Iliias' research interests include the role of microfinance, trust, informal economy, economic anthropology, and economic psychology in community development projects in post-Soviet Central Asia. Previously, Iliias has worked as a scientific assistant at IFEAC (2016–2019) and as the Head of the International Office of the American University of Central Asia (AUCA) (2013–2016).

Jessica Neafie is an Assistant Professor of International Relations at Nazarbayev University. She writes on China's soft power, investment and aid impact. She has conducted qualitative and quantitative research in Asia and Africa, and her expertise is centered at the intersection of foreign investment and society. Her work on investment and the environment in developing countries is published in Politikon. She is currently working on several projects in Kazakhstan examining the impact of Chinese economic investment and soft power.

David Orlov is a cofounder and CEO of "Turar" Center for Research in Humanities and Social Sciences. As a Ph.D. student in Eurasian Studies at Nazarbayev University, he researches the ethnic consciousness of the Kazakh diaspora in Iran, Turkey, and Sweden.

Dana Rice is a doctoral scholar at the Australian National University. She completed her undergraduate and Honors degrees at the University of Tasmania and the European University at Saint Petersburg. Her research interests include China–Russia and China–Central Asia relations, oil/gas in Central Asia, the Eurasian Economic Union, the Belt and Road Initiative, and critical geopolitics. Her work has been published in the *ASAN Forum, Australian Outlook, Calvert Journal, Eurasianet,* and *Russian International Affairs Council,* among other outlets. Outside of her studies, Dana has worked in the policy section of the Tasmanian Department of Health and at the Australian Institute of International Affairs. She is currently the Editor-in-Chief of *ENERPO (Energy Politics of Eurasia) Journal,* published by the European University at Saint Petersburg.

Wilder Alejandro Sánchez is an international security analyst who focuses on geopolitics, trade, defense, and security issues in the Western Hemisphere and post-Soviet regions. He writes for *Janes, Shephard Media,* and he is the Washington DC correspondent to *The Indepth Investing Podcast with Gavin Graham.* His research on Kazakhstan includes the country's role in peacekeeping operations and the AIFC's International Arbitration Centre. His analyses have been published in numerous refereed journals including *Small Wars and Insurgencies, Defence Studies, Polar Journal,* the *Journal of Slavic Military Studies, European Security, Studies in Conflict and Terrorism,* and *Perspectivas.* His most recent book chapter is a co-authored analysis about separatism in Moldova. Mr. Sánchez holds a Master's degree in International Peace and Conflict Resolution from the School of International Service at American University. He has also attended the National Defense University's Perry Center (formerly the Center for Hemispheric Defense Studies) in Washington DC.

Hélène Thibault is assistant professor in the department of Political science and international relations at Nazarbayev University (NU) since 2016. She holds a Ph.D. from the University of Ottawa (2014). She is also a co-investigator in the Political Economy of Education Research (PEER) Network. She specializes in issues of religion, gender, and sexuality in Central Asia.

List of Figures

Fig. 3.1	Semantic network of the most commonly used concepts	48
Fig. 6.1	Poverty rate (national estimate) and GDP growth—Kyrgyz Republic (2007–2020) (Graph by authors based on the following sources: 1. World Bank [2021], "Data Bank", March 17, https://data.worldbank.org/indicator/SI.POV.NAHC?locations=KG [page accessed on March 20, 2021]; 2. World Bank (2021). "One Year Later in the Kyrgyz Republic's Battle Against COVID-19", March 17, https://www.worldbank.org/en/news/feature/2021/03/17/one-year-later-in-the-kyrgyz-republic-s-battle-against-covid-19 [page accessed on March 20, 2021])	116
Fig. 6.2	COVID-19 in Kyrgyzstan, cumulative number of total death and total cases due to COVID-19 (2020–2021) (Graph by authors based on the following sources: 1. John Hopkins Coronavirus Resource Center (2021). "Kyrgyzstan". May 5, Johns Hopkins University & Medicine from https://coronavirus.jhu.edu/us-map [page accessed on April 30, 2021])	119
Fig. 6.3	Number of deaths from all causes, Kyrgyzstan (2006–2020) (*Source* Graph by authors based on the open data available at National Statistical Committee of the Kyrgyz Republic [NSC], http://www.stat.kg/ru/opendata/category/47/, accessed on March 22, 2021)	120

Fig. 6.4	Percentage of female microcredit borrowers in Kyrgyzstan (2003–2019) (*Source* Chart by authors based on: (1) Annual reports [2000–2019] of National Bank of Kyrgyz Republic, https://www.nbkr.kg/index1.jsp?item=136&lang=RUS [accessed on January 20, 2021]. (2) Statistical Committee of the Kyrgyz Republic, [accessed on January 20, 2021])	125
Photo 6.1	A speech delivered by one of the members of a Kyrgyz political party to the protestors at Ala-Too square, Bishkek. October 5, 2020 (Photo by authors)	105
Photo 6.2	A group of protestors gather and debate before the central administrative building, White House, at Ala-Too square, Bishkek, on October 5, 2020 (Photo by authors)	111
Photo 6.3	A queue formed before the only office of Aeroflot Russian Airlines in Bishkek that provides ticket reimbursement in case of passenger's flight cancellation caused by COVID-19 positive test results 72 hours before the flight departure. As air travel remains the sole means of travelling to Russia from Kyrgyzstan, high demand for tickets make it rather difficult to purchase them with tickets' availability limited to only two months from the date of purchase. March 29, 2021 (Photo by authors)	115
Photo 6.4	The White House in free access. June 14, 2021 (Photo by authors)	131

List of Tables

Table 2.1	Question: Are you familiar with the word "uyat"?	16
Table 2.2	Question: How important is it for you to avoid having one of your behavior labelled as shameful?	17
Table 2.3	Question: According to you, are these behaviors shameful?	19
Table 2.4	Question: Since mid-May, have you participated in large family gatherings with your relatives?	22
Table 2.5	If avoiding having one of your behavior to be labelled as shameful is either "extremely important" or "important", how would you feel if someone from the following groups would qualified one of your behaviors as being shameful ("uyat")? would you be "extremely affected", "affected", "not affected", "don't care/prefer not to answer"	24
Table 3.1	Psychological and physiological state of participants before and after the COVID-19 outbreak (in June 2020)	42
Table 3.2	List of the most commonly used concepts used by interviewees	47
Table 5.1	Which country do you think has the greatest influence in Asia?	83
Table 5.2	Does China bring more benefit or harm to Asia?	84
Table 5.3	In general, does China have a positive or negative influence on Kazakhstan?	85
Table 5.4	Have you heard of the "Health Silk Road"?	87
Table 5.5	Have you heard of the Belt and Road Initiative?	88

Table 5.6	During COVID-19, how helpful has China been in Kazakhstan?	88
Table 5.7	Generally speaking, COVID-19 has made the relationship of China and Kazakhstan?	89

CHAPTER 1

Introduction

Jean-François Caron and Hélène Thibault

Abstract This chapter introduces some key features of how the Covid-19 pandemic has affected Central Asia and summarizes the various chapters of the book.

Keywords Covid-19 · Central Asia · Sinophobia · Kazakhstan · Kyrgyzstan

In late 2019, a coronavirus (which is now known as the COVID-19 virus) shocked the world and led to unprecedented measures: lockdowns of entire cities were ordered, curfews were imposed, borders were closed and international trade suffered a major setback, leading some to believe that this sanitary crisis will end up having long-lasting effects on global exchanges and production of goods (Caron, 2020). Unfortunately, the Central Asian region has not been sparred by this pandemic. Despite claims from the Turkmen authorities that the country has been miraculously spared by the virus and from the Tajik authorities that the country has not experienced a single positive case between the end of December 2020 and the end of June 2021, as well as the low number of people who have died from the virus (4042 in Kazakhstan; 696 in Uzbekistan, 1842 in Kyrgyzstan; and 90 in Tajikistan as of June 5, 2021) (WHO), it is clear that these claims and official numbers have more to do with fiction than reality. This rhetoric hides the fact that the Covid-19 pandemic has had a heavy impact on the people of Central Asia just like anywhere else in the world. Indeed, it is important to recall that Kazakhstan and Uzbekistan were the first countries in the world to suffer from a second wave of infections in early July 2020 and had to re-impose lockdowns after they experienced an exponential rise of the number of infected people after the rules were loosened up a few weeks before. For those who were in these countries at that time, the situation was indeed serious. In Kyrgyzstan, the already underperforming health care system quickly reached its breaking point (Eshaliyeva, 2020). Despite governments' attempts to control the information, reports showed images and footages of crowded hospitals with people left on the floors or in the parking lots due to a lack of available beds as well as makeshift graveyards that clearly showed that the number of reported deaths was highly underestimated (Kaiyrtayuly, 2020): a reality that seems to be validated by comparing the excess mortality rates of Central Asian countries to their respective official Covid counts. More precisely, compared with the 5 previous years (2015–2019), Tajikistan experienced a 27% increase of the number of deaths per 100,000 people, while that percentage reached 25% in Kazakhstan, 23% in Kyrgyzstan and 13% in Uzbekistan (World Mortality Dataset); thereby making the five Stans some of the countries in the world that have suffered the heaviest death toll in proportion to their population in the course of this—still ongoing—global sanitary crisis.

Moreover, the political consequences of the COVID-19 pandemic were also very significant. While being the most democratic country in the region, Kyrgyzstan is also the most unstable and has experienced no less than three popular revolutions in the last 15 years, with the latest occurring in the middle of the pandemic. If the two previous political crises have been linked with the country's elite and ethnic divides, the latest one that saw the overthrow of the government in October 2020 seems to have been a direct result of people's grievances against their regime that had been unable to protect them and incapable of maintaining their already precarious standards of living. Alongside these immediate political consequences, needless to say that the future remains largely uncertain for the five Stans, especially when it comes to the geopolitical orientation of their economic policies. If international trade does not resume to its pre-pandemic course, all options must be considered with one of them being a drastic change in the politics of developments these countries have been pursuing since the collapse of the Soviet Union which can bring them closer to Beijing's sphere of influence. With the clear paradigmatic shift of the post-Cold War world order that appears to be opening a new era of global confrontations in which China will unequivocally be a dominant player, we may also wonder how the coronavirus pandemic will contribute to enhance or decrease Beijing's influence in the region. One major element to take into account in this regard is the rather negative popular perception of China held by citizens of Central Asia that the Covid-19 pandemic has exacerbated. Similarly, Sinophobia has been on the rise in Western countries where many citizens are blaming China for being responsible (inadvertently or not) of the pandemic. Knowing that these anti-Chinese sentiments can rhetorically be used to justify sanctions against Beijing's regime, a similar pattern may lead the five Stans to distance themselves from China and threatens its future economic projects, with the most important being the Belt and Road Initiative (BRI) which success requires the participation of the Central Asian republics. In light of the popular skepticism that was already apparent before the pandemic with regards to China's attempts to gain influence in the region and that have led some of the governments to adopt legislations designed to prevent the acquisition of lands by foreigners following large and unusual popular protests in these authoritarian regimes, the geopolitical impacts of Sinophobia cannot be ignored.

This book aims at shedding lights on these aforementioned aspects, namely by explaining the reasons why the death rates during the pandemic were so high in Central Asia. More specifically, this book will analyse the reasons why many individuals did not follow the sanitary rules imposed by their respective government and on the role played by misinformation in this regard. Secondly, it will also examine the impact of Sinophobia in Central Asia and the future challenges these sentiments may pose on the authorities in the near future. Lastly, this book will look at how the pandemic has contributed to expose the inherent geopolitical vulnerabilities of Kazakhstan and Kyrgyzstan by focusing on its immediate and future geopolitical consequences.

In the first chapter, Jean-François Caron and David Orlov are focusing on the sociological reasons behind the large and underestimated number of individuals who were infected during the pandemic because of people's unwillingness to abide by the sanitary directives imposed by the authorities. They are investigating the role played in this regard by the prevalent concept of "uyat", or shame, in the region that created a form of social pressure on people who felt obligated to ignore the rules forbidding large gatherings outside of family bubbles. They are arguing that the fear of being shamed by family members for refusing their invitations to participate in various meetings is a fundamental reason why the infection rate in the region has been so high in Kazakhstan. For their part, Deniza Alieva and Asal Dadakhonova are exploring in the second chapter the impact misinformation had on people in Uzbekistan. On the one hand, the release of information on social and official media during the pandemic left people overwhelmed, anxious, and disoriented because of their constant exposure to alarming news reports. On the other hand, the fact that a great amount of the information generated was spreading false rumors inevitably left some people unable to assess the reliability of the information regarding the virus. In times of a pandemic, this lack of trust toward information is a fundamental problem as individuals' self-perception of the seriousness of the situation can end up differing from the reality, thereby leading to irresponsible behaviors and a tendency to live in a parallel world.

In the third and fourth chapters, Dana Rice and Jessica Neafie are respectively investigating how the pandemic has played a role in the development—or rather, the reinforcement—of anti-Chinese sentiments in Kyrgyzstan and in Kazakhstan. Apart from providing a well-needed historical overview of how Sinophobia has evolved in Central Asia over the last centuries, these two chapters are discussing the complexity of anti-Chinese sentiments. Rice's chapter focuses on how this feeling has been felt and expressed by the Kyrgyz people who tend to associate the China with diseases, would they be biological or cultural. The author also shows how this perception is often intertwined with people's perceptions of their own political elites. Prior to the pandemic, anti-Chinese sentiments were also fueled by the political repression of Muslim Uyghur communities and ethnic Kazakhs in China's Xinjiang.

For her part, Neafie's chapter provides data that tend to show how Kazakhstanis' perceptions of China are changing, and that the pandemic has contributed to exacerbate the negative perceptions of China in Central Asia. As China is trying to become more involved in the region with the BRI, needless to say that authorities will have to reconcile their economic interests and this potential epidemic of Sinophobia to ensure socio-political stability and remain legitimate in the eyes of their own populations.

Finally, the fifth and sixth chapters, are respectively discussing the direct economic and political consequences of the pandemic on Central Asia, more specifically on Kyrgyzstan and Kazakhstan. Julien Bruley and Iliias Mamadiiarov are especially interested to show how the deep reasons of the 2020 political revolution that led to the election of Sadyr Japarov as Kyrgyz President differed from the two previous similar events that occurred in 2005 and 2010. Indeed, if the elite divide between politicians coming from the Northern and Southern parts of the country played a significant role in these two political events, the revolution that took place in October 2020 was rather the result of grievances associated with the profound disruptions and injustices caused by the pandemic. Lastly, Wilder Alejandro Sánchez seeks to determine how the pandemic will affect Kazakhstan's strategy of economic diversification and objective of becoming one of the world's 30 most developed countries by 2050. In order to achieve this goal, the Kazakhstani government has displayed numerous efforts and initiatives in the past to diversify its economy as well as its trading partners. However, just like many other countries, Kazakhstan's economy has suffered major disruptions because of this sanitary crisis. Largely because of the drastic fall of oil prices that accompanied the pandemic, as well as a decline of its global trade, the Kazakhstani economy has contracted in 2020. One of the big questions is whether this downturn will incite Kazakhstan to turn to China as a destination for goods and services, and for more investment. Is the increase in trade between Kazakhstan and China that we have witnessed in 2019 and in 2020 a forewarning sign of a failure of these diversification efforts and of a growing dependency towards Beijing and of a region slowly but surely drifting away from Moscow's sphere of influence? Finally, one aspect of the consequences of the pandemic in Central Asia that has not been covered in this volume but that is worth attention concerns the information battles being played online during the pandemic. The spread of false information "fake news" and the struggle of authorities to impose sanitary measures such as vaccination revealed a worrying proclivity: many citizens do not trust their government. Even though misinformation and suspicion towards authorities can be witnessed in many countries of the world, this trend was particularly strong in Central Asia and Russia and exposes the limits of authoritarian rule in the region.

References

Caron, J.-F. (2020). The resurgence of the nation-state and the future of globalization. In *A sketch of the world after the Covid-19 crisis: Essays on political authority, The future of globalization and the rise of China* (pp. 23–40). Palgrave Macmillan.

Eshaliyeva, K. (2020). *Is Kyrgyzstan losing the fights against coronavirus?* https://www.opendemocracy.net/en/odr/kyrgyzstan-losing-fight-against-coronavirus/. Accessed 3 June 2021.

Kaiyrtayuly, M. (2020). *Kazakh Covid-19 cemetery has more graves than reported coronavirus victims.* https://www.rferl.org/a/kazakh-covid-cemetery-has-more-graves-than-reported-coronavirus-victims/30634039.html. Accessed 3 June 2021.

World Health Organization (WHO). https://covid19.who.int. Accessed 3 June 2021.

World Mortality Dataset. https://raw.githubusercontent.com/dkobak/excess-mortality/main/img/all-countries.png. Accessed 3 June 2021.

CHAPTER 2

Uyat or the Culture of Shame as a Vector of Covid-19 Contamination in Kazakhstan

Jean-François Caron and David Orlov

Abstract In early July 2020, Kazakhstan became the first country worldwide to impose a second nationwide lockdown to stop the spread of Covid-19. According to reports, this was the consequence of individuals not respecting social distancing rules. Indeed, as noted by both state officials as well as representatives of international organisations, large family gatherings continued to be organised despite being banned. This study attempts to identify the fundamental reason why such gatherings continued in the Spring of 2020 and argues that the prevalent custom of shame (or *uyat*) in Kazakhstan played a role, as it contributed to making people's participation in social gatherings an obligation that took precedence over respect for publicly known sanitary rules in a time of pandemic. Based upon a survey conducted in August 2020 with 803 respondents in the cities of Almaty, Nur-Sultan, Petropavlovsk and

J.-F. Caron (✉) · D. Orlov
Nazarbayev University, Nur-Sultan, Kazakhstan
e-mail: jean-francois.caron@nu.edu.kz

Shymkent, this text shows that peoples' decision to ignore the authorities' directives and to gather with their relatives was not only a voluntary decision, but also one that resulted from their fear of being shamed for their refusal to participate in these meetings.

Keywords Uyat · Shame · Covid-19 · Kazakhstan

Introduction

On July 5, 2020, Kazakhstan became the first country worldwide to reintroduce a nationwide lockdown. This was the result of an incredible surge in the Covid-19 infection rate throughout this country of 18 million that saturated the country's hospitals. For residents of Kazakhstan, this decision was not surprising; it was obvious that the loosening of restrictions at the end of the first lockdown in mid-May did not change people's actions. On the contrary, basic rules of social distancing that were strongly advocated by the Kazakhstani government as well as international organisations in the country—namely, the World Health Organization (WHO)—were ignored by individuals who continued to organise large family gatherings despite them being forbidden by the authorities. Not only were such gatherings publicly denounced by the head of the WHO Country Office, Caroline Clarinval,[1] but also by the Kazakhstani Deputy Prime Minister, Yeraly Tugzhanov, who was quoted as saying that 'It is no secret that people have been secretly performing weddings, meeting with their families, and doing get-together events. Because of their thoughtless actions, people end up in hospital beds, to say nothing of the fatal cases. Each of us should be responsible not only for our own health but also for the health of our loved ones' (Satubaldina, 2020b). The outcome of this irresponsibility turned out to be tragic as expected, although we may very well never know for sure how many people ended up dying from the virus, but there are reasons to believe that the official number of 5620 people as of May 2021 is largely underestimated. In fact, based upon the mortality

---

[1] As she said: 'At the same time, we are deeply concerned by the behavior of the population. After easing the restrictions, not all people have been following the necessary precautionary measures, including maintaining social distance from, especially one's family' (Satubaldina, 2020a).

rate of 2020 compared with those from previous years, Kazakhstan (and other countries, such as Russia, Iran or Peru) have experienced what has been referred to as "excess mortality", which gives credibility to the estimate that almost 82,000 people have died from the coronavirus from March 2020 to May 2021, which represents almost 0.5% of the Kazakhstani population: a proportion that would place Kazakhstan as having one of the highest death ratio of the Covid-19 (Measuring What Matters, 2021).

The attitude of the Kazakhstani population reflected the same lack of regard for political authority as that observed in Western societies, where many individuals also chose to disregard the sanitary measures advocated by their respective governments. However, this lack of obedience to authority finds its origins in two different sources: if in Western countries the lack of respect for sanitary rules was more the result of thoughtless and careless individuals who refused to limit their own negative freedom (Caron, 2020a, 2020b; 2021a, 2021b), the main cause of the spread of the virus in Kazakhstan was different. Based upon the aforementioned observations, its spread in the Central Asian Republic seemed to be more collective in nature, resulting from the numerous large family gatherings that were organised in the interval between the first and second lockdowns. This illustrates how the main challenges to political authority differ between Liberal societies and societies where the remnants of tribalism continue to play a role in social life. Indeed, as noted by Zhanna Shayakhmetova, 'Social isolation and the phenomenon of "living on your own" probably sound quite bizarre to most Kazakhs' (2016) and being hospitable to one's family members (even to unexpected visitors who are referred to as a *kudaiy konak* or as 'a guest sent by God') plays a fundamental role for them.

This cultural feature is by no means a surprise; many authors have previously described and explained the prevalence of family ties and obligations between members that find their roots in the traditions of Kazakhs' former nomadic life, when the family unit (as well as the broader clan unit) was essential to their survival (Rigi, 2004; Schatz, 2000, 2004). This cultural norm, which bears the ethical obligation of helping one's family members, penetrates all levels of Kazakhstani society, and has been identified as one of the principal reasons for the country's systemic corruption and nepotism, which Edward van Roy (1970) refers to as 'the ethnocentric factor'. In light of the aforementioned testimonies of public officials and of our own findings, it appears that the pervasiveness of this cultural feature has played a major role in the large family gatherings that continued in Kazakhstan, despite the presence of Covid-19.

However, the importance of these gatherings cannot be fully appreciated without considering another important aspect of Central Asian culture; namely, the fear of being labelled as having a *uyat* or 'shameful' behaviour. More precisely, we believe that participation in large family gatherings during the pandemic was not only the result of voluntarism by people who saw such participation as a positive obligation, but also stemmed from a fear of being seen by one's family members as displaying *uyat* by refusing to attend these events. As a result, these two distinct, yet complementary cultural beliefs, were detrimental to the recommended practices of social distancing advocated by the state authorities. Consequently, these beliefs were the prime vectors of contamination throughout the Spring of 2020.

This study will focus on the importance of the second factor and will test how the fear of being perceived negatively by one's family was directly connected with people's participation in large family gatherings, often against their will. In fact, based upon the existing literature, we already know that the fear of *uyat* plays a role in dictating peoples' behaviours. Through our research, we hope to achieve two main goals. Firstly, since the existing research has mainly focused on how this tradition affects peoples' sexual orientation and romantic conducts (Levitanus, 2020; Sataeva, 2017; Zhanabayeva, 2018), we wish to provide a broader view of the impact of *uyat* on the Kazakhstani society by highlighting how it impacts peoples' sense of hospitality, namely their participation to large family gatherings. Secondly, we are also intending to show how the fear of *uyat* can have more influence of peoples' behaviours than their obligations as citizens to obey the law and can therefore be a custom that is detrimental to the respect of political authority.

This study will test this claim by providing empirical data regarding the essential role played by the notion of *uyat* in Kazakhstan and how it has led to family obligations that are seen as unavoidable by a very significant portion of the population. To do so, we collected the largest sample of empirical data about this notion to date and use it to illustrate (a) the ramification and degree of fear of having one's behaviour labelled as *uyat*; and (b) how this fear may lead people to behave in a way they would otherwise not prioritise, including participating in large family gatherings even at the cost of contracting or infecting other members of their families.

Methods

In August 2020, a survey was conducted on his own by one of the co-authors in four Kazakhstani cities: Nur-Sultan, Almaty, Shymkent, and Petropavlovsk. A total of 803 respondents (199 in Nur-Sultan, 204 in Almaty, 200 in Shymkent, and 200 in Petropavlovsk) aged 18 and older who were randomly selected in public places accepted to answer in person a questionnaire composed of eleven closed-ended multiple choice questions and the interviews that lasted on average 5–7 minutes. The results were then filtered by cross-tabulating subgroups in order to have a better view of the impact of *uyat* between age, gender and ethnic groups. In addition, 9 open-ended interviews were conducted with respondents who confirmed to have disobeyed the law by attending large family gatherings in the Spring of 2020. These interviews lasted on average an additional 15 minutes. All participants were provided informed consent before they agreed to take part in the survey.

These four cities were selected in order to evaluate attitudes toward *uyat* in both the Northern (Nur-Sultan and Petropavlovsk) and Southern (Almaty and Shymkent) parts of Kazakhstan. Geographical variation could have explained the variations in people's attitudes because while Northern Kazakhstan is closer to Russia in terms of both language and culture, Southern Kazakhstan is perceived as the centre of Kazakh culture; that is, it is more conservative and closer to Islam. Studying these two different regions was a way to determine if the notion of *uyat*, which is fundamentally a Kazakh custom, has more importance among members of this ethnicity than amongst ethnic Russians. Indeed, considering the ethnic diversity of Kazakhstan[2] the selection of respondents purposely included in the sample approximately 20% of respondents who identified as ethnic Russians (14.7% identified as such in Almaty, 24% in Nur-Sultan, 21% in Shymkent, and 30% in Petropavlovsk).[3] This allowed for the analysis of intercultural differences between ethnic Kazakhs and ethnic Russians to determine if *uyat* custom is widely shared between these two ethnic groups or if this tradition is exclusively associated with the ethnic Kazakhs

---

[2] 68.5% of the population identify as ethnic Kazakhs, while 18.9% are ethnic Russian (3.3% identify as Uzbek, 1.5% as Uyghur, 1.4% as Ukrainians, 1.1% as Tatars, 1.0% as Germans, and 4.5% as belonging to other nationalities).

[3] Being closer to the Russian border than Almaty and Shymkent, it was easier to find ethnic Russians in Nur-Sultan and Petropavlovsk.

as argued in the literature. It also allowed to see if there are significant gaps between individuals from the same ethnic groups based on their geographical location. More specifically, if being in a more Kazakh-centric environment (that is, in Southern Kazakhstan) contributed to making *uyat* a more prevalent cultural norm among the ethnic Russians living there and, in return, if being closer to the Russian culture (in Northern Kazakhstan) contributed to decreasing the importance of this custom for the ethnic Kazakhs living in this part of the country. Secondly, not only did the survey attempt to ensure a gender balance between respondents, but as much as possible, it also established an equilibrium between individuals aged below and above the age of 45. These criteria allowed for a better idea of men's and women's respective attitudes toward *uyat*, as well as allowing a better understanding as to whether this custom is evenly shared across age groups or if it has more weight for one generation than another.

These objectives served to assess the following hypotheses:

a) *Uyat* is essentially a Kazakh custom that has significantly less importance for ethnic Russians;
b) The fear of having one's behaviour labelled as *uyat* plays a significant role in the lives of Kazakhs;
c) *Uyat* has significantly more importance for people aged over 45 years old than for the younger generation;
d) The fear of deceiving one's family and being labelled as *uyat* by family members plays a significant role in people's sense of obligation to participate in large family gatherings in a period of pandemic, despite being aware that these gatherings increase the risk of contamination by Covid-19.

Results

The Meaning and Impact of Uyat in Kazakhstani Society

Uyat, or shame, is a traditional custom in Central Asian republics and is used to regulate individuals' behaviours and to encourage them to conform to the dominant social norms.[4] Any deviations may lead the

---

[4] In line with what has been argued by anthropologist Collette Harris in her ethnographic research conducted in Tajikistan, the notion of shame (known there as 'aye') also

transgressor to be publicly shamed, stigmatised, and ultimately to lose the social connections upon which a great deal depends (namely, finding a job) (Sataeva, 2017, p. 25). When this custom is prevalent, public shaming will take the form of what John Stuart Mill once referred to as social tyranny, forcing people to change their preferred actions and abide, rather, by a certain set of rules and norms to avoid being judged and shamed in front of other people (Sataeva, 2017, p. 25).

In the recent past, a number of well-publicised events have demonstrated the prevalence of this custom in Central Asian culture and the impact it may have. For instance, in December 2017, 22-year-old Aizhan Baizakova was jailed for encouraging women in her Almaty nightclub to strip naked on stage. Her sentence was immediately followed by a wave of moral indignation led by men who resorted to threats and intimidation against her. In a widely shared video, a group of men issued a statement against these sorts of behaviours and encouraged their counterparts to prevent Kazakh women from copying such conduct. Several days later, a large group of men showed up to protest in front of the nightclub, which ultimately led to Baizakova closing it down. She had fallen victim to *uyat*.

One year previously, in Nur-Sultan (at the time known as Astana), a man named Talgat Sholtayev gained recognition when he publicly denounced the unveiling of a statue depicting a man and a woman holding each other, because it was possible to see the outline of the female body. Outraged by this artwork which he felt was shameful for women, he covered the female body in a colourful robe to protect her dignity (Kumenov, 2018). This protest led a young artist, Murat Dilmanov, to create a new cartoon hero named 'Uyatman' whose physical traits aped those of Sholtayev and whose role it was to 'patrol Kazakhstan to stop women from behaving indecently' (Kumenov, 2018)—Dilmanov's way of mocking these moral guardians. However, nobody is safe from such public accusations of *uyat*. In 2017, for example, the Kyrgyz President's 20-year-old daughter was accused of shaming her family for posting on Instagram photos of her bump and of her breastfeeding her new-born child (McLaughlin, 2017).

Women are clearly more affected by this custom which reinforces the patriarchal Central Asian culture and its conservative value system that emphasises the importance of a traditional family where the wife

plays a central role and exposes individuals who are its victims to social exclusion (Harris, 2004).

is subordinate to her husband (Beyer, 2016; Werner, 2009). It is from this perspective that Begimai Sataeva writes the following about Kyrgyz culture:

> [The] Kyrgyz culture is a culture of guilt, the force of which drives the performance of public shaming. This mechanism is especially meant to shame women, as they play crucial roles in Kyrgyz society as reproducers of both children and culture. There are various forms of public shaming in Kyrgyz culture—physical, emotional, and public—all of which explicitly limit both genders/sexes, but especially women, in their choices. "Uyat!"— "Shame on you!"—is a commonly heard expression, and most women coming from this culture have experienced the effects of public shaming at least once in their lives. (Sataeva, 2017, pp. 25–26)

Consequently, the fear of *uyat* may prevent women from leaving their homes alone without the accompaniment of a male family member due to the fear and anxiety that she may tarnish her family's honour (Rubinov, 2014, p. 204). Inevitably, this fear contributes to preventing women from procuring jobs outside of their households and ultimately leads to some tragic situations. For instance, since pre-marital sex resulting in pregnancy is considered by many a shameful behaviour, it is not rare to hear reports of new-borns that have been abandoned in garbage bins or public toilets (Kabatova, 2018; CAP Fellows Paper 200, 2018). Moreover, the moral pressures preventing premarital sex, other shameful behaviours, and the fear of teenage pregnancy play an important role in the high rate of suicide among teenage girls (aged 15–19), with Kazakhstan sadly known to have one of the highest rates in the world (Bagayeva, 2012).

However, despite the fact that women are usually the primary victims of this custom, shame is used in a variety of ways and its weight is also felt by men, especially homosexuals who are targeted and shamed for their 'deviant' behaviour (Kudaibergenova, 2019). The same can be said in cases where family members see a failure to help one's relative as *uyat*. In his empirical work on Kyrgyzstan, David Gullette wrote that:

> "Obligation" is the expectation and duty to render help, particularly between family members. There are, of course, instances when, despite the desire to support others and all obligations, a person cannot provide help that is expected. For example, one man I knew was castigated by his father for not helping his step-brother get into university. Despite his willingness to help, the man was contacted late and could not help his

step-brother. In addition, it was not clear when and what course his step-brother wanted to study. The man would have had to call on other people, but by the time his step-brother asked him for help it was too late for him to get in contact with the people he knew as they had either moved away or were no longer at the university. The relationship between this man and his father, which was already difficult, suffered considerably because of this. Yet, the expectation of what is to be done is a significant factor in these relations. If a person is seen as not fulfilling their obligations, it can, as in the example above, create further problems between family members. Obligations are also emphasized in other ways. Marriage constitutes another area where notions of shame (in Kyrgyz, *uyat*) are employed to reinforce duty, obligation and the place of help. (Gullette, 2010, pp. 102–103)

Obviously, despite the weight this custom may have on people, it would be misleading to pretend that everybody in Central Asia is affected by this form of social pressure. For those who have spent time in the region, it is clear that many people refuse to abide by the norms imposed by those who would act as moral guardians. The whole question now, however, is to determine who is more prone to being affected by this fear of social stigmatisation. More especially, is it a custom that has more impact on members of the older generation than on younger individuals? Is it more prevalent amongst people whose cultural background is not Russian? Moreover, what sorts of behaviour are considered *uyat* and can differences be seen between men and women as well as between people living in major urban centres compared to those living in smaller towns?

The survey supports hypothesis A and shows that this custom is intimately connected with ethnic Kazakhs more than ethnic Russians. More precisely, the data reveal that in Nur-Sultan only 1.3% of Kazakhs are not familiar with the notion and meaning of *uyat*, while this proportion reaches 3.4% in Almaty, 1.2% in Shymkent, and 13.5% in Petropavlovsk. In return, 34% of ethnic Russians living in Nur-Sultan are not familiar with this notion, and this proportion reaches 26.6% in Almaty, 24% in Shymkent, and 46.6% in Petropavlovsk (Table 2.1).

This divide between ethnic Kazakhs and ethnic Russians is further reinforced by the importance that avoiding having one's behaviour labelled as *uyat* has for these two ethnic groups. For 57.2% of Kazakhs living in Nur-Sultan, it is either extremely important or important not to have their behaviour labelled as *uyat*, while this proportion reaches 46.8% for ethnic Russians. In Almaty, this proportion reaches 77% for Kazakhs and only 30% for ethnic Russians. In Shymkent, 81% of Kazakhs believe that

Table 2.1 Question: Are you familiar with the word "uyat"?

Nur-Sultan (199 respondents)
Yes: 181 (150 Kazakhs, 31 ethnic Russians)
No: 18 (2 Kazakhs, 16 ethnic Russians)
34% of ethnic Russians are not familiar with this notion
1.3% of Kazakhs are not familiar with this notion
Almaty (204 respondents)
Yes: 190 (168 Kazakhs, 22 ethnic Russians)
No: 14 (6 Kazakhs, 8 ethnic Russians)
26.6% of ethnic Russians are not familiar with this notion
3.4%% of Kazakhs are not familiar with this notion
Shymkent (200 respondents)
Yes: 188 (156 Kazakhs, 32 ethnic Russians)
No: 12 (2 Kazakhs, 10 ethnic Russians)
24% of ethnic Russians are not familiar with this notion
1.2% of Kazakhs are not familiar with this notion
Petropavlovsk (200 respondents)
Yes: 153 (121 Kazakhs, 32 ethnic Russians)
No: 47 (19 Kazakhs, 28 ethnic Russians)
46.6% of ethnic Russians are not familiar with this notion
13.5% of Kazakhs are not familiar with this notion

it is either extremely important or important not to have their behaviour labelled as *uyat*, while this proportion reaches 64.3% for ethnic Russians, while the respective proportions are 73.6% and 62% in Petropavlovsk.

The data also show a significant generational gap between those aged below and above 45. Indeed, almost two-thirds of the respondents in Nur-Sultan aged above 45 said it was either extremely important or important to avoid having their behaviour labelled as *uyat*, while this proportion reached 42.5% for respondents aged below 45. In Almaty, these proportions reached 82.3% and 57.7% respectively; and in Petropavlovsk, 77.7% and 58.8% respectively. The only exception was Shymkent, where more individuals aged below 45 replied that it is either extremely important or important not to have their behaviour labelled as *uyat* than their counterparts aged above 45 (79.8% and 74.3%). These data tend to validate in part hypothesis C (Table 2.2).

While these data show the ethnic divide between Kazakhs and Russians as well as the differences between people aged above and below 45, they nonetheless reveal the prevalence of this notion amongst the Kazakhstani people and show the significant weight it places on people's lives

Table 2.2 Question: How important is it for you to avoid having one of your behavior labelled as shameful?

Nur-Sultan (199 respondents)

Extremely important: 35 (26 Kazakhs, 9 ethnic Russians)
Important: 74 (61 Kazakhs, 13 ethnic Russians)
Not important/I don't care: 91 (66 Kazakhs, 25 ethnic Russians)
For 43% of Kazakhs, it is not important or they don't care if one of their behavior is labelled as shameful, while this proportion reaches 53% for ethnic Russians
People aged 45 and above: 85
Extremely important: 12 (14%)
Important: 41 (48.2%)
Not important/I don't care: 32 (37.6%)
People aged below 45: 101
Extremely important: 10 (9.9%)
Important: 33 (32.6%)
Not important/I don't care: 58 (57.4%)
Almaty (204 respondents)
Extremely important: 35 (34 Kazakhs, 1 ethnic Russian)
Important: 108 (100 Kazakhs, 8 ethnic Russians) 30 Kazakhs
Not important/I don't care: 61 (40 Kazakhs, 21 ethnic Russians)
For 23% of Kazakhs, it is not important or they don't care if one of their behavior is labelled as shameful, while this proportion reaches 70% for ethnic Russians
People aged 45 and above: 102
Extremely important: 23 (22.5%)
Important: 61 (59.8%)
Not important/I don't care: 18 (17.6%)
People aged below 45: 102
Extremely important: 12 (11.7%)
Important: 47 (46%)
Not important/I don't care: 43 (42%)
Shymkent (200 respondents)
Extremely important: 76 (66 Kazakhs, 10 ethnic Russians)
Important: 79 (62 Kazakhs, 17 ethnic Russians)
Not important/I don't care: 45 (30 Kazakhs, 15 ethnic Russians)
For 19% of Kazakhs, it is not important or they don't care if one of their behavior is labelled as shameful, while this proportion reaches 35.7% for ethnic Russians
People aged 45 and above: 86
Extremely important: 33 (38.3%)
Important: 31 (36%)
Not important/I don't care: 22 (25.5%)

(continued)

Table 2.2 (continued)

Nur-Sultan *(199 respondents)*
People aged below 45: 114
Extremely important: 43 (37.7%)
Important: 48 (42.1%)
Not important/I don't care: 23 (20%)
Petropavlovsk (200 respondents)
Extremely important: 36 (32 Kazakhs, 4 ethnic Russians)
Important: 104 (71 Kazakhs, 33 ethnic Russians)
Not important/I don't care: 60 (37 Kazakhs, 23 ethnic Russians)
For 26.4% of Kazakhs, it is not important or they don't care if one of their behavior is labelled as shameful, while this proportion reaches 38% for ethnic Russians
People aged 45 and above: 117
Extremely important: 27 (23%)
Important: 64 (54.7%)
Not important/I don't care: 26 (22.2%)
People aged below 45: 83
Extremely important: 9 (10.8%)
Important: 40 (48%)
Not important/I don't care: 34 (41%)

and actions. This can be observed from the respondents' answers (see Table 2.3), who were asked whether or not the following behaviours were considered *uyat*: having sexual relations outside of wedlock; refusing to welcome to one's house a relative who stops by unannounced; being homosexual; being drunk in public; and being dressed carelessly in public. In this regard, hypothesis B is also confirmed.

The Impacts of 'Uyat' on the Spread of Covid-19 in Kazakhstan

As mentioned above, large family gatherings have been identified by state authorities as well as international organisations as a determining factor in the spread of Covid-19, forcing the Kazakhstani government to impose a second lockdown in early July 2020 after a surge in the contamination rate in the country. In light of the significant fear of having one's behaviour labelled as *uyat*, the survey wanted to test whether the weight of this custom played a role in people's decisions to attend family gatherings, despite being aware of the ongoing global pandemic and that participating in such events was contrary to the advice on social distancing and, therefore, constituted a threat to their own lives or those of their relatives. Hypothesis D was partly confirmed as 35.6% of respondents in

Table 2.3 Question: According to you, are these behaviors shameful?

***Nur-Sultan** (199 respondents)*

-Having a sexual relation out of wedlock:
yes 62 (31%)
no 114 (57.2%)
prefer not to answer 23 (11.5%)
-Refusing to welcome to your house a relative who is stopping by unannounced:
yes 105 (52.7%)
no 85 (42.7%)
prefer not to answer 9 (4.5%)
-Being homosexual:
yes 110 (55%)
no 51 (25.6%)
prefer not to answer 38 (19%)
-Being drunk in public:
yes 98 (49.2%)
no 81 (40.7%)
prefer not to answer 20 (10%)
-Being dressed carelessly in public:
yes 90 (45.2%)
no 93 (46.7%)
prefer not to answer 15 (7.5%)

Almaty (204 respondents)

-Having a sexual relation out of wedlock:
yes 118 (57.8%)
no 73 (35.7%)
prefer not to answer 13 (6%)
-Refusing to welcome to your house a relative who is stopping by unannounced:
yes 138 (67.6%)
no 51 (25%)
prefer not to answer 15 (12.2%)
-Being homosexual:
yes 110 (54%)
no 47 (23%)
prefer not to answer 47 (23%)
-Being drunk in public:
yes 140 (68.6%)
no 52 (25.4%)
prefer not to answer 12 (5.8%)
-Being dressed carelessly in public:

(continued)

Table 2.3 (continued)

Nur-Sultan (199 respondents)

yes 113 (55.3%)
no 83 (40.6%)
prefer not to answer 8 (3.9%)
Shymkent (200 respondents)
-Having a sexual relation out of wedlock:
yes 120 (60%)
no 53 (26.5%)
prefer not to answer 27 (13.5%)
-Refusing to welcome to your house a relative who is stopping by unannounced:
yes 99 (49.5%)
no 79 (39.5%)
prefer not to answer 22 (11%)
-Being homosexual:
yes 112 (56%)
no 40 (20%)
prefer not to answer 48 (24%)
-Being drunk in public:
yes 136 (68%)
no 36 (18%)
prefer not to answer 28 (14%)
-Being dressed carelessly in public:
yes 128 (64%)
no 45 (22.5%)
prefer not to answer 27(13.5%)
Petropavlovsk (200 respondents)
-Having a sexual relation out of wedlock:
yes 71 (35.5%)
no 82 (41%)
prefer not to answer 47 (23.5%)
-Refusing to welcome to your house a relative who is stopping by unannounced:
yes 121 (60.5%)
no 67 (33.5%)
prefer not to answer 12 (6%)
-Being homosexual:
yes 78 (39%)
no 61 (30.5%)
prefer not to answer 61 (30.5%)
-Being drunk in public:

(continued)

Table 2.3 (continued)	Nur-Sultan (199 respondents)
	yes 117 (58.5%)
	no 64 (32%)
	prefer not to answer 19 (9.5%)
	-Being dressed carelessly in public:
	yes 126 (63%)
	no 61 (30.5%)
	prefer not to answer 13 (6.5%)

Nur-Sultan answered 'yes' to the following question: 'In order to avoid being labelled as *uyat*, are you willing to do things that you would otherwise not do? For instance, you have nonetheless decided to attend a large family gathering contrary to your wishes in order to avoid your absence/refusal to attend being labelled as *uyat*?'. The proportion of affirmative responses reached 64% in Almaty, 48% in Shymkent, and 54.5% in Petropavlovsk.

Accordingly, the variable weight of this family obligation between the four cities has played an undeniable role in the organisation of large family gatherings since the end of the first lockdown in mid-May 2020, as can be observed in Table 2.4. Because of the important role played by families ties in Kazakhstan, it is more than evident that many individuals wilfully participated in these gatherings in a period when the virus was very active in Kazakhstan. We must consider the possibility that the fear of *uyat* played an important role, as many respondents reported attending these gatherings to avoid disappointing their family members and being judged as *uyat*.

Although a similar survey has not been conducted in Kyrgyzstan, we cannot ignore the possibility that there was a direct correlation between the surge in the number of infected individuals in June and July 2020 that pushed the country's health care system to its limits (Eshaliyeva, 2020). The weight of family obligations is supported by the fear of accusation of *uyat* which, based on the existing literature, appears to be as prevalent as it is in Kazakhstan. After all, although the label of *uyat* can come from various individuals, Table 2.5 shows that such an accusation is most fearful when it comes from close family members.

The connection between fear of *uyat* and unwillingness to respect social distancing can be further demonstrated from interviews conducted

Table 2.4 Question: Since mid-May, have you participated in large family gatherings with your relatives?

Nur-Sultan (199 respondents)

Since mid-May, have you participated in large family gatherings with your relatives?
Yes: 104 (52%)
No: 95 (48%)
If yes, how many people were present?
6 or less: 61 (58.6%)
7–12: 25 (24%)
more than a dozen: 18 (17.3%)
If yes, how many times?
1 or 2 times: 59 (56.7%)
3 to 5 times: 30 (28.8%)
more than 6 times: 15 (14.4%)

Almaty (204 respondents)
Since mid-May, have you participated to large family gatherings with your relatives?
Yes: 119 (58%)
No: 81 (40%)
If yes, how many people were present?
6 or less: 48 (40%)
7–12: 23 (19.3%)
more than a dozen: 48 (40%)
If yes, how many times?
1 or 2 times: 89 (74.7%)
3 to 5 times: 22 (18.4%)
more than 6 times: 8 (6.7%)

Shymkent (200 respondents)
Since mid-May, have you participated in large family gatherings with your relatives?
Yes: 95 (47.5%)
No: 105 (52.5%)
If yes, how many people were present?
6 or less: 51 (53.6%)
7–12: 24 (25.3%)
more than a dozen: 20 (21%)
If yes, how many times?
1 or 2 times: 41 (43%)
3 to 5 times: 31 (32.6%)
more than 6 times: 23 (24.3%)

Petropavlovsk (200 respondents)

(continued)

Table 2.4 (continued)

Nur-Sultan (199 respondents)
Since mid-May, have you participated in large family gatherings with your relatives? Yes: 104 (52%) No: 96 (48%) *If yes, how many people were present?* 6 or less: 40 (38.4%) 7–12: 37 (35.6%) more than a dozen: 27 (26%) *If yes, how many times?* 1 or 2 times: 58 (55.7%) 3 to 5 times: 30 (28.9%) more than 6 times: 16 (15.4%)

in August 2020 with nine individuals who chose to participate in large family gatherings during the pandemic to avoid being shamed by their relatives.

One of the survey questions asked study participants whether they believe there is an on-going global pandemic in the form of Covid-19, to which 91.5% of respondents gave an affirmative answer. This clearly demonstrates the population's awareness of the existence of this virus and its attendant dangers. Nevertheless, 52.5% of the study participants confirmed that during the period of quarantine they disobeyed the law by attending large family gatherings.[5] In-depth interviews were conducted with 9 of the participants who had participated in these family events despite being aware of the potential dangers to themselves and others. Many of their testimonies demonstrated that the fear of *uyat* played a major role in their decision-making.

To begin with, almost all interviewees attempted to justify their actions by saying that the event had been small and only their closest relatives and friends were invited. The criteria for justifying the size of the event varied between respondents, with different numbers of guests mentioned, from

---

[5] This number must be taken with a grain of salt, as this question in our survey led people to openly admit to a stranger that they had violated a government directive: a violation which came with a fine of 83,340 tenge (205 USD). We can therefore presuppose that this percentage may have been higher as some respondents may have been wary to admit having had an unlawful behavior.

Table 2.5 If avoiding having one of your behavior to be labelled as shameful is either "extremely important" or "important", how would you feel if someone from the following groups would qualified one of your behaviors as being shameful ("uyat")? would you be "extremely affected", "affected", "not affected", "don't care/prefer not to answer"

Nur-Sultan (109 respondents)

From a friend:
extremely affected: 24 (22%);
affected: 58 (53%);
not affected: 12 (11%);
don't care/prefer not to answer: 15 (13.7%)
From a colleague:
extremely affected: 12 (11%);
affected: 23 (21%);
not affected: 49 (44.9%);
don't care/prefer not to answer: 14 (12.8%)
From a member of your immediate family (father, mother, brother or sister):
Extremely affected: 46 (42%),
affected 48 (44%);
not affected: 4 (3.6%);
don't care/prefer not to answer: 4 (3.6%)
From a member of your extended family (aunt, uncle, cousin, in-laws):
extremely affected: 16 (14,6%);
affected: 43 (39.4%);
not affected: 40 (36.6%);
don't care/prefer not to answer: 10 (9%)
From a state representative (police officer, judge, civil servant):
extremely affected: 12 (11%);
affected: 25 (22.9%);
not affected: 59 (54%);
don't care/prefer not to answer: 13 (11.9%)
From a foreigner:
extremely affected: 8 (7%);
affected: 23 (21%);
not affected: 66 (60%);
don't care/prefer not to answer: 12 (11%)

Almaty (143 respondents)
From a friend:
extremely affected: 21 (14.6%);
affected: 100 (69.9%);
not affected: 10 (6.9%);
don't care/prefer not to answer: 12 (8.3%);
From a colleague:

(continued)

Table 2.5 (continued)

Nur-Sultan (109 respondents)
extremely affected: 10 (6.9%);
affected: 80 (55.9%);
not affected: 31 (21.6%);
don't care/prefer not to answer: 22 (15.3%);
From a member of your immediate family (father, mother, brother or sister):
Extremely affected: 65 (46.1%);
affected 75 (52.4%);
not affected: 1 (0.6%);
don't care/prefer not to answer: 2 (1.3%);
From a member of your extended family (aunt, uncle, cousin, in-laws):
extremely affected: 34 (23.7%);
affected: 78 (54.5%);
not affected: 17 (11.8%);
don't care/prefer not to answer: 14 (9.7%)
From a state representative (police officer, judge, civil servant):
extremely affected: 0 (0%);
affected: 13 (9%);
not affected: 92 (64.3%);
don't care/prefer not to answer: 38 (26.5%);
From a foreigner:
extremely affected: 0 (0%);
affected: 19 (13.2%);
not affected: 101 (70.6%);
don't care/prefer not to answer: 23 (16%);
Shymkent (155 respondents)
From a friend:
extremely affected: 47 (30%);
affected: 78 (50%);
not affected: 17 (11%);
don't care/prefer not to answer: 13 (8.4%);
From a colleague:
extremely affected: 39 (25.2%);
affected: 73 (47%);
not affected: 33 (21.3%);
don't care/prefer not to answer: 10 (6.5%);
From a member of your immediate family (father, mother, brother or sister):

(continued)

Table 2.5 (continued)

Nur-Sultan (109 respondents)
Extremely affected: 80 (51.7%)
Affected: 59 (38%)
not affected: 11 (7%)
don't care/prefer not to answer: 5 (3.3%)
From a member of your extended family (aunt, uncle, cousin, in-laws):
extremely affected: 37 (23.9%)
affected: 71 (45.9%)
not affected: 40 (25.8%)
don't care/prefer not to answer: 7 (4.5%)
From a state representative (police officer, judge, civil servant):
extremely affected: 35 (22.5%)
affected: 60 (38.8%)
not affected: 44 (28.4%)
don't care/prefer not to answer: 16 (10.4%)
From a foreigner:
extremely affected: 22 (14.2%)
affected: 50 (32.3%)
not affected: 70 (45%)
don't care/prefer not to answer: 13 (8.4%)
Petropavlovsk (140 respondents)
From a friend:
extremely affected: 34 (24.3%)
affected: 87 (62.2%)
not affected: 13 (9.3%)
From a colleague:
extremely affected: 13 (9.3%)
affected: 66 (47.2%)
not affected: 36 (25.8%)
don't care/prefer not to answer: 25 (17.9%)
From a member of your immediate family (father, mother, brother or sister):
Extremely affected: 67 (47.9%)
Affected: 67 (47.9%)
not affected: 4 (2.9%)
don't care/prefer not to answer: 2 (1.5%)
From a member of your extended family (aunt, uncle, cousin, in-laws):
extremely affected: 21 (15%)

(continued)

Table 2.5 (continued)

Nur-Sultan (109 respondents)
affected: 62 (44.3%) not affected: 10 (7.1%) don't care/prefer not to answer: 19 (13.6%) From a state representative (police officer, judge, civil servant): extremely affected: 10 (7.1%) affected: 48 (34.2%) not affected: 61 (43.6%) don't care/prefer not to answer: 21 (15%) From a foreigner: extremely affected: 4 (2.9%) affected: 26 (18.6%) not affected: 58 (41.4%) don't care/prefer not to answer: 52 (37.1%)

20 to 80. Indeed, in Kazakhstan a wedding with less than 100 guests would be considered small.

One respondent who was invited to a wedding by her aunt's husband said the following:

> It was super inconvenient for me to go there because I was not feeling well that day. I was at work and I needed to go home to change my clothes and then go to the party. Anyway, I couldn't refuse even this kind of invitation from my aunt's husband because he is a very respected person in our family, and he does a lot for me. Finally, just because it was shameful (*uyat*) to say no, I went to this party.

One of the participants from Nur-Sultan stated that he had abided by the norms throughout the period of quarantine, but when his close friend asked him to be his groomsman at his wedding he could not refuse. The wedding was held in the bride's family's house. At the beginning, everyone was wearing masks and used fist bumping instead of traditional handshaking. Nevertheless, the situation quickly changed when someone said, 'Come on, we are a family now'. The masks were taken off and the guests started shaking hands and hugging as usual. The groomsman could not protest. As he said, 'if an older man at your friend's wedding gives you a hand to welcome you, you simply cannot refuse'.

Another participant from Shymkent shared the story of one of her relatives who had had Covid-19 and left the hospital on the day of a wedding. Despite the fact that she was supposed to isolate for two more weeks, she went to the party anyway because she did not want other relatives to think that she did not respect them. This case demonstrates the power of *uyat*. The interviewee tried to explain such behaviour as follows: 'It was shameful to skip the party of the oldest sister in the family, so she took a risk and chose to attend the wedding where there were about 40 people'. Another participant shared a similar story. Again, a respondent's aunt was organising the marriage of her son. Her sister in law had just checked out from the hospital and was recovering from Covid-19. The day of the marriage was just a week after she checked out. Initially, she refused to attend the wedding, but the groom's mother felt aggrieved by her decision. Realising that their future relationship would suffer if she refused to go, she finally changed her mind and went.

Weddings are among the most frequent events for large family gatherings that one 'must' attend when invited, as are funerals—respect should be paid to the person who has died as well as to his or her family. A man in Shymkent shared a story about the loss of his uncle at a period when cases of Covid-19 in Shymkent were growing rapidly. The interviewee and his brother tried to persuade their father who had lost his elder brother to abnegate a traditional funeral. However, not only did their father refuse but he even stated that he 'must' go with the traditions. Not only was it important for him to pay respect to his brother, he also 'had to' invite their friends and relatives to avoid *uyat*. The study participant and his brother persuaded their father to at least reduce the number of guests and ultimately 'only' 80 people were invited.

One of the stories that we collected describes not only a family gathering organised due to the death of a relative or friend, but someone who died due to Covid-19:

> In May 2020, my father's uncle died as a result of coronavirus in Karaganda city. We were very close. According to our traditions, all of the relatives and friends of the deceased person should visit his relatives and share their loss with them. Since my father's uncle was very close to our family, we all went to Karaganda to support them. On our way, we realised that we were going to visit a house where a person had died due to Covid-19, filled with his relatives who had been in direct contact with him. Nevertheless,

it would have been shameful (*uyat*) for my father if he did not go and pay his respects.

General Conclusions

Based on these findings, we can explain the reasons why a second national lockdown was imposed in Kazakhstan in early July 2020 after the country saw a surge in Covid-19 infection rates. Indeed, despite being formally forbidden by the state, a majority of respondents admitted—except in Shymkent where the proportion reached 47.5%—to having participated in large family gatherings where people mutually infected one another. In this regard, and contrary to what many would have thought, the lack of trust towards government which is so typical in post-Soviet societies did not play a significant role in peoples' disobedience to their government's directive. Indeed, out of the 803 respondents, 724 acknowledged that the world was indeed facing a global pandemic. In light of available data, this level is higher than the one in other countries. Indeed, in Poland, 25% of people believed that the Covid19 was definitely or probably a complete myth created by what was labelled as "powerful forces". Similar proportions were found in Turkey, Egypt and Saudi Arabia, while it reached 13% in the United States (Henley & McIntyre, 2020). Rather, these findings suggest that the fear of deceiving one's family and of being labelled *uyat* by refusing to attend these gatherings played a significant role. This pressure to abide by social conventions—including participating in these gatherings among other quasi obligations—plays a fundamental role in Kazakhstani society. Indeed, with its roots in Kazakh culture, this pressure can be observed primarily among Kazakh respondents for whom the importance of not being labelled *uyat* plays either an extremely important or important role in their lives. Consequently, this belief contributes to shaping their everyday choices, even those that are known to be hazardous such as gathering with family members during a pandemic. Even amongst ethnic Russians, this fear of not abiding by social norms plays an important role, albeit to a lesser degree than for ethnic Kazakhs, which means that Kazakh culture is transcending the country's ethnic divisions and shows the effect of 'Kazakhstanization' on people's minds and its effectiveness as a form of majoritarian nationalism (Caron, 2019).

Moreover, in light of the weight played by *uyat* in the Kazakhstani society, we can also venture the hypothesis that since public officials and foreigners are generally not perceived by individuals as the main source of shame, public denunciations by government officials or international organisations cannot counterbalance the embarrassment associated with not obeying the wishes and expectations of one's family members. If people have to choose between obeying the law or avoiding *uyat* from one family member, the latter choice will prevail over the former which of course translates into a problematic questioning of political authority in a time when government imposed sanitary norms ought to be followed. In this sense, our findings validate hypotheses A, B, and D.

When it comes to hypothesis C, the fear of *uyat* generally seems to play a bigger role for people aged over 45 years than for the younger generation in Nur-Sultan, Almaty, and Petropavlovsk. Many factors can explain this trend. For example, we may consider that younger people have more to lose from such a custom that regulates individuals' freedom and prevents them from enjoying their youth in a liberal manner. This feeling may be reinforced by the fact that these individuals have also been able to travel more extensively abroad—sometimes to study abroad thanks to the *Bolashak* program that provides full scholarships—than their older countrymen who have spent their youth in the closed environment of the Soviet Union. By doing so, they have been exposed to different, namely Liberal, values, which may have contributed to changing their conception of the good life. Another reason may be the growing urbanity that the country has known since its independence. Because of the anonymity usually associated with the urban environment, individuals' behaviours are less scrutinised by their relatives than in rural environments or in cities where people enjoy fewer opportunities to move away from their family circles. Nur-Sultan, formerly known as Astana until March 2019, is a good example of this. This planned city has become the prime destination for young professionals since becoming the country's capital in 1997. It is now the headquarters for many international companies operating in Kazakhstan and its population has increased fivefold in the last 30 years (from 280,000 in 1989 to 1.1 million in 2020), allowing many individuals to move out of the family nest to seek job opportunities and, consequently, enjoying a greater capacity to make life choices out of their relatives' sight and to enjoy greater contacts with individuals from abroad. This may explain why Nur-Sultan is the city where the percentage of respondents who believe it is not important or do not care if one of their behaviours is labelled as shameful is the highest amongst the four cities visited.

It is, of course, impossible to predict whether this tradition is doomed to fade away with time if individuals aged below 45 maintain the same attitude towards it throughout the course of their lives. However, despite *uyat* having less influence on this age group than on individuals aged over 45, it continues to play a determining role for a majority of people aged under 45 (with the exception of Nur-Sultan, where it is only the case for 43% of respondents) and, consequently, it may survive over time. This possibility may be reinforced by the Kazakhstani government's active strategy to revive Kazakh culture through a program called 'Ruhani Zhangyru' (or 'рухани жаңғыру' in Kazakh). It is not impossible to believe that the pressure associated with cultural revival may ultimately offset the willingness and capacity of members of the younger generation to enjoy a more Liberal way of life in the future. This tendency will obviously need further investigation in the future.

The only exception when it comes to the perception of people aged above or below 45 is Shymkent where this trend is inverted (74% of respondents aged above 45 years old believe it is either extremely important or important to avoid having one of their behaviours labelled as shameful, while this proportion reaches 79% for people aged below 45 years old). This is an important finding that illustrates how this important part of Kazakh culture is transmitted from generation to generation and can give weight to the general perception of Shymkent as a very conservative city. As noted by Hanks (2019), Shymkent's youth are more conservative than their counterparts as they are less keen to have interethnic marriages or to befriend individuals from other ethnic groups. This phenomenon can explain why Kazakh conservative values—including *uyat*—tend to reproduce themselves more easily in this city than elsewhere in the country.

Overall, the weight of *uyat* as a cultural tradition of Kazakh culture is a tangible reality for a majority of people living in Kazakhstan. As the data have shown, it has a widespread impact on people's behaviours and conceptions of the good life. During the Covid-19 pandemic, this fear of being shamed by one's family members seems to have played a determining role in the large gatherings that occurred from the end of the first nationwide quarantine in mid-May 2020 until the implementation of the second quarantine a few weeks later in early July. From this perspective, we can assume that people attend these frequent gatherings that occur for various reasons in Kazakh culture not only out of personal desire, but also from a fear of being shamed and of suffering the associated consequences.

Of course, one of the remaining questions that ought to be answered is why the fear of being shamed by refusing an invitation that was discouraged by public authorities played a bigger role than the fear of being shamed for potentially transmitting the virus to other family members (which may also have deadly consequences). Like we have already argued, the data is showing that people were very much aware of the presence of the virus and it is therefore hardly possible to infer that denial played a role in this regard. Unfortunately, we cannot identify clear reasons for the choice people privileged as they were not questioned about it in the survey. We can only venture on possible reasons, such as the fact that, although aware of the presence of the virus, people assumed that it was nothing more than a "very bad cold" that did not prove deadlier than any other similar infection. Indeed, when the government reintroduced lockdown measures in early July 2020, the country had (officially) been spared the disaster other countries had previously experienced or were experiencing with only a total of less than 45,000 cases and with only 35 confirmed deaths (out of a population of 18 million). However, as we said previously, this reason is only speculative, but nonetheless seems as the most obvious one why people were globally not fearful of being shamed for infecting family members when participating to large gatherings. Although this research was limited to Kazakhstan, we can postulate that this custom—which can be found elsewhere in the Central Asian region—may also have played a role in the other republics that also had to reimpose a second lockdown at the beginning of July 2020 when their numbers of infected people started to rise rapidly as well. But this hypothesis would of course need to be validated with additional empirical studies.

References

Bagayeva, E. V. (2012). *Devochki Kazakhstana: Pravo na zhizn: analiticheskiy document*. Institute of Equal Rights and Equal Opportunities of Kazakhstan.

Beyer, J. (2016). *The force of custom: Law and the ordering of everyday life in Kyrgyzstan*. Pittsburgh University Press.

CAP (Central Asian Program). (2018). 'Overcoming a Taboo: Normalizing Sexuality Education in Kazakhstan', CAP Fellow Paper 200, January.

Caron, J.-F. (2019). The contemporary politics of Kazakhization: The case of Astana's Urbanism. In J.-F. Caron (Ed.), *Kazakhstan and the Soviet legacy: Between continuity and rupture* (pp. 181–205). Palgrave Macmillan.

Caron, J.-F. (2020a). The Western model of liberal democracies and the need for authority. In *A sketch of the world after the Covid-19 crisis: Essays on political authority, the future of globalization and the rise of China* (pp. 5–21). Palgrave Macmillan.

Caron, J.-F. (2020b). *Pandémie: une esquisse politique et philosophique du monde d'après*. Presses de l'Université Laval.

Caron, J.-F. (2021a). *Irresponsible citizenship: The cultural roots of the crisis of authority in the time of a pandemic*. Peter Lang.

Caron, J.-F. (2021b). *La citoyenneté irresponsable: les racines culturelles de la crise d'autorité en temps de pandémie*. Presses de l'Université Laval.

Eshaliyeva, K. (2020, July 13). Is Kyrgyzstan losing the fight against coronavirus? *Open Democracy*. https://www.opendemocracy.net/en/odr/kyrgyzstan-losing-fight-against-coronavirus/?fbclid=IwAR0mm3bLlSF1I1dGhu7Vw7GGHzj5iIX2OCIBIRhYwGmHS_K_9Fr3kdIoOgs

Gullette, D. (2010). *The genealogical construction of the Kyrgyz Republic*. Brill.

Hanks, R. R. (2019). Contours of ethnonational landscapes in three cities: Youth's perspectives on ethnic and social integration. In M. Laruelle (Ed.), *The Nazarbayev generation: Youth in Kazakhstan* (pp. 153–164). Lexington Books.

Harris, C. (2004). *Control and subversion: Gender relations in Tajikistan*. Pluto Press.

Henley, J., & McIntyre, N. (2020, October 26). Survey uncovers widespread belief in 'dangerous' Covid conspiracy theories. *The Guardian*. https://www.theguardian.com/world/2020/oct/26/survey-uncovers-widespread-belief-dangerous-covid-conspiracy-theories

Kabatova, K. (2018, August 3). No shame: How an online initiative in Kazakhstan is helping youth protect their sexual health. *Global voices*. https://globalvoices.org/2018/08/03/no-shame-how-an-online-initiative-in-kazakhstan-is-helping-youth-protect-their-sexual-health/

Kudaibergenova, D. T. (2019). The body global and the body traditional: A digital ethnography of Instagram and nationalism in Kazakhstan and Russia. *Central Asian Survey*, *38*(3), 363–380.

Kumenov, A. (2018, January 25). Kazakhstan: Morality mavens monitoring women. *Eurasianet*. https://eurasianet.org/kazakhstan-morality-mavens-monitoring-women

Levitanus, M. (2020). *Regulation and negotiation of queer subjectivities in post-Soviet Kazakhstan*. University of Edinburgh.

Measuring What Matters. (2021, May 6). Estimation of Total Mortality Due to Covid-19. http://www.healthdata.org/special-analysis/estimation-excess-mortality-due-covid-19-and-scalars-reported-covid-19-deaths?fbclid=IwAR17QEXsBXBuuw3AJt03JHjHBsUXmgJsnJdzA5k7Ujud-tTO-Rz73NYdzbg

McLaughlin, K. (2017, April 17). Kyrgyzstan's president's daughter is accused of "shaming" her family by sharing breastfeeding photos in the 75% Muslim country. Daily Mail. https://www.dailymail.co.uk/news/article-4418160/Kyrgyzstan-president-s-daughter-posts-breastfeeding-photos.html

Rigi, J. (2004). Corruption in Post-Soviet Kazakhstan. In I. Pardo (Ed.), *Between morality and the law: Corruption, anthropology and comparative society* (pp. 101–117). Ashgate Pub Ltd.

Rubinov, I. (2014). Migrant assemblages: Building postsocialist households with Kyrgyz Remittances. *Anthropological Quarterly, 87*(1), 183–215.

Sataeva, B. (2017). *Public shaming and resistance in the context of bride kidnapping phenomenon in Kyrgyzstan*. University of Utrecht.

Satubaldina, A. (2020a, July 16). People's continued negligence of social distancing must be addressed, says WHO Director in Kazakhstan. *The Astana Times*. https://astanatimes.com/2020/07/peoples-continued-negligence-of-social-distancing-must-be-addressed-says-who-director-in-kazakhstan/

Satubaldina, A. (2020b, July 3). Kazakhstan to reintroduce two week lockdown to deal with COVID-19 spike. *The Astana Times*. https://astanatimes.com/2020/07/kazakhstan-to-reintroduce-two-week-lockdown-to-deal-with-covid-19-spike/

Schatz, E. (2000). The politics of multiple identities: Lineage and ethnicity in Kazakhstan. *Europe-Asia Studies, 52*(3), 489–508.

Schatz, E. (2004). *Modern clan politics: The power of 'blood' in Kazakhstan and beyond*. University of Washington Press.

Shayakhmetova, Z. (2016, November 1). Family hospitality traditions keeps Kazakhstan strong. *Astana Times*. https://astanatimes.com/2016/11/family-hospitality-tradition-keeps-kazakhstan-strong/

Van Roy, E. (1970). On the theory of corruption. *Economic Development and Cultural Change, 19*(1), 86–110.

Werner, C. (2009). Bride abduction in post-Soviet Central Asia: Marking a shift towards patriarchy through local discourses of shame and tradition. *Journal of the Royal Anthropological Institute, 15*(2), 314–331.

Zhanabayeva, N. (2018). *Restrained by Uyat [Shame]: Culture of dating and romantic relationships among urban Kyrgyz Youth*. Nazarbayev University.

CHAPTER 3

Understanding the Impact of Misinformation on Psychological State of Uzbekistani Citizens During the COVID-19 Outbreak

Deniza Alieva and Asal Dadakhonova

Abstract The COVID-19 outbreak affected countries differently. The pandemic hit them economically, socially and politically, influencing on day-to-day life and causing deaths and economic losses. In the present chapter we would like to study the case of the Republic of Uzbekistan. The first case of COVID-19 registered in Uzbekistan dates to March 15, 2020. The government took measures to prevent the spread of the virus, declaring a national lockdown and making citizens respect more or less strict quarantine measures starting from the end of March until now. We

---

D. Alieva (✉) · A. Dadakhonova
Management Development Institute of Singapore in Tashkent, Tashkent, Uzbekistan
e-mail: dalieva@mdis.uz

A. Dadakhonova
e-mail: adadakhonova@mdis.uz

© The Author(s), under exclusive license to Springer Nature Singapore Pte Ltd. 2022
J.-F. Caron and H. Thibault (eds.), *Central Asia and the Covid-19 Pandemic*, The Steppe and Beyond: Studies on Central Asia,
https://doi.org/10.1007/978-981-16-7586-7_3

have applied a survey to Uzbekistani citizens in order to evaluate the effects of misinformation on them. The results of the study conducted confirm the idea that misinformation during such a crisis as was caused by the pandemic can have a very negative effect on people's psychological and emotional state. There is a difference between the strength of impact provoked by the information spread via local sources and the one distributed through international channels. The age and gender of respondents also demonstrated correlation with the level of stress and negative emotions provoked by misinformation.

Keywords Covid-19 · Psychological effects · Physiological effects · Infodemic · Uzbekistan

INTRODUCTION

Social Media and Their Usage in Misinformation Spread

Advancements in Internet technologies have immensely enhanced access to information during times of health emergencies (Cole et al., 2016). It enables people to easily share the information and effectively seek information. According to the Freberg et al. (2013), social media can also be effectively used to communicate health information to the general public during a pandemic. Emerging infectious diseases, such as COVID-19, almost always result in increased usage and consumption of media of all forms by the general public for information. Therefore, social media has a crucial role in people's perception of disease exposure, resultant decision making, and risk behaviors (Giustini et al., 2018). Additionally, real-time surveillance from social media about COVID-19 can be an important tool in the armamentarium of interventions by public health agencies and organisations (Tsao et al., 2021).

The latest observations suggest that the enormous amount of COVID-19 information generated on social media has overwhelmed users and had a strong impact on their psychological well-being (Islam et al., 2020). Therefore, COVID-19 is not only a global pandemic, but also an 'infodemic' (Laato et al., 2020b). For COVID-19, accurate and reliable information through social media platforms can have a crucial role in tackling infodemics, misinformation, and rumors. Infodemic, according to the World Health Organization, is false or misleading information that is published or articulated in digital or physical environment during a disease outbreak (WHO, 2021). The negative consequences of infodemic on psychological and mental health are noted by researchers and international organizations (WHO, 2021).

However, social media also became one of the most effective channels for misinformation. As information on social media is generated by users, such information can be subjective or inaccurate, and frequently includes misinformation and conspiracy theories (Bridgman et al., 2020). Misinformation involves information that is inadvertently false and is shared without intent to cause harm, while disinformation involves false information knowingly being created and shared to cause harm (Wardle & Derakhshan, 2017). Before discussing the macro-phenomenon of misinformation spread, we first conceptualize the potential mechanism following Wardle and Derakhshan (2017). Three major components are involved in the creation, production, distribution and re-production of misinformation—agent, message and interpreter (Wardle & Derakhshan, 2017). At the micro-level, individuals who receive misinformation form judgement about the believability of the message, depending on information source, narrative and context, while the tendency to spread depends on the degree to which receivers suspect such misinformation (Karlova & Fisher, 2013). At the macro-level, we observe patterns of misinformation cascade and characteristics of networks.

In recent years, misinformation has been a vital issue in health ecosystems (Li et al., 2019; Zhao et al., 2019). According to Chou et al. (2018), health-related misinformation is defined as a health-related claim that is false because a lack of scientific evidence. Recently, the dissemination of misinformation on social media in health emergencies has gained increasing attention because dissemination can pose threats to public health. When facing health emergencies, people often experience health anxiety (Oh & Lee, 2019); thus, they wish to find information about disease prevention and treatment and gain social support to deal with the disease (Chen et al., 2018).

During health emergencies, the number of people who use social media and internet to seek health-related information, such as health advice, prevention and treatment information, appears to be high (Chu et al.,

2017). To date, social media has increasingly influenced people's daily lives and their health behaviors (Zhao et al., 2020).

Such an enormous volume of health information causes difficulties for users, however, in locating, processing and managing the required valuable information effectively (Zhang et al., 2016). This intensive use of social media leads to information overload, meaning that social media users are exposed to information but it exceeds their ability to digest it (Bright et al., 2015). Information overload phenomena occur when users have difficulties in processing and handling the volume of information presented on social media (Maier et al., 2015). Although social media plays an important role in information dissemination today, information overload has been confirmed as one trigger of the negative consequences of social media usage (Bright et al., 2015; Laato et al., 2020a).

Social Networks and Internet Coverage in Uzbekistan

About 96% of the population of Uzbekistan has access to mobile technology (Alieva & Makovskaya, 2021). There are 265 thousand mobile stations deployed throughout the republic's territory, with coverage distribution varying based on location and population density. According to the figures, 22 million people have access to the internet, but only about 3 million of them use it from a phone. Others would either use a wired internet service or just use a mobile connection (Alieva & Makovskaya, 2021).

Uzbekistan is starting to extend its wired high-speed network infrastructure, which is projected to reach 48 thousand kilometers by the end of 2020.

The quarantine resulted in a drop in internet service quality, especially in rural areas. Companies were required to revise electromagnetic radiation requirements and raise capacity, according to Alieva and Makovskaya (2021). In addition, all mobile operators operating in Uzbekistan have upgraded nearly 300 base stations to allow internet access. However, the consistency and speed began to deteriorate as the infrastructure was not prepared for increased Internet traffic that occurred suddenly.

Companies are currently renovating and modernizing equipment and base stations in order to improve Internet speed.

In most cases for Uzbek people social networks and messenger became the main source of information rather than looking for information in official websites or newspapers/magazines. According to the IWPR (2019), such a trend increases the country's vulnerability to the spread of misinformation since it is impossible to analyze, study and control the content distributed in instant messengers. According to IWPR (2019) data, Facebook ranked first among social networks, and Telegram among messenger apps.

Methodology

Objectives

The present study aims to analyze the psychological impacts of infodemic that appeared during the COVID-19 pandemic on Uzbekistani youth.

We focus on the psychological factors and potential health consequences. The general objective in this case can be determined as follows: to measure psychological impact of infodemic and suggest practical solutions based on relevant literature to decrease that influence and deal with short-, medium- and long-term consequences.

Following the outline of the general objective, the particular objectives were established:

- To determine types of negative impacts that COVID-19 infodemic had on Uzbekistani youngsters;
- To present practical solutions for the youngsters, their families, community and practitioners to leverage on consequences and decrease the negative effect caused;
- To determine if there were positive influences of infodemic on Uzbekistani youngsters.

Data Collection

The data for present study was collected in June 2020, at a moment when the majority of lockdown measures were weakened and people could already share the experience they had. The questionnaire was created in three languages: English, Russian and Uzbek in order to include as many potential respondents as possible. The researchers created electronic questionnaires that were distributed among their lists of contacts and via Telegram channels of several universities in Uzbekistan.

The questionnaire is composed of two parts. The first part collects information on participants' demographic characteristics, while the second one measures lockdown and infodemic influences on psychological and physiological state of participants. Both positive and negative impacts are measured, using two types of scales: the dichotomous and Likert scale that collected information on agreement and disagreement levels.

The measurement is done through self-evaluation made by respondent of his/her before and after pandemic psychological and physiological states.

With help of the questionnaire, we determine the level of stress experienced in the beginning and during the lockdown, analyze the factors that also played role on information perception and the way governmental creation of official information channels influenced on emotional and psychological state of participants. We measured the effect of information received both from Uzbek and international sources that had been talking about situation in Uzbekistan.

On the other hand, thirty-seven in-depth semi-structured interviews were conducted in order to evaluate the impact of misinformation more profoundly. The researchers chose randomly the interviewees, the request for an interview was sent to fifty-seven people (one-fifth of the total number of participants), the response rate reached 64.91%. Each interview lasted one hour—one hour and a half and was conducted in Zoom by one of the researchers.

The interviews helped to create a semantic map of terms used by participants to describe their emotions and feelings caused by information received from different channels in several phases of lockdown. In addition, the perception of role of government in regulation of misinformation cases was measured.

We tried to minimize the mediation effect that could be caused by factors other than misinformation: for instance, psychological state of the participant prior to lockdown, the way he or she spent quarantine at home (actively or passively resting, working, etc.) and so on.

The questionnaires analysis was conducted with IBM SPSS Statistics 23, for the semantic analysis of interviews the researchers used AutoMap and ORA, the visualization of network was done with Gephi 0.9.2.

Participants

To reach the objectives stated we collected data from 284 participants using the questionnaires designed. 5.92% of them are 17–19 years old, 27.11%—20–21 years old, 28.52%—22–24 years old, and the rest are older than 25 years old. We almost could reach gender balance in present research, having 48.24% males and 51.76% females.

As we have included in our study only the youngsters, placing the bar between 17 and 30 years old, the majority of our participants are still studying in undergraduate or graduate programs (96.83% or 275 people). Due to that fact 64.08% of total sample reported to be unemployed, while the others—to be part-time employees.

In Uzbekistan, people tend to get married at an early age. Taking this into consideration we had to determine whether our participants are married. The results show that 4.93% of them are currently married, while the others were single in the moment of filling out the questionnaire. We consider that characteristic to be important, as marital status and obligations that are related with family issues can also impact psychological state during the pandemic.

The other factor we needed to control in the number of people living in participant's household. Traditional Uzbek families have many members, and we had to take this fact into account, as the lockdown with big family could produce different impact on the participant, probably suppressing the effects of infodemic.

In addition, we used self-reports of survey participants on having a chronic disease as a control variable, as that condition can also impact the psychological health. Thirty-five participants reported having a chronic disease.

Results

Psychological and Physiological Impact of COVID-19

The comparison of participants' psychological and physiological characteristics before and after the COVID-19 outbreak shows negative shifts that can be potentially caused by pandemic and infodemic (Table 3.1). The mean is calculated on the basis of the Likert scale from 1 to 5, where 1 meant "not at all", and 5—"constantly". The respondents had to evaluate the frequency of experiencing of the conditions listed in the table.

Table 3.1 Psychological and physiological state of participants before and after the COVID-19 outbreak (in June 2020)

Characteristic	Before COVID-19		In June 2020		Difference
	M	SD	M	SD	
High level of stress	1.26	0.31	3.09	1.21	+1.83
High level of anxiety	0.71	0.24	4.12	0.78	+3.41
Problems with digestion	1.12	1.01	3.31	2.09	+2.19
Severe headaches	0.96	1.09	4.19	1.19	+3.23
Low level of concentration	1.59	1.71	3.80	1.41	+2.21
Low level of performance	1.83	0.85	3.12	1.38	+1.29

As it can be noticed, the biggest change is observed in case of anxiety level (increase from $M = 0.71$ to $M = 4.12$) and severe headaches (increase from $M = 0.96$ to $M = 4.19$).

If we analyze the results more in detail, we can observe that the results of the study conducted show that among young people there is a high level of several psychological problems: about 49.51% reported having anxiety, 56.70%—frustration and 24.07%—sense of helplessness. First, it is associated with anxiety about the health of their family members and friends (35.72%). In particular, the greatest concern is caused by the health of elderly parents and the desire to protect them from the virus (46.51%). In the second place is the concern about the respondents' health (28.12%), in the third place is concern about the situation in the country (22.91%).

The data show that the level of anxiety in female respondents is higher than that of males (52.61 versus 43.12%). One of the reasons that can explain that situation is the increased volume of household duties women found themselves with during the lockdown. Other differences on the gender basis are related with day-to-day activities: females reported more discomfort in going to the street (71.98%) and interacting with people (67.02%) in comparison with males (43.10 and 30.05% respectively).

The marital status of the respondents, according to the results of our study, also affects the psychological state during a pandemic. Married participants in the survey showed a higher level of anxiety (78.15%) compared with single ones (54.06%), while indicating a greater isolation from the outside world (65.49 versus 40.15%). It should be noted that this indicator is directly related to the level of anxiety and disappointment ($r = 0.702$ and $r = 0.894$ respectively).

The stress level experienced by survey participants increased during lockdown in Uzbekistan at 27.40%. At the same time, 39.59% reported more frequent migraines and headaches, 14.80%—problems with digestion and 62.60%—emotional disorders and difficulties in controlling emotions. Levels of concentration and attention also suffered, especially in the case of female respondents. In particular, 43.09% of women noted decreased levels of concentration and attention, while among men this indicator reached 20.15%.

Problems with understanding and perceiving information also arose in 67.12% of respondents. It should be noted that in this issue we controlled the factor associated with the nature of the perceived source. As the respondents were young people, students in their majority, they were asked to provide information regarding their perception of the material. The questionnaire clarified that it is not about understanding the material of an online lesson, but about the perception of information itself. In particular, two questions on that topic were asked: *(a) Do you feel that information you get during online classes is difficult to understand and remember? (b) Do you feel that online classes are more difficult to understand and remember than offline classes?* We consider this remark important and necessary, since the transfer of the lesson to the online mode in itself reduces the concentration levels and attention of students, therefore, it would be unreasonable to evaluate these factors from the point of view of the direct influence of the lockdown within its framework.

Female respondents identified as one of the problems of lockdown the impossibility of direct communication with friends and isolation from them (43.59%), while among the male respondents the number of those who felt this effect is much lower (11.16%). The support women received from communicating with friends in person was of a different quality from that received through communication over the Internet and through telephone calls.

Male respondents reported improved relationships with household members during the lockdown period (48.11%), increased feelings of loneliness (39.79%) and the desire to break off relations with relatives because of contact with them 24 hours 7 days a week (10.41%). Females also reported improved relationships with household members (32.09%) and an opportunity to take care of themselves and listen to themselves (42.70%).

We identified a relationship between improved relationships and feelings of anxiety ($r = -0.629$) and fear ($r = 0.943$). As we can see, with an increase in the quality of relationships with household members, the level of fear increased, since, most likely, an awareness of their vulnerability was added with fear and worries for them. On the other hand, the level of anxiety decreased.

In the following paragraphs we will evaluate the relationships between all these psychological and physiological states, source of information used for receiving news about the situation with COVID-19 in Uzbekistan and the quality of the information. We will also try to assess whether the additional effect of misinformation arises in those cases where we have already established correlations.

The Psychological Impacts of Misinformation

The participants in our study named two main sources of information about the current situation in the country during the COVID-19 pandemic: internet (100%) and relatives/friends (92.32%). Among internet-sources the following were indicated: (1) official governmental Telegram channels (95.52%); (2) non-official Telegram channels (82.81%); (3) social networks—Facebook, Twitter, etc. (63.09%), and (4) newspapers (15.19%). In has to be noted that 100% of the survey participants said that they received news about what is happening in the country and the world from local news sources, 93.81% in parallel followed the news about Uzbekistan in the foreign press.

The respondents noted the high influence of information received from all sources, while they found it difficult to say what indicators they used to determine the reliability of the information provided or to assess its quality. On the other hand, the survey participants noted that the abundance of different, and sometimes contradictory data, led to a deterioration in their psychological state and to a feeling of confusion, anxiety and fear.

> At the beginning of the quarantine, when it was not clear what was happening and how long it would take, I tracked all the news, followed the statistics on the number of cases and deaths. Then I realized that I could

not change anything, but only drove myself into a panic, and decided to stop tracking this information. It immediately became a relief for me.

(Female respondent, unmarried, 19 years old)

If something is published on a channel opened by the government, this is probably reliable information, right? I also convinced myself that way, and then opened Facebook and read messages from users who denied this information. And it became very bad, because it was not clear what and whom to believe.

(Male respondent, married, 24 years old)

The respondents noted that the information they received from relatives and friends during the entire lockdown was assessed more critically by them than what was disseminated on social networks (trust level reached 2.6 out of 5 and 4.3 out of 5, respectively). As a result, we can conclude that people are more likely to trust the information found online than information provided directly by their relatives or acquaintances.

93.71% of respondents were able to recall the experience of more than fifteen cases of misinformation during the lockdown period, 5.12%—more than ten. In particular, this concerned data related to the number of cases and deaths in the country, the readiness of hospitals and hospitals to receive patients for treatment and the availability of necessary drugs and equipment. This situation gave rise to uncertainty, misunderstanding of what was happening and, as a result, led to increased levels of psychological stress. After the information was refuted by official sources, the level of anxiety did not decrease in 34.01%, but increased in 15.93%; the level of fear remained the same at 43.76%, and increased at 2.93%.

When I read the refutation in the official Telegram channel, it seemed to me that this was not true, and that something was being hidden from us. If you see the same information in three sources and the fourth tells you that this is not true, you still start to think that something fishy is going on. And then the parents come and say that they also read something, and it starts to seem to you that everyone has different information and you do not know who to believe.

(Female respondent, non-married, 22 years old)

The respondents also noted the deterioration in physical health, attributing this both to the general state of panic and tension, and to the abundance of information and confusion among the population. According to their reports, refusing to track any information did not help to cope with the symptoms, as they received it, without even controlling the process, from family members.

> At some point in the quarantine, I decided that it would be better to sit in complete isolation and not know what was happening around. I tried to stop tracking the data on the number of cases, but it did not help, because my household was constantly discussing these statistics. I unsubscribed from all channels, tried not to participate in discussions, but this also did not change the situation in any way.
> (Male respondent, 22 years old, married)

It should be noted that we found a strong correlation between the negative effect provoked by misinformation, lockdown and pandemic, and the age of the respondents ($r = 0.801$). In particular, 17–19-year-old participants in the survey showed greater uncertainty caused by misinformation ($M = 4.2$ out of 5 possible), while showing lower levels of stress ($M = 2.6$ out of 5 possible). A survey of 20–21-year-old participants revealed a lower level of uncertainty ($M = 3.9$ out of 5), while stress rises to $M = 3.2$. Respondents aged 22 and over showed an average level of misinformation-provoked uncertainty ($M = 2.6$ out of 5), but a high level of stress ($M = 4.8$ out of 5).

It is important to mention that 67.01% of respondents stated that the voluminous information they were processing each day looking for news and even cases of misinformation helped them to develop their critical abilities and to approach more with more skepticism any data or information they get.

Semantic Analysis of Interviews Conducted

Semantic analysis of thirty-seven interviews conducted allowed us to determine the following. The most common concepts turned out to be the ones presented in the Table 3.1. Predictably, COVID-19/pandemic and lockdown, mentioned by all thirty-seven respondents, took the top spot on the list. The second position was taken by the negative effects of the pandemic, which we also described in the previous parts of the analysis—anxiety and fear. Concerns about health, as well as about family and relatives, moved to third and fourth places, respectively.

Since our respondents were mostly full-time or part-time University students, concerns about these aspects of life are also reflected in the frequency of usage these concepts. Online (study or work) and self-study were also mentioned. The next group was made up of concepts related to leisure and/or with free time—friends, travel and communication. Interestingly, information sources (news and social networks) showed almost equal number of mentions by the respondents—22 and 21 people, respectively, spoke about them (Table 3.2).

In Fig. 3.1, we can see a network showing the frequency of mentioning together the most common concepts by the same interviewee. We can see that the themes of the first group present in all interviews—COVID-19/pandemic and lockdown connect all other concepts into a single network. The strong connection that is present confirms the results presented above on the relationship of the pandemic and lockdown with information and psychological consequences.

Table 3.2 List of the most commonly used concepts used by interviewees

Concept	Number of interviews	%
COVID-19/pandemic	37	100.00
lockdown	37	100.00
anxiety	36	97.30
fear	36	97.30
health	35	94.59
family/relatives	33	89.19
studies	32	86.49
work	31	83.78
friends	31	83.78
travel	24	64.26
communication	22	59.46
news	22	59.46
self-study	22	59.46
online	21	56.76
social media	21	56.76

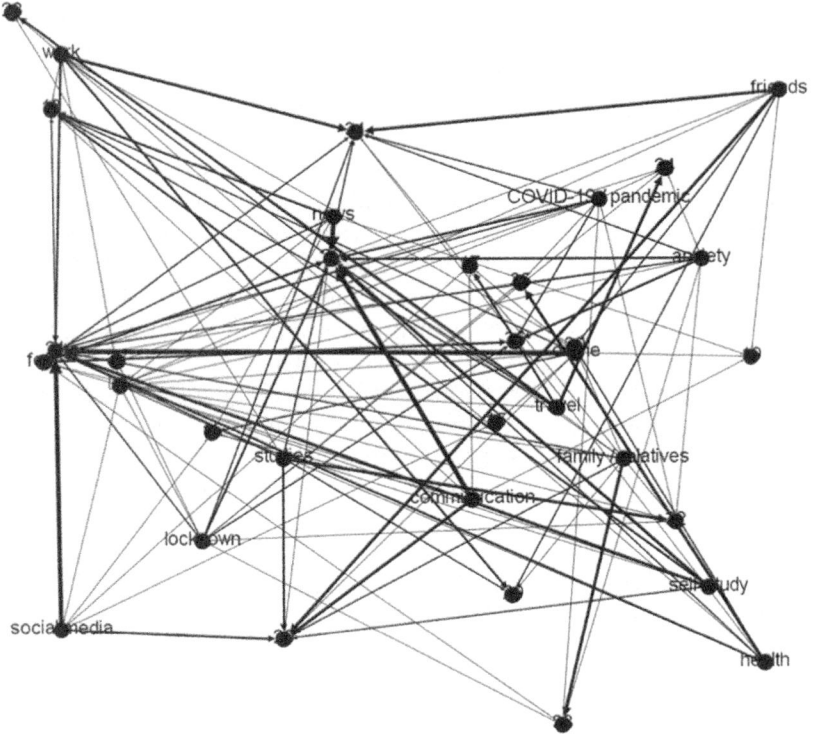

Fig. 3.1 Semantic network of the most commonly used concepts

Conclusions

Against the backdrop of the rapid spread of the coronavirus disease pandemic to an increasing number of countries around the world, the general population has a feeling of anxiety, fear and stress, which is a completely natural and normal reaction to the ever-changing and unpredictable situation in which the planet is.

Job loss, isolation, family troubles, endless news about the increase in the number of people infected with the coronavirus and deaths, as well as the uncertainty of the future amid a pandemic, can affect a person's psychological state and mental health.

Psychological fatigue and exhaustion, insomnia, depression and fear, as well as suicidal moods can arise against the backdrop of global turmoil. The coronavirus pandemic is no exception, and the youngsters are traditionally one of the most vulnerable groups in the society that can be easily affected by such dramatic events.

The study conducted helped to evaluate different aspects related to mental and psychological health of Uzbekistani youngsters. As we have seen, the COVID-19 pandemic, misinformation and infodemic had a huge impact on them. On the one hand, the study has determined the increased level of anxiety, specifically among females. In our opinion, this higher impact happened due to the fact that the economic impact of COVID-19 is especially affecting females. In Uzbekistan, as in many other countries, females traditionally tend to have lower earnings and less savings, which led them to higher levels of fear of future and more perceived risks associated with it. In addition, they also had to face an increased volume of household work, which has resulted from children not attending school, and the elderly having a greater need for home care due to the congestion of the health care system.

On the other hand, we have identified that the effect of misinformation or excess of information, viral spread of news and many different sources impacted negatively in different levels the youngsters. This is confirmed by the results of the survey and interviews conducted. However, part of the respondents could have found a positive effect of misinformation and existence of many sources on them and their personal and professional capabilities.

Due to the fact that data collection was conducted online, the study centered more on those who live in places with Internet access. It led to the situation where the majority of participants were receiving information from internet sources. However, the gossips from relatives, friends and neighbors could have had different effect on our participants, as they would had been receiving them from people of their environment. The level of trust could have played a mediator role in that case and we would like to measure it in future studies. On the other hand, as a short period of time has passed after the major lockdown and the country is currently still under partial quarantine, we couldn't have measured long-lasting effect of infodemic. Third, as the psychological and emotional state were measured by participants themselves, however, there is a risk that self-perception differs from the reality.

In future studies we would like to use more objective measures (physiological indicators, official diagnosis, etc.) to compare the results obtained with self-evaluation of participants and measure more effectively the influence of infodemic on participants.

From a practical perspective, our findings prove the importance of development of strong skills that can be helpful in order to control the spread of misinformation, specifically in such an emergent cases, like pandemic, natural disasters, etc. We should provide our youngsters the tools and instruments needed to evaluate critically the data they get from different sources. The critical thinking and analytical skills development integrated in educational programs and school and university curricula are crucial in that case.

In addition, it is recommended to create specific psychological units dedicated to work with youngsters and young adults during and after emergent situations. The sense of support and understanding from the part of the society and authorities can become helpful for their mental state and psychological health.

REFERENCES

Alieva, D. & Makovskaya, L. (2021). *Feasibility study on scaling innovation: Project "Edu Market"*. KIX EAP Learning Cycle, KIX Europe-Asia-Pacific Hub.

Bridgman, A., Merkley, E., & Loewen, P. J. (2020, June 18). The causes and consequences of COVID-19 misperceptions: Understanding the role of news and social media. *Misinformation Review*. https://misinforeview.hks.harvard.edu/article/the-causes-and-consequences-of-covid-19-misperceptions-understanding-the-role-of-news-and-social-media. Accessed 15 Sept 2020.

Bright, L. F., Kleiser, S. B., & Grau, S. L. (2015). Too much Facebook? An exploratory examination of social media fatigue. *Computing Human Behavior, 44*, 148–155.

Chen, X., Hay, J. L., Waters, E. A., Kiviniemi, M. T., Biddle, C., & Schofield, E. (2018). Health literacy and use and trust in health information. *Journal of Health Communication, 23*(8), 724–734.

Chou, W. Y. S., Oh, A., & Klein, W. M. (2018). Addressing health-related misinformation on social media. *JAMA, 320*(23), 2417–2418.

Chu, J. T., Wang, M. P., Shen, C., Viswanath, K., Lam, T. H., & Chan, S. S. C. (2017). How, when and why people seek health information online: Qualitative study in Hong Kong. *Interactive Journal of Medical Research, 6*(2), 1–10.

Cole, J., Kleine, D., & Watkins, C. (2016, June). Internet discussion forums: Maximizing choice in health-seeking behaviour during public health emergencies. In *2016 International Conference On Cyber Situational Awareness, Data Analytics And Assessment (CyberSA)* (pp. 1–4). IEEE.

Freberg, K., Palenchar, M. J., & Veil, S. R. (2013). Managing and sharing H1N1 crisis information using social media bookmarking services. *Public Relations Review, 39*, 178–184.

Giustini, D., Ali, S., Fraser, M., & Kamel Boulos, M. (2018). Effective uses of social media in public health and medicine: A systematic review of systematic reviews. *Online Journal of Public Health Informatics, 10*, 215.

Islam, A. K. M. N., Laato, S., Talukder, S., & Sutinen, E. (2020). Misinformation sharing and social media fatigue during COVID-19: An affordance and cognitive load perspective. *Technological Forecasting and Social Change, 159*, 1–14.

IWPR CA. (2019). *Report on social networks as a source for news*. Institute for War & Peace Reporting (IWPR).

Karlova, N. A., & Fisher, K. E. (2013). A social diffusion model of misinformation and disinformation for understanding human information behaviour. *Information Research, 18*(1), 1–12.

Laato, S., Islam, A., Islam, M., & Whelan, E. (2020a). What drives unverified information sharing and cyberchondria during the COVID-19 pandemic? *European Journal of Information System, 29*, 288–305.

Laato, S., Islam, A. K. M. N., Farooq, A., & Dhir, A. (2020b). Unusual purchasing behavior during the early stages of the COVID-19 pandemic: The stimulus-organism-response approach. *Journal of Retailing and Consumer Services, 57*, 1–12.

Li, Y. J., Cheung, C. M., Shen, X. L., & Lee, M. K. (2019). Health misinformation on social media: A literature review. In *23rd Pacific Asia Conference on Information Systems (PACIS 2019)*.

Maier, C., Laumer, S., Eckhardt, A., & Weitzel, T. (2015). Giving too much social support: Social overload on social networking sites. *European Journal of Information System, 24*, 447–464.

Oh, H. J., & Lee, H. (2019). When do people verify and share health rumors on social media? The effects of message importance, health anxiety, and health literacy. *Journal of Health Communication, 24*(11), 837–847.

Tsao, S.-F., Chen, H., Tisseverasinghe, T., Yang, Y., Li, L., & Butt, Z. A. (2021). What social media told us in the time of COVID-19: A scoping review. *The Lancet Digital Health, 3*(3), e175–e194.

Wardle, C., & Derakhshan, H. (2017). Information disorder: Toward an Interdisciplinary framework for research and policy making. *Council of Europe Report, 27*, 1–107.

World Health Organization. (2021). *Infodemic.* https://www.who.int/health-topics/infodemic. Accessed 31 May 2021.

Zhao, Y., Da, J., & Yan, J. (2020). Detecting health misinformation in online health communities: Incorporating behavioral features into machine learning based approaches. *Information Processing & Management, 58*(1), 1–24.

Zhao, Y., Zhang, J., & Wu, M. (2019). Finding users' voice on social media: An investigation of online support groups for autism-affected users on Facebook. *International Journal of Environmental Research and Public Health, 16*(23), 4804.

Zhang, S., Zhao, L., Lu, Y., & Yang, J. (2016). Do you get tired of socializing? An empirical explanation of discontinuous usage behaviour in social network services. *Journal of Information Management, 53,* 904–914.

CHAPTER 4

The "Sick Man of Asia": Exploring Popular Perceptions of China in Kyrgyzstan

Dana Rice

Abstract Since the collapse of the Soviet Union, interaction between the Chinese and Kyrgyz governments has rapidly increased. The two countries have cooperated over territory/border delineation, trade, investment and security among other spheres. However, not everyone in Kyrgyzstan is happy about China's growing influence, with concerns being raised among the general populace over possible land takeovers, ecological degradation by Chinese firms and the persecution of ethnic Kyrgyz in China's Xinjiang region. In recent years, a number of anti-Chinese rallies have taken place across the country, where demands have included a moratorium on Kyrgyz passports to Chinese citizens, deportation of Chinese citizens living illegally in Kyrgyzstan, prohibition of Kyrgyz-Chinese intermarriage and further scrutiny of Chinese companies operating in the country. This chapter explores these popular perceptions of

D. Rice (✉)
The Australian National University, Canberra, ACT, Australia
e-mail: dana.rice@anu.edu.au

© The Author(s), under exclusive license to Springer Nature Singapore Pte Ltd. 2022
J.-F. Caron and H. Thibault (eds.), *Central Asia and the Covid-19 Pandemic*, The Steppe and Beyond: Studies on Central Asia, https://doi.org/10.1007/978-981-16-7586-7_4

China in Kyrgyzstan, particularly their development in response to the COVID-19 pandemic. More specifically, the chapter examines the *noso-symbolic* discourses (that is, the *associations with disease*) that have evolved in Kyrgyzstan in connection to China, the proverbial "Sick Man of Asia".

Keywords China · COVID-19 · Kyrgyzstan · Sinophobia · Yellow Peril

Introduction

From the bubonic plague to SARS, China and disease have long been intertwined in the discourse of "Yellow Peril". The COVID-19 pandemic, which is thought to have originated in the Chinese city of Wuhan, has renewed this association once more. This chapter seeks to explore how, if at all, anti-Chinese sentiment has manifested in Kyrgyzstan in response to the coronavirus.

Currently, only a small body of literature exists on sinophobia in Central Asia (see Burkhanov & Chen, 2016; Chen & Günther, 2020; Grozin, 2019; Kulintsev et al., 2020; Owen, 2017; Peyrouse, 2016). Providing the first in-depth analysis of anti-Chinese sentiment in Kyrgyzstan since COVID-19, this chapter offers a contribution to this conversation. The chapter will primarily rely on analysis of news articles and social media as well as interviews with local experts and community leaders.

In examining the *noso-symbolic* elements (that is, the *associations with disease*) of global sinophobia back in 2018, Lynteris stressed that historic and modern sinophobia should be understood as two distinct phenomena. In the 1800s, the fear of Chinese bodies as carriers of disease was linked to China as a place of "degeneration" and "decay", a civilisation on its deathbed, encircled by greedy imperial powers (Lynteris, 2018, p. 38). In the past few decades, however, a new epidemiological discourse has arisen. China has become the land of "emergence", where disease becomes imagined as the product of the country's "unrestrained capitalist production and exploitation" (Lynteris, 2018, pp. 50–54).

This new discourse is increasingly playing out in Central Asia, even more so since the outbreak of COVID-19. In unravelling these various strands of anti-Chinese sentiments, this chapter begins by providing a background to Sino-Kyrgyz relations; then discusses the history of sinophobia both globally and in Kyrgyzstan; and finally examines how COVID-19 has affected perceptions of China in Kyrgyzstan. Ultimately, I argue that anti-Chinese sentiments both prior to and during the pandemic tie into a more general distrust of the Kyrgyz government.

A Background to Sino-Kyrgyz Relations

Before exploring popular perceptions of China in Kyrgyzstan and how these perceptions have evolved since COVID-19, a brief background to Chinese-Kyrgyz relations is first needed. This chapter begins by examining the key, overlapping areas of interaction between China and Kyrgyzstan: territory/borders, trade, investment and security.

Following the Soviet Union's collapse in 1991, the newly independent Kyrgyz Republic, a small, mountainous country of just four million, suddenly had to reckon with the massive industrial powerhouse at its doorstep. Sharing a border over 1000 kms in length raised numerous issues for both Kyrgyzstan and China. Number one on the agenda was determining where that border actually lies, as numerous land disputes from the Soviet era remained unresolved. One of Kyrgyzstan's first official dealings with China was as part of the Shanghai Five, a grouping of five states—China, Russia, Tajikistan, Kazakhstan and Kyrgyzstan—established to settle this boundary issue. Demarcation of the Sino-Kyrgyz border would, however, take nearly two decades to finally be completed—and not without its share of political controversy. In 1999, Kyrgyzstan signed a deal to hand over 1250 square kilometres of land to China, resulting in calls for then-President Askar Askaev to be impeached. Only in 2009, following more handovers, was the boundary considered settled.

In these intervening years, however, the Shanghai Cooperation Organisation (SCO), the Shanghai Five's reincarnation as a permanent body, "became China's vehicle for entering Central Asia economically" (Pannier 2016). From having almost no economic exchange in Soviet times, China has now displaced Russia—Kyrgyzstan's traditional economic, military and political partner—in bilateral trade figures. This development is particularly visible in Kyrgyzstan's bazaars—a study by the Central Asia Free Market Institute suggests that over 75 percent of goods at Dordoi bazaar and 85 percent at Kara-Suu come from China (Rickleton, 2011). Dordoi and Kara-Suu are the largest bazaars in the country as well as two of the main employment centres. The re-exportation of Chinese goods to neighbouring countries has also been a major contributor to the Kyrgyz economy. Already in 2007, Peyrouse (p. 17) noted that this re-exportation of Chinese goods had "become one of the two largest economic activities in Kyrgyzstan".

China has also invested in numerous economic projects in Kyrgyzstan. According to China Global Investment Tracker (CGIT), the most comprehensive publicly available dataset on China's global investment and construction transactions, Chinese investments and contracts in Kyrgyzstan since 2005 total at least $4.73 billion USD—CGIT's list is not exhaustive, so in all likelihood the figure is higher. In addition, China has offered massive "no strings attached" loans to Kyrgyzstan; a reported $1.8 billion is owed to the Export–Import Bank of China alone, making the bank Kyrgyzstan's largest creditor (Rickleton, 2020). Since 2013, these projects—many of them already completed or under construction by that time—have been bundled into Xi Jinping's grand strategy, the Belt and Road Initiative (initially referred to as "One Belt, One Road" and still referred to by that name in post-Soviet countries). According to a National Bureau of Economic Research whitepaper, Kyrgyzstan is one of the countries with the most hidden Chinese debt relative to its population (Horn et al., 2019). Like in Kazakhstan, a significant amount of China's investment in Kyrgyzstan is in the energy sector. Shaanxi Coal and Chemical's $430 million investment in the Kara-Balta oil refinery marks one of the largest Chinese investments in the country. Another major sector of Chinese investment in Kyrgyzstan is mining. Zijin Mining, for instance, invested $150 million in the Taldybulak Levoberezhny gold mine in 2015.

In addition to these aforementioned areas of cooperation and contention around which Sino-Kyrgyz relations are built (territory, trade and investment), another important reason for Chinese interest remains: that of Xinjiang, the restive province on China's Western frontier. This autonomous region, which borders three of the post-Soviet Central Asian states (Kazakhstan, Kyrgyzstan and Tajikistan), has an ethnic Uyghur majority in addition to ethnic Kyrgyz, Kazakh, Hui (Dungan), Tajik and other Muslim minorities. A long history of migration exists between what is now the borders of modern-day Kyrgyzstan and China. Many of the ethnic Kyrgyz in Xinjiang arrived in the region during "Urkun" in 1916. "Urkun" (also known as the Semirechye Revolt) was a popular uprising in Central Asia against Tsarist Russia, the harsh suppression of which led to mass deaths and exodus. Although many Chinese Kyrgyz have returned to Kyrgyzstan since the collapse of the USSR through the Kyrgyz government's Kairylman ("Returnee") program, approximately 200,000 remain in China today, primarily in Kizilsu Kyrgyz Autonomous Prefecture. Likewise, waves of Hui (a Chinese-speaking Muslim people from north-west China, known in Central Asia as Dungans) and Uyghurs have migrated westward to Kyrgyzstan over the centuries, embedding themselves in the country's complex, multi-ethnic landscape.

Along with Taiwan, Tibet and Hong Kong, the Chinese government sees Xinjiang as a problem region, where ethnic- and religious-motivated separatism is a threat. Indeed, parts of Xinjiang have broken away previously, albeit both attempts at independence were short-lived: the First East Turkestan Republic lasted from 1933 to 1934 while the Second East Turkestan Republic survived from 1944 to 1949. In various reincarnations, movements pushing for Uyghur or pan-Turkic independence have continued in the region, occasionally culminating in civil clashes and violence. One response of the Chinese authorities has been to introduce further measures of religious repression aimed at countering this alleged terrorism and separatism. Since 2017, accounts have emerged of Uyghurs and various minority groups—including Kyrgyz—being detained en masse in what are officially termed "Vocational Education and Training Centres".[1]

Within these internment camps, political indoctrination, torture, rape and compulsory sterilisation have been reported to take place, leading to widespread condemnation and accusations of genocide from various human rights groups and scholars. Estimates vary as to the number of detainees. However, Adrian Zenz, one of the leading researchers on the Xinjiang camps and an individual recently sanctioned by the CCP for his activism on this issue, suggests the number at any given time since 2016 is up to 1.5 million. Among these reported detainees are those with family in Kyrgyzstan as well as residents, and even citizens, of Kyrgyzstan. In one highly publicised case, Turgunaly Tursunaly (the grandson of the last great "manaschy", or reciter of Kyrgyzstan's national epic Manas)

---

[1] Much of this documentation has been undertaken by Atajurt (see Footnote 2), Gene Bunin's Xinjiang Victims Database, and Adrian Zenz (see, for instance, Zenz, 2019). One of the better-known personal accounts comes from Sayragul Sauytbay, an ethnic Kazakh woman whose book-length testimony of the Xinjiang re-education facilities was originally published in German in 2020 and in English in 2021 under the title *The Chief Witness: Escape from China's Modern-Day Concentration Camps*.

crossed the border from Kyrgyzstan into Xinjiang during a short university break and was not heard from again, leading some to speculate that he was detained by Chinese authorities. Many similar stories to Tursunaly's exist. However, unlike Atajurt in neighbouring Kazakhstan (which itself faces government difficulties),[2] no equivalent organisation to raise public awareness on missing Kyrgyz has developed in Kyrgyzstan.

Ensuring domestic security and stability in Xinjiang has become a key rationale behind China's engagement with Central Asia, both in the economic and security spheres. Since the late 1990s, China has embarked on a "Develop the West" campaign, aimed at improving living standards in the Western regions of China—but part of ensuring that the Turkic populations in Xinjiang are "deradicalised" has meant looking further west, to Central Asia, and preventing any pan-Turkic movements from arising there. The CCP believes that Xinjiang could be at risk should any radical Islamic organisations find a footing in neighbouring Kazakhstan, Kyrgyzstan or Tajikistan. As a result, China has taken great interest in Central Asia's development path long prior to the official announcement of BRI. Since 2001 and the 9/11 terrorist attacks, the SCO's focus has likewise shifted more towards security cooperation and jointly fighting the so-called "Three Evils": terrorism, separatism and religious extremism. While the reports mentioned above suggest that China's measures against the Three Evils have gone far beyond fighting the "radical" elements of society and more towards indiscriminate persecution of non-Han ethnic groups, the Kyrgyz government, both under the previous Jeenbekov administration and the current Japarov leadership, has been extremely reticent on such matters. Massive unpaid loans from China to Kyrgyzstan make the issue a delicate matter, especially given Kyrgyzstan's ongoing requests for debt relief (Rickleton, 2020).

Current research on Central Asia is disproportionately focused on issues of great power rivalry, viewing the region as a pawn caught in a

---

[2] Founded in Kazakhstan by Serikzhan Bilash in 2017, the human rights organisation Atajurt Eriktileri (Volunteers of the Fatherland) has compiled testimonies of former re-education camp detainees and relatives of those still missing in Xinjiang. With no equivalent organisation in Kyrgyzstan, Bunin (2019) notes how Kyrgyz citizens with missing relatives have had to make the day-long trip to the Atajurt headquarters in Almaty. In 2019, Bilash was arrested by Kazakh authorities for inciting ethnic hatred. A Kazakh government-approved splinter organisation continues to operate without Bilash's involvement under the original Atajurt Eriktileri name. Bilash later fled to Turkey and then America where he started a new group called Naghyz (the Real) Atajurt.

game between China, Russia and other regional players. Comparatively few studies seek to understand how Central Asian governments themselves interact with bordering powers, and even fewer have given a voice to the individuals living under these regimes. Yet, as Catherine Owens (2018, p. 461) notes, "Central Asian states are sovereign states with the capacity to shape international alliances and undermine hegemonic schemes. The views of their citizens ... are therefore not to be dismissed". Understanding perceptions of China is even more important considering the emphasis that China itself places on national image and cultural interaction in its overseas activities. Xi Jinping understands that his ability to appeal to the general public has the potential to impact the overall success of his flagship Belt and Road Initiative (BRI). People-to-people exchange is therefore one of the five official pillars of BRI.

Exploring Popular Perceptions of China

As explored at length in Billé and Urbansky's edited volume *Yellow Perils* (2018), sinophobia is far from a new phenomenon. In the book's introduction, Billé charts the history of anti-Chinese sentiment over the centuries. China, he writes, has traditionally been viewed as the cultural antithesis, the ultimate Other to civilised Europe. China was a land "[a]ssociated with violent invaders such as Genghis Khan (Zhou, 2006), with deadly diseases such as the bubonic plague (Watts, 1997), and occasionally depicted as the location of hell in medieval cartography" (Billé, 2018, p. 5). Indeed, though not noted by Billé, the Land of Gog and Magog—apocalyptic figures in Christian and Islamic tradition—has long been tied by some to this distant, volatile region of Eurasia (see Tchen & Yeats, 2014).

As waves of Chinese émigrés spread into Western cities from the 1800s onwards and set up Chinatowns, various popular stereotypes and fears have been generated and reproduced over the years. The sheer size of the Chinese population presents one reason for these fears, yet India has almost as large a population and rarely does one hear of the "India Threat". The Mongloid "Otherness" of the Chinese people may evoke xenophobia among Caucasians, but the same phenotypical "Otherness" may be said to be true for Africans and yet sinophobia is decidedly different from "afrophobia". Sinophobia is more than mere demographics or racial difference—there are unique characteristics which distinguish perceptions expressed towards the Chinese compared to other racial or ethnic groups.

As discussed at length by Frayling (2014) and Mayer (2014) among others, popular representations such as Dr. Fu Manchu (the evil Chinese mastermind of an early twentieth century book series which sold 20 million copies in the author's lifetime) have contributed to a perception of Chinese as wickedly smart yet soulless. In such books, comics, films and other examples of popular culture, the Chinese evoke a sense of almost superhuman, alien futurity, as though automatons. Accordingly, they are capable only of duplication, of copying, never creation—a standard conception further developed in the stereotype of Chinese having big brains and small genitalia. As Billé (2018, p. 17) explains, "[w]hereas much of anti-black narratives hinge around the notion that they are less cultured, less 'evolved', and more 'animalistic' than whites, ... on the contrary, Asians are often depicted as highly intelligent, less sexual and physical (i.e., less animalistic), and rational to the point of complete emotional detachment".

As certain authors note, sinophobia and the related race-colour metaphor of "Yellow Peril" is an ever-shifting concept, as new paradigms on who is "yellow" and what "peril" is faced are generated. Sometimes perceptions of the Chinese become enmeshed with or even obscured by a more generic fear of the "Eastern" Other (see Said, 1978). This often "unbridgeable" Otherness has generated not only fears and hatred but also, at times, a sense of intense fascination where Asia and the Orient are positioned as "a site of sophistication and exoticism" (Billé, 2018, p. 5). Yellow Peril has, as Tchen and Yeats (2014, p. 16) so perfectly capture, "a complex and sweeping genealogy ... connecting Mongols and Muslims, Jews and Japanese, the West and the East from the twelfth-century past to a horrific dystopic future ... suggest[ing] the scale and topography of [these] recurring fears". In other words, defining this Asian or Eastern Other has had an integral role in creating the European or Western Self. But what of those societies that lay outside the so-called Western sphere?

What makes sinophobia unique in Central Asia is that it may be one of the only regions in the world where the concept of "Chinese" does not conjure up the usual image of an ethnic Han. Does the large Dungan population (Muslim people of ethnic Hui origin) also count as "Chinese"? Are the Uyghurs (a Turkic people affiliated with the Far West of China) Chinese? What about the Chinese Kairylman (ethnic Kyrgyz who have "returned" to Kyrgyzstan, often after multiple generations overseas)? Along with neighbouring Kazakhstan, the concept of "Chinese" in Kyrgyzstan is multi-dimensional and fluid.

The growing economic engagement between Kyrgyzstan and China following the collapse of the Soviet Union has brought increased interaction with these Chinese and China-connected communities, including an influx of ethnic Han traders and workers. In fact, the belief that Chinese workers are taking away jobs from Kyrgyz citizens has been repeatedly brought up in anti-Chinese rhetoric and interethnic violence in Kyrgyzstan. However, even putting a number on the Chinese citizens living in the country proves difficult as government sources themselves vary wildly. For instance, the 2009 nationwide census of Kyrgyzstan (the most recent census at the time of writing) showed only 1813 Chinese citizens in the country, while police records for 2008 suggested this number was actually 60,000. A more recent report, prepared by the Kyrgyz Ministry of Labour, Migration and Youth in 2014, cites a figure of 20,000 Chinese citizens in Kyrgyzstan as the official statistic provided by the Chinese Embassy in Bishkek but admits that, according to experts, the actual figure is likely to be much higher. It is possible that many are living and working in the country illegally.

As the presence of "China" is increasingly felt in the country's economy and blamed for certain grievances, "Chinese" workers—whether new migrants or Dungans/Uyghurs with several generations' ties to Kyrgyzstan—have been the target of several interethnic clashes and attacks. Amid the ethnic riots of the 2010 Kyrgyz revolution, for example, the shops of ethnic Dungans and Uyghurs in northern Kyrgyzstan were ransacked, and two people died in a Dungan café set afire in Gidrostroitel. During the same period, the Goin Center, a symbol of Chinese traders' presence in Bishkek, was targetted by gangs and looters.

In subsequent years, nationalist group Kyrk Choro (Kyrgyz for "Forty Knights", a reference to the Manas epic) has taken it upon itself to enact vigilante justice against what it sees as Chinese interference and corruption of local morals. In December 2014, for instance, Kyrk Choro raided a Bishkek night club, detaining 17 Chinese citizens and 22 Kyrgyz women whom they accused of providing sexual services to the Chinese. Although the organisation had no authority to make these detentions, they did not face any legal repercussions.

Kyrgyzstan's citizens have also expressed resentment towards specific Chinese companies and their projects. In May 2013, for instance, protesters blocked the Chinese gold mining company Kaidi's operations in Osh Province, resulting in over 150 police officers being sent in to quell the violence. Among a number of other more recent incidents, dozens were also injured in clashes in 2019 against China's Zhong Ji Mining-operated Solton-Sary gold mine, which local residents claimed was polluting the environment and killing livestock en masse. However, it should be noted that other foreign companies operating in Kyrgyzstan—such as Canadian gold mining company Centerra—have also been the object of protests, suggesting that foreign interference in general (opposed to China alone) may concern segments of the population.

More recently, in February 2020, hundreds of Kyrgyz protested against China's proposed industrial, trade, logistics and cultural centre in At-Bashi. Many of the protestors rode on horses (a symbol of the Kyrgyz nation) with banners reading "No Kyrgyz Land to China!", echoing the earlier 2016 land protests in Kazakhstan.[3] Among the demands made at this protest and others are a moratorium on Kyrgyz passports to Chinese citizens, deportation of Chinese citizens living illegally in Kyrgyzstan, prohibition of Kyrgyz-Chinese intermarriage and further scrutiny of Chinese companies operating in the country.

An Epidemic of Yellow Peril?

Popular perceptions of China and fears of disease have long been intertwined. Yet, as Lynteris, one of the leading authorities on this topic, notes, the nature of this connection has changed over time. In examining the *noso-symbolic* elements (that is, the *associations with disease*) of global sinophobia, Lynteris stresses the differences between epidemic discourses present in historic and modern sinophobia. In the nineteenth century, China was perceived as a civilisation on its deathbed, existing at the edge of the modern, learned world. Seen as a place of "degeneration" and "decay" (Lynteris, 2018, p. 38), China was referred to as the "Sick Man

---

[3] In 2016, protests began in the Western Kazakh city of Atyrau and spread throughout the country in response to proposed legislation which would have allowed foreign entities to lease Kazakh land for 25 years at a time. The rallies were largely directed against China and Chinese-owned companies. In the end, the government caved to public pressure and shelved the proposed reforms.

of Asia", a term used throughout the latter half of the 1800s.[4] The association became literal with the so-called "third plague pandemic", which began with the 1894 bubonic plague outbreak in Hong Kong and led to the death of over 12 million people around the world (Lynteris, 2016). The fear of Chinese bodies and objects as carriers of disease led to various xenophobic attacks such as the Chinatown pogroms and stigmatisation of Chinese communities in the United States.

In the past few decades, however, a new epidemiological discourse has arisen. Taking on the role of a global superpower at the centre of world commerce and politics, China has become the land of "emergence". Here disease becomes imagined as the product of the country's "unrestrained capitalist production and exploitation" (Lynteris, 2018, pp. 50–54). In this new discourse, disease is especially linked to the imaginary of the wet market and the live, exotic animals which are sold there for human consumption: the civets, the snakes, the rats and so on. The very name "wet market" is evocative of the poor sanitation and the lack of separation between human and animal worlds, creating an environment ripe for zoonotic spread. The chaotic, contaminated wet market exists in distinct opposition to the organised, sterile supermarket. In this way, the wet market becomes a spatial representation of the barbaric soul which is perceived to endure beneath the modern, high-tech skin of Chinese society. The wild animals which populate the wet markets likewise become a reflection of this society—exotic, non-domesticated, licentious, a source of what Lynteris refers to as "hedonistic-cum-pathogenic peril" (Lynteris, 2016, p. 121). Such images are not just relayed in the media of the West but in other parts of the "East" as witnessed through examination of Kyrgyz media. Just as in many other countries, the now famous image of a Chinese woman eating a bat went viral in Kyrgyzstan at the beginning of COVID-19's emergence.

In majority-Muslim societies like that of the Kyrgyz people, this connection between Chinese food and disease can be taken a step further. In Islam, like Judaism, pork is considered *haram* ("forbidden"). Al-Māʾidah 5:3 in the Quran declares that "prohibited to you are dead animals, blood, the flesh of swine, and that which has been dedicated to other than Allah", while Al-ʿAnaʿām 6:145 similarly pronounces that

---

[4] Note that the earlier term "Sick Man of Europe" was coined in 1853 to refer to the decline of the Ottoman Empire, again linking discourses of sinophobia to a more pervasive relationship with the Eastern Other.

"a dead animal or blood spilled out or the flesh of swine ... is impure". According to Islamic tradition, animals must be killed by a throat cut and then bled out, but as pigs have no throat, there is no halal way to slaughter them, thus polluting their meat both physically with the blood and spiritually. Numerous Islamic websites aimed at the post-Soviet Muslim populations (such as islam.ru) warn of the health dangers for the "pig-eater"—including the transfer of parasitic worms and influenza between species. Such websites detail how pigs are one of the filthiest animals on the planet, scavengers who "cannot resist" eating unhygienic substances like feces, dirt, rotting carcasses and even their own babies (islam.ru 2013). Not only is pork the most consumed meat in China, but China is also the world's leading consumer, importer and producer of pork. This pork-centric society lends to a popular imagination where Chinese are seen as dirty and polluted.

In December 2019, the first case of a new, highly infectious disease caused by severe acute respiratory syndrome coronavirus 2 (SARS-CoV-2) was reported in Wuhan in Hubei Province, China. While the Chinese government has resisted investigations on the origins of the virus, it is widely believed that the COVID-19 pandemic is linked to the Huanan Seafood Wholesale Market, a wet market in Wuhan. Named "COVID-19" by the World Health Organisation (WHO), the virus quickly spread through the country and abroad. By March 2020, as the WHO declared COVID-19 a pandemic, the Kyrgyz government confirmed that the virus had reached their borders, carried by a citizen returning from Islamic pilgrimage to Mecca. Kyrgyz authorities quickly limited or forbid large public gatherings and banned Friday worship at mosques altogether. Starting from March 22nd, a state of emergency came into effect in which public transport ceased operation in Bishkek, and beginning two days later, curfews were enforced in the three most populous cities in Kyrgyzstan—Bishkek, Osh and Jalalabad.

During these difficult times, China was quick to offer aid. The idea of the "Health Silk Road", already a strand of the Belt and Road Initiative prior to COVID, suddenly took on new relevance. In June 2020, Osh, for instance, received 90,000 masks, 5000 respirators, 80 thermometers, 1750 protective suits, 700 protective glasses, 420 medical caps, 5000 pairs of gloves and 1 lung ventilator donated by the cities of Foshan, Xi'ian, Shijiazhuang and Lanzhou. Donations also came from private Chinese sponsors and companies such as the Jack Ma Foundation and the Alibaba Foundation. Then, in September 2020, Chinese foreign minister Wang

Yi met with his Kyrgyz, Kazakh, Mongolian and Russian counterparts, agreeing to work together to "build an 'anti-pandemic fortress, a Health Silk Road', to share medical supplies and vaccines, and even to promote traditional Chinese medicines"—although as Meirkhanova (2021) notes, the words cited in the Central Asian media were always Wang's, never the local representatives. More recently, on February 5th 2021, Chinese Ambassador to Kyrgyzstan, Du Dewen, announced that the Chinese government would provide Kyrgyzstan with free Chinese vaccines. All of these efforts have undoubtedly been aimed at improving China's image among the general public.

Temur Umarov suggests that "for the part of the population that supports closer relations with China, Beijing's successful fight with COVID-19 became another proof that Kyrgyzstan should imitate Chinese practices in governance and other spheres. [But for] those who were against China—the fact that the pandemic started in Wuhan and that the Chinese authorities were not quick to publicly talk about the pandemic, is and will be in the future used as an example of how China is unreliable and irresponsible" (Umarov, 2021, personal communication, February 12). Unfortunately, however, there is no regular opinion poll conducted on perceptions of China in Kyrgyzstan or even in Central Asia at large. The few surveys that have been conducted, usually of university students due to their relative ease of access, are not periodic and lack external validity, making it impossible to know quantitatively whether feelings towards China in Kyrgyzstan have declined or improved since the emergence of COVID-19.

One starting point, however, for understanding sinophobia during COVID-19 is to explore the numerous stories that have spread on Kyrgyz social media. According to factcheck.kg, a Kyrgyz fake news reporting website funded by Hungarian-American billionaire George Soros' Open Society Foundations, many conspiracies that have abounded in other countries during COVID-19 have also found fertile ground in Kyrgyzstan. These stories include COVID-19 being an electronic virus transmitted via 5G networks or being a man-made disease linked to American billionaire Bill Gates (factcheck.kg, 2021, personal communication, March 23). However, 2020 also saw the spread of other stories specific to the cultural landscape in Central Asia. Some of these stories, often circulated on Telegram channels as well as Facebook and WhatsApp, are directly aimed at the Chinese and China's government.

The Central Asian Bureau for Analytical Reporting suggests that some of the most viral stories in Central Asia since the beginning of COVID have been related to Islam—for instance, that COVID-19 was God punishing China for its oppression of Muslims or that Chinese were converting to Islam en masse as COVID didn't affect Muslims (Akayeva, 2020). A related story, investigated by factcheck.kg (2020a), was that the Chinese prime minister had been found praying in a mosque. Upon closer investigation, factcheck.kg found that the misleading video actually showed the Malaysian prime minister visiting a Beijing mosque back in 2015, not as the Chinese prime minister as had been claimed.

Another China-related story doing rounds on Kyrgyz social media was entitled "How Xi Jinping Fooled the US and the EU". The story claimed that China had used COVID-19 for economic gain, earning $20 billion and returning 30% of shares in its own companies to itself in the span of a few days (thanks to the panic which led foreign shareholders to sell out cheaply) (factcheck.kg, 2020b). Meanwhile, yet another fake news story in Kyrgyzstan claimed that Chinese traders at the Bishkek market "Madina" were forced out and had their wares taken from them.

It was also during the pandemic that the timely movie *Meken* was released by Kyrgyzstan's Borbor Asia studio. The film tells of a confrontation between local residents and a Chinese company developing their bucolic village. As a result of harmful emissions from the company's project, the villagers' cattle begin to die and the people themselves fall ill. While the movie would have been filmed prior to the pandemic, these central images are very much related to the noso-symbolic discourse that has existed around China for centuries. For some, China's rise has become equated with using its neighbours as a dumping ground for excess, unclean industries—polluting both the land and people (see, for instance, Imanaliyeva, 2020). The material linkage between disease and contaminated land/soil is a long-time trope in the popular imagination on China (see Lynteris, 2017). Having failed to achieve any results from petitions to government agencies, the townsfolk in the film take matters into their own hands, marching to the company's property with pitchforks—echoing the real-life protests in Kyrgyzstan. In the end, the residents are successful in expelling the Chinese. Finally backing down, the villainous Chinese investor angrily shouts, "I gave them [the bureaucrats] all the money. For winning a tender, for obtaining a license, for field development, for an inspector, I paid for everything. If not for these bribes, we would have spent this money on the safe storage of hazardous substances"

(*Kaktus*, 2020). Ironically but perhaps not surprisingly given the content, the government authorities dragged out a decision on the film's general distribution license. In the end, Borbor Asia studio decided to upload the film to YouTube for free in an effort to circumvent the bureaucracy.

The *Meken* example highlights how fear and anger around China's activities in Kyrgyzstan are part of an overarching distrust of corrupt bureaucrats and government authorities. Likewise, according to one Bishkek-based researcher spoken to, the skepticism around COVID-19 did not necessarily have to do with fears around a Chinese government conspiracy but concerns that Kyrgyzstan's own government was not being transparent and was using the coronavirus to exert more control over the population.

In fact, the second wave of the virus swept through the country alongside the October 2020 revolution. On October 4th 2020, parliamentary elections were held in which pro-government factions received a supermajority of seats, a result widely deemed to be rigged. Citizens thronged together in the streets—with little regard for COVID restrictions—protesting the results and alleged vote-buying. Over the next ten days, the political situation changed dramatically—protests swelled in size, former lawmaker Sadyr Japarov was broken out of jail by loyal supporters, key government buildings were seized (causing then-President Sooranbay Jeenbekov to declare a state of emergency), violent clashes occurred on the streets and Japarov eventually declared himself both acting Prime Minister and acting President.

In the midst of all of this upheaval and unrest, numerous Chinese businesses were targeted. Chinese "women were threatened with rape, [Chinese] men were savagely beaten and the Chinese flag set alight" (Yau, 2020). Among these incidents was the story of 35 Chinese executives forced to take refuge in a Bishkek hotel on October 6th, "only to be surrounded by an armed mob seeking ransom" (Yau, 2020). In another region of Kyrgyzstan, more than 100 Chinese mine workers fled into the woods and spent the night amidst the snow after a different mob occupied their worksite. The following day a Chinese oil refinery in the country was approached by a group of men with Kalashnikovs, threatening to burn the facility to the ground and demanding a $350,000 "protection fee" (Yau, 2020).

Sadyr Japarov's own connections to China are complicated. On the one hand, Japarov has long been supported by nationalist groups including Kyrk Choro. It should be noted that one of Japarov's earlier campaign promises was to nationalise the Chinese gold mines in Kyrgyzstan as well as other foreign ventures such as the Canadian-owned Kumtor gold mine. On the other hand, Japarov has maintained close political and business ties with Chinese nationals throughout his working career. In fact, it is believed that at least part of the $560,000 that his campaign raised came from China and Chinese donors (Umarov, 2021). Interestingly, Japarov's father was an ethnic Kyrgyz who was born and raised in China and returned to Kyrgyzstan several years prior to Japarov's birth, again highlighting the extent of cross-border flows mentioned earlier in this chapter.

On this point, it is also worth considering how COVID-19 have affected relations with China-connected communities in Kyrgyzstan such as Uyghurs and Dungans. In February 2020, for instance, almost a dozen people were killed and nearly two hundred injured in clashes between Kazakh and Dungan villages in southern Kazakhstan, on Kyrgyzstan's border. Hours later fake news circulated on social media using images from the conflict. The focus had shifted from Kazakh-Dungan to anti-Chinese as stories spread about Chinese restaurants being burned and "'ruthless pogroms in Kazakhstan around the spreading of coronavirus' … fueling hysteria in other parts of the country" (Sorbello, 2020). The clashes had cross-border effects and saw 26,000 Dungans stream across into Tokmok on the Kyrgyz side, seeking the comparative safety of relatives' homes there (to give an idea of the scale of this temporary migratory flow, the entire population of Dungans in Kyrgyzstan is only 73,000). While anti-Chinese sentiment did not necessarily fuel the conflict, the event's aftermath suggests a conflation between xenophobia expressed towards ethnic Han Chinese who are citizens of China and other ethnic and ethno-cultural groups residing in Central Asia with connections to China. Commenting on this episode and others, a blogger and activist in Kazakhstan, Malika Moldakhanova (2020), summed up existing tensions in Central Asia, saying that "we will definitely die from an epidemic", but an epidemic "of sinophobia", not coronavirus.

As part of the research for this chapter, I attempted to interview leaders of both the Uyghur and Dungan communities in Kyrgyzstan. I was able to speak with a representative from *Ittipak*, the Kyrgyz Uyghur organisation which is part of the People's Assembly of Kyrgyzstan and runs a Uyghur-language newspaper in the country, also funded partially by Soros' Open Society Foundations. However, the informant was extremely reticent about providing information and did not wish to be named—perhaps not surprisingly given the organisation has been labelled a separatist threat by the CCP which regularly pressures the Kyrgyz government to "monitor" the group more closely.[5]

The chairman for the Dungan Association of Kyrgyzstan, Mr. Karim Lemzarovich Khandzheza, was more willing to talk and discussed the great difficulties faced by Dungan people in Kyrgyzstan because of COVID-19. Mr. Khandzheza said that July 2020, known as "Black July", had witnessed numerous deaths in the Dungan community and that the livelihood of many Dungans had also been affected, given that many engage in trade. However, he did not comment on the ethnic riots in Kazakhstan which had led so many Dungans to seek refuge in Kyrgyzstan temporarily. Instead, he affirmed that Dungans in Kyrgyzstan faced no hate and had instead united with other Kyrgyz citizens, helping each other out. The Dungan Association had received aid and had even sent their own aid to the south of Kyrgyzstan and Issyk-Kul region.

Perhaps the difficulty in receiving answers over the phone and the reservation of those who did answer speaks to the challenges of conducting virtual ethnography. While speaking about such sensitive topics, it is important to gain the trust of the informants and it is my feeling that this would have been better achieved had it been possible to conduct the interviews in person. Yet, COVID-19 has restricted not only movement between countries for researchers but also the possibility for meetings within a given country, therefore making on-the-ground fieldwork exceedingly difficult.

Conclusion

Following the Soviet Union's collapse, the Chinese government has become increasingly involved in Kyrgyzstan, with their cooperation expanding over areas including territory, trade, investment and security. Yet, in recent years, attacks against Chinese and China-connected peoples, protests against Chinese companies and the rise of groups such as Kyrk Choro suggest that not everyone in Kyrgyzstan is happy with China's growing influence.

Most research, however, has been concentrated solely on aspects of great power rivalry in Central Asia, ignoring what the citizens themselves

---

[5] In 2000, the group's chairman Nigmat Bazakmat was assassinated, a job that some in the local Uyghur community believe was carried out by Chinese government operatives.

think. This chapter aimed to help fill that gap by exploring how elements of sinophobia have manifested in Kyrgyzstan in response to the coronavirus. Although impossible to definitively measure sinophobia given that no regularly administered surveys exist, this chapter tried to gain an essence of Kyrgyz perceptions through analysis of local news and social media as well as interviews with regional experts and community leaders.

For some, Beijing's successful example in the COVID fight and their aid to Kyrgyzstan will no doubt increase already positive feelings towards China. Yet, as the sinophobic social media stories, the popular culture productions such as *Meken* and the opportunistic attacks against Chinese during the latest revolution arguably highlight, the pandemic has served to reinforce sinophobic sentiment among the segments of the community who had previously espoused anti-Chinese views. As China becomes more involved in Kyrgyzstan, Kyrgyz authorities will have to deal with this potential epidemic of sinophobia on their hands.

Yet, the sinophobia expressed since the pandemic's beginning has been as much a vote of no confidence in the Kyrgyz government itself as it has been in China's activities in the country. Despite being seen by many in the West as the beacon of democracy in Central Asia, Kyrgyz society is permeated by a deep lack of trust in the government. Sinophobia ties into these more general fears of the Kyrgyz government selling out the country and lying to the people, as the events of October 2020 attest.

More work needs to be done to give Kyrgyz citizens a voice and to understand their perspectives, including regular surveys and detailed ethnographic research and interviews. Perhaps, as academics, we are too focused on the "big picture" politics of great power rivalry to notice the sentiments of ordinary citizens. Yet, as the wise old Chinese saying goes, "mosquito legs are also meat"—in other words, individuals have the power to add up and become a great force. The Kyrgyz revolutions of 2005, 2010 and 2020, largely unpredicted by academics and politicians alike, show just how out of touch many of the "expert sphere" are with the common man.

Acknowledgements I would like to thank the scholars and community members who took the time to help with my research. Special thanks goes to Aiperi for assisting with the interviews.

Bibliography

Akayeva, K. (2020, April 3). Fake news on the coronavirus pandemic: What do Central Asians believe in? *CABAR.* https://cabar.asia/en/fake-news-on-the-coronavirus-pandemic-what-do-central-asians-believe-in (page accessed on March 5, 2021).

Billé, F. (2018). Introduction. In F. Billé & S. Urbansky (Eds.), *Yellow perils: China narratives in the contemporary world* (pp. 1–34). University of Hawai'i Press.

Bunin, G. A. (2019, July 4). How Kyrgyzstan abandoned its own in Xinjiang while Kazakhstan didn't. *The Art of Life in Chinese Central Asia.* https://livingotherwise.com/2019/07/04/gene-a-bunin-how-kyrgyzstan-abandoned-its-own-in-xinjiang-while-kazakhstan-didnt/ (page accessed on March 5, 2020).

Burkhanov, A., & Chen, Y. (2016). Kazakh perspective on China, the Chinese, and Chinese migration. *Ethnic and Racial Studies, 39*(12), 2129–2148.

Chen, Y., & Günther, O. (2020). Back to normalization or conflict with China in Greater Central Asia? Evidence from local students' perceptions. *Problems of Post-Communism, 67*(3), 228–240.

factcheck.kg. (2020a, February 4). *The Chinese prime minister prays in a mosque? We investigate* [translation by the author]. https://factcheck.kg/kitajskij-premer-molitsya-v-mecheti-proveryaem/ (page accessed on March 5, 2021).

factcheck.kg. (2020b, May 3). *China earned $20 billion from coronavirus—fake?* [translation by the author]. https://factcheck.kg/kitaj-zarabotal-na-koronaviruse-20-milliardov-dollarov-fejk/ (page accessed on March 5, 2021).

Frayling, C. (2014). *The yellow peril: Dr. Fu Manchu and the rise of Chinaphobia.* Thames and Hudson.

Grozin, A .V. (2019). Sinophobia in Central Asia: From mythology to instrument [translation by the author]. *Russia and China: History and Prospects of Cooperation* [translation by the author]. Conference Proceedings.

Horn, S., Reinhart, C. M., & Trebesch, C. (2019). *China's overseas lending.* National Bureau of Economic Research. Whitepaper.

Imanaliyeva, A. (2020, October 22). Kyrgyzstan: Living in the shadow of a sleeping Chinese oil refinery. *Eurasianet.* https://eurasianet.org/kyrgyzstan-living-in-the-shadow-of-a-sleeping-chinese-oil-refinery (page accessed on October 23, 2020).

Kaktus. (2020, August 4). *Patriotic or Sinophobic? Controversial film "Meken" received mixed reviews* [translation by the author]. https://kaktus.media/doc/418190_patrioticheskiy_ili_sinofobskiy_skandalnyy_film_meken_polychil_neodnoznachnye_otzyvy.html (page accessed on November 7, 2020).

Kulintsev, Y. V., Mukambaev, A. A., Rakhimov, K. K., & Zuenko, I. Yu. (2020). Sinophobia in the post-soviet space: A reaction to expansion or a challenge to integration? *Russia in Global Affairs, 18*(3), 128–151.

Lynteris, C. (2016). The prophetic faculty of epidemic photography: Chinese wet markets and the imagination of the next pandemic. Special issue, Medicine, Photography and Anthropology. *Visual Anthropology, 29*(2), 118–132.

Lynteris, C. (2017). A 'suitable soil': Plague's breeding grounds at the dawn of the third pandemic. *Medical History, 61*(3), 343–357.

Lynteris, C. (2018). Yellow peril epidemics: The political ontology of degeneration and emergence. In F. Billé & S. Urbansky (Eds.), *Yellow perils: China narratives in the contemporary world* (pp. 35–39). University of Hawai'i Press.

Lynteris, C. (2020, June 23). Sinophobia, epidemics, and interspecies catastrophe. *Cultural Anthropology*. https://culanth.org/fieldsights/sinophobia-epidemics-and-interspecies-catastrophe (page accessed on March 3, 2021).

Mayer, R. (2014). *Serial Fu Manchu: The Chinese supervillian and the spread of yellow peril ideology*. Temple University Press.

Meirkhanova, A. (2021, March 30). Perspectives | Beijing's "health silk road" abandons Central Asia. *Eurasianet*. https://eurasianet.org/perspectives-beijings-health-silk-road-abandons-central-asia (page accessed on April 1, 2021).

Ministry of Labour, Migration and Youth of the Kyrgyz Republic. (2014). *Single report on migration in the Kyrgyz Republic* [translation by the author]. http://ssm.gov.kg/wp-content/uploads/2018/01/6085ac55f5312eedfe985ed7b374466d.pdf (page accessed on May 30, 2021).

Moldakhanova, M. (2020, February 13). We will definitely die from an epidemic: But not from the virus [translation by the author]. *Esquire.kz*. https://esquire.kz/m-odnoznatchno-umrem-ot-pidemii-no-ne-ot-virusa/ (page accessed on October 23, 2020).

Owen, C. (2017). 'The sleeping dragon is gathering strength': Causes of sinophobia in Central Asia. *China Quarterly of International Strategic Studies, 3*(1), 101–119.

Owen, C. (2018). Making friends with neighbors?: Local perceptions of Russia and China in Kyrgyzstan. *China Quarterly of International Strategic Studies, 4*(3), 457–480. https://doi.org/10.1142/S2377740018500185

Peyrouse, S. (2007). *Economic aspects of the Chinese-Central Asia rapprochement*. Silk Road Paper, Central Asia-Caucasus Institute Silk Road Studies Program.

Peyrouse, S. (2016). Discussing China: Sinophilia and sinophobia in Central Asia. *Journal of Eurasian Studies, 7*, 14–23.

Rickleton, C. (2011, April 28). Kyrgyzstan: China's economic influence fostering resentment. *Eurasianet*. https://eurasianet.org/kyrgyzstan-chinas-economic-influence-fostering-resentment (page accessed on March 2, 2021).

Rickleton, C. (2020, November 17). Kyrgyzstan's China debt: Between crowdfunding and austerity. *Eurasianet*. https://eurasianet.org/kyrgyzstans-china-debt-between-crowdfunding-and-austerity (page accessed on March 3, 2021).

Said, E. (1978). *Orientalism*. Routledge & Kegan Paul Ltd.

Sorbello, P. (2020, February 11). Violence in Kazakhstan turns deadly for dungans. *Diplomat*. https://thediplomat.com/2020/02/violence-in-kazakhstan-turns-deadly-for-dungans/ (page accessed on October 23, 2020).

Tchen, J. K. W., & Yeats, D. (Eds.). (2014). *Yellow peril! An archive of Anti-Asian fear*. Verso.

Umarov, T. (2021, January 29). *Dangerous liaisons: How China is taming Central Asia's elites*. Carnegie Moscow Center. https://carnegie.ru/commentary/83756 (page accessed on December 15, 2021).

Yau, N. (2020, November 3). China business briefing: Not happy with Kyrgyzstan. *Eurasianet*. https://eurasianet.org/china-business-briefing-not-happy-with-kyrgyzstan (page accessed on November 4, 2021).

Zenz, A. (2019). Brainwashing, police guards and coercive internment: Evidence from Chinese Government documents about the nature and extent of Xinjiang's 'vocational training internment camps'. *Journal of Political Risk, 7*(7).

CHAPTER 5

Anti-Chinese Sentiment, the BRI, and COVID-19: Kazakhstani Perceptions of China in Central Asia

Jessica Neafie

Abstract China's Belt and Road Initiative (BRI) brought commodity-rich Kazakhstan many new economic opportunities and investment projects over the last 7 years, however, the global pandemic may be threatening Kazakhstan's development and its relationship with China. COVID-19 not only reduced Kazakh oil exports to China and put many of the infrastructure projects and investment opportunities from China on hold but exacerbated tensions between the citizens of Kazakhstan and the Chinese. Surveys in 2014 and 2016 found generally positive feelings about the rise of China amongst future elites, but the respondents seemed to have a limited understanding of China's presence in Kazakhstan. During the pandemic, China has been at the forefront of international news as the source of the pandemic and a source for foreign

---

J. Neafie (✉)
Nazarbayev University, Astana, Kazakhstan
e-mail: jessica.neafie@nu.edu.kz

contagion. This study replicates these earlier studies, with new questions related to COVID-19, to find out if perceptions of China are changing in Kazakhstan and the effect that COVID-19 had on those perceptions. The survey was distributed to students around Kazakhstan at the beginning of 2021, with 186 respondents. These surveys show evidence to suggest that perceptions of China are changing, and preliminary evidence that COVID-19 has exacerbated the negative perceptions of China in Central Asia.

Keywords China · FDI · COVID19 · Central Asia · Kazakhstan

Introduction

The COVID-19 pandemic has not only led to mass illness and economic problems but also the rise of stigmatization and prejudice towards particular groups. The pandemic was first detected in China in late 2019 (Zhang et al., 2020), and as states became unable to provide health care and enforce restrictions there was an increase of fear and uncertainty across many populations around the world that colored their perceptions, particularly of China (Nicomedes & Avila, 2020; Penn, 2020; Yoon et al., 2021). During the global pandemic, China's actions have both helped and hurt the way it is perceived. On one hand, as the source of the COVID-19 virus, China may be perceived as a bio-hazard threat. Many Chinese and foreign businesspeople going into other countries were seen as sources of the spread of the virus into those countries (Pantucci, 2020). China was also largely criticized in the international media for its early handling of the disease and unwillingness to work with other countries. Mixed with rising tensions over the handling of Xinjiang, China has been struggling to repair its international brand. On the other hand, China has been sending aid and technology to assist countries, like Kazakhstan, in fighting the pandemic. When its investment into its Belt and Road initiative BRI was flagging due to pandemic related economic declines, China attempted to establish its "Health Silk Road" as a diplomatic tool for easing tensions in investment recipient countries. Understanding the changing nature of local perceptions considering an international pandemic and Beijing's strategic narrative can help states better understand the complexities of public opinion and understand current shifts in the political environment.

Kazakhstan is an important location for surveys on perceptions of China because it is central to the Belt and Road Initiative (BRI) and has not only been affected by the COVID-19 pandemic but has also seen growing apprehension over ethnic Kazakhs in China who are in custody in Xinjiang (RFE/RL's Kazakh Service, 2021b). While Kazakhstani officials continue to maintain friendly relations with China, the Kazakhstani population seems to present more variegated viewpoints, individuals are starting to question political relationships with its great neighbor causing China to struggle to repair its brand in Kazakhstan. China has responded to some of the criticism in Kazakhstan through programs of soft power—such as the Health Silk Road, that includes the sharing of technology, medical personnel, and vaccines in Kazakhstan to alleviate the rising tensions (*Tengrinews*, 2020). Previous surveys (Chen, 2015; Chen & Günther, 2020; Chen & Jiménez-Tovar, 2017) completed in Kazakhstan in 2014 and 2016 show a surging influence of China on locals, and the authors felt that continued Chinese interact with locals through infrastructure projects would embed China even further into the local psyche and improve perceptions over time. However, this was before a global pandemic would reduce Kazakhstani oil exports to China and put many of the infrastructure projects and investment opportunities on hold.

In winter 2021, a survey on perceptions of China was administered at universities throughout Kazakhstan. The survey is based on previous studies performed before COVID-19 on university students in Kazakhstan and allow me to investigate how the local perceptions have changed over time and how world events may be affecting these perceptions. These surveys are designed with questions targeting perceptions of China's influence in Kazakhstan and the wider Asian continent, and the survey I performed in 2021 adds not only another data point to test changes in Chinese sentiment over time but also how the actions of the Chinese during the pandemic have helped or hurt local opinions of China.

BACKGROUND: CHINA AND KAZAKHSTAN

Kazakhstan is a leading player in geopolitical and geoeconomic strategies between China, Russia, and the USA as well as being an important land bridge for the transportation of goods from East Asia to Europe. In terms of economics, Kazakhstan is a central location for transporting goods and resource extraction. For China, using train routes though Kazakhstan can take goods to Europe over 35 days faster than by ship (Furlong & Kupka, 2018). Even before the Belt and Road Initiative (BRI), China has had a long standing economic and security relationship with Kazakhstan, and when many Western countries reduced investment following the 2008 economic crisis, China's investment increased. After the announcement of the BRI in Kazakhstan, China has financed and built a series of infrastructure projects and has further strengthened its trade relationship (Chazan, 2020). This has given commodity-rich Kazakhstan many new opportunities and investment projects. Kazakhstan is also important to security in the region and is seen as a stabilizing force in Central Asia and has been important to the promotion of anti-terrorism and non-proliferation issues. In both economics and security, Kazakhstan has had a growing relationship with China and been increasingly important for China's strategic narrative.

Even before the Belt and Road Initiative (BRI), China has had a long standing economic and security relationship with Kazakhstan. But with the announcement of the BRI project, China poured millions of dollars into Kazakhstan, to build influence through infrastructure and investment, following a geoeconomic approach of "win–win" strategies for China and the recipient countries. Where the Chinese seek to benefit from the vast energy wealth nearby with claims that they will share their wealth and development, while making the global order responsive to the needs of developing countries, like Kazakhstan. The BRI has provided Kazakhstan with new infrastructure investment projects, financing for local businesses, and become a strategic balance for Kazakhstan's relationship with Russia, while China receives access to resources, and increased access and more influence in Central Asia and other countries that Kazakhstan has partnered with. For example, Kazakhstan has strategic partnerships with Europe and Russia that China can capitalize on, and overland train routs that provide China with the means to get goods to Europe faster and cheaper than by sea (Furlong & Kupka, 2018). Additionally the economic relationship between China and Kazakhstan, while imbalanced in terms of total number, is complementary in terms of goods, about 80% of imports to Kazakhstan are finished consumer goods (shoes, appliances, toys, etc.) while 85% of exports to China are raw materials (Chazan, 2020). This relationship has generally favored Kazakhstani elites who have financially benefited from bilateral exchanges and development led by Chinese investment. As a result, many of the elites are taking a more favorable stance on China, as was seen in earlier surveys done in Kazakhstan (Chen, 2015; Chen & Günther, 2020; Chen & Jiménez-Tovar, 2017).

While government has maintained amiable relations with China, the public opinion of China in Kazakhstan has become increasingly more strained in which locals feel threatened by the Chinese presence, and find them unreliable (Plakhina, 2021). Just before the COVID-19 pandemic caused economic problems worldwide, the Chinese BRI projects were already flagging, and Kazakhstani citizens are concerned about the ramifications of Chinese presence and influence in Kazakhstan. Their concerns are based on a fear of Chinese land grabs, a perceived lack of transparency or accountability for Chinese investment projects in Kazakhstan and a growing apprehension over ethnic Kazakhs who they believe are in custody in Xinjiang (RFE/RL's Kazakh Service, 2021b). Fear of China acquiring Kazakh land goes back to the secession of land in the late 1990s, when critics of a disputed territory agreement with Kazakhstan, condemned a decision by the Kazakhstani government to give up 43.1% of the contested territory that had considered to be Kazakhstan's land (Pannier, 2016). These tensions flared up again 20 years later, when, in 2016, protests spread across Kazakhstan to object to changes in the Kazakhstani Land Code, in which the government was going to allow the rent of unused agriculture land by foreigners to increase from 10 to 25 years (Putz, 2021). Protestors fear giving land to the Chinese, because, as one protestor stated "If they come they won't leave" (Abdurasulov, 2016). This fear is built around the idea that China is going to expand into Kazakhstan and come for their farmland, their companies, and their jobs.

At the government level rhetoric from Kazakhstani officials demonstrated how the BRI has matched up with Kazakh development, but locals see the increasing debt that is growing with their neighbor, a lack of transparency, and local workers fear China ruining the local labor economy (Jardine, 2019; Plakhina, 2021; Vidyanova, 2020). The locals believe that Chinese companies are coming in and taking advantage of Kazakhstan, hiring very few locals and when they do hire locals paying them less than foreign workers (Reuters Staff, 2019b). A 2021 protest of the investment in the construction of 56 Chinese factories in Kazakhstan, is being protested for this reason, as locals believe it will be built mostly by Chinese workers who "will settle in Kazakhstan" (Shaku, 2021). They believe that land grabs mixed with these investment plans exist so that China may claim economic control over Kazakhstan. Chinese investment projects are also associated with environmental pollution (Shaku, 2021) and local government scandals, such as the Astana Light Rail project (Koskina, 2019), that have a negative effect on the way that that locals see these projects.

A fear of China also exists in Kazakhstan because of the internment-camp system targeting its Muslim population, that includes ethnic Kazakhs (Standish, 2019). Kazakhs protest at Chinese consulates in Kazakhstan saying that they have relatives that are missing, jailed, or detained by China's crackdown (Standish & Toleukhanova, 2021), and as these stories increase, there is a strengthening of anti-Chinese sentiment in Kazakhstan. This anti-Chinese sentiment has led to increased criticism of the Kazakhstani government's growing ties to Beijing, and the growing detainment of anti-Chinese protestors is creating concerns that China has too much power over the local government (Reuters Staff, 2019a).

During the COVID-19 pandemic, as oil demand from China decreased, and China's shrinking economy led to a 54% reduction of investment in 2020, affecting over 50% of BRI projects, citizens of Kazakhstan became even more concerned for the country's economic reliance on China (*Business Standard*, 2021; Rapoza, 2020). Because countries started to feel like they could no longer rely on Chinese support, China responded to the pandemic and apprehension from international governments, like Kazakhstan's, with the "Health Silk Road" initiative (*Tengrinews*, 2020). The goals of this project were two-fold: to set up a cooperative to fight the pandemic but also to continue Chinese influence along the BRI in spite of loses due to economic decline (Xinhua, 2020). However, there is not much evidence that this "Health Silk Road" initiative has had any effect on the thinking of locals. While the government continues to back China, individuals are questioning Kazakhstan's reliance on China as a source of COVID-19 relief (Meirkhanova, 2021).

Research Design and Methodology

This survey instrument is modified from earlier surveys in Kazakhstan to include questions relevant to COVID-19 (Chen, 2015; Chen & Günther, 2020; Chen & Jiménez-Tovar, 2017) and based on the Asian Barometer and Afro barometer surveys. These are both well-known large-scale survey projects that investigate public opinions about politics in Africa and East and Southeast Asia. Using a similar survey instrument, I am able to have a systematic basis of comparison to early studies done by

Chen, Jimenez-Tovar, and Gunther, to see how opinions of university students in Kazakhstan have changed overtime. I use the same questions for the first part of the survey given to a similar survey sample (university students in Kazakhstan), those questions are analyzed using the results from the original surveys, but I also add additional questions to the survey pertaining to COVID-19 that will allow me answer questions about the impact this event has had on China's presence in Kazakhstan. My surveys contain a larger sample of students from universities in Kazakhstan compared to the original surveys.

The survey was given to students in January to March 2021. Because Kazakhstan was still under COVID restrictions, there were limitations in the ability to distribute the survey. All survey respondents were recruited through university emails listservs, and were asked to complete the survey using Qualtrics, an online survey system. Measures were instituted to prevent respondents from making duplicate responses.

The study of university students allows us to consider the opinions of potential elites. Chen and Jiménez-Tovar (2017) identify university students as a group of at least a middle-class background with family and relatives who may be political, business, or intellectual elites as they have access to higher education. These potential elites are important to study because they have more capacity to affect sociopolitical change that would direct Kazakhstan's future developments. They were also much easier to conduct surveys with during a pandemic as they can be easily communicated with through academic networks.

This questionnaire was prepared in both Russian and English and contained 22 questions and, due to the COVID-19 pandemic, was only available online. In the winter of 2021, the survey was distributed to university students throughout Kazakhstan though scholarly networks at universities throughout the country, including Nazarbayev University, Al Farabi Kazakh National University, Astana IT University, Kazguu University, Satbayev Kazakh National Technical University, Kimep University, and International IT University. In addition to demographic questions (e.g., citizenship, age, gender), the respondents were asked about their perception of influence by select counties that have been active in the regional politics of Asia (e.g., Russia, United States [US], China, Japan) as well as a better understanding of their views of China and how those views may have changed due to the COVID-19 pandemic. While this short survey, only 22 questions, may not provide a completely comprehensive understanding of the respondents' opinions of China, given the difficulty of distribution and time individuals are willing to commit to these types of surveys, but it should be able to increase the understanding about how individuals' views may be changing since the original surveys were done in 2014 and 2016 and what effect, if any, COVID-19 may have had.

The survey respondents identified as undergraduate (67.7%, 126 respondents) or graduate students (32.3%, 60 respondents) at universities in Kazakhstan. Of the survey respondents, 33.9% (63 respondents) are younger than 20 years old, 58.6% (109 respondents) are in their 20s, 6% (11 respondents) are older than 30, and 2 respondents did not reply. Of these, 80% are between 17 and 22 years old. 98.4% of the respondents are Kazakhstani citizens, and most of the respondents identified as Kazakhs (90.9%, 169 respondents), with only 3% identifying as Russian or Russian mixed, and the other 6.1% identifying as mixed or of another ethnicity. This survey is skewed in terms of gender, I received responses from 126 self-identifying females (67.7%) and 60 self-identifying males (32.3%). However, this aligns with Asian Development Bank statistics on female university enrollment in Kazakhstan (Asian Development Bank, 2018).

What Country Has the Most Influence in Asia?

The 2021 survey results maintain some of the findings from the earlier studies, see Table 5.1. China is still seen by most respondents as having the most influence in Asia. Not unusual given Chinese growing presence in the region due to the BRI and proximity of Kazakhstan to China. However, 2021 marked the first-time respondents of the survey started to see the influence of China wane over time in the region and see the potential of other countries to have more influence in Asia over the next ten years. This may be influenced by the effects of COVID-19, which due to economic declines in the region, has led the Chinese to pull back on their investments in Asia (*How China's Flagship Belt & Road Project Stalled Out*, 2021). This means that more respondents are seeing the potential for instability in Chinese influence moving forward, and that they are expecting to see some amount of change in relationships on the continent.

In the earlier surveys, respondents' attention was limited to Russia and China, but in the 2021 survey there is an increase in awareness of the US and Japan in Kazakhstan. The largest difference seems to be in

Table 5.1 Which country do you think has the greatest influence in Asia?

	2014		2016		2021	
	Now	In 10 years	Now	In 10 years	Now	In 10 years
Japan	1 (1.2%)	4 (4.7%)	2 (2.7%)	6 (8.2%)	9 (4.8%)	31 (16.7%)
China	65 (75.6%)	72 (83.7%)	48 (65.8%)	49 (67.1%)	125 (67%)	111 (59.7%)
India	0 (0%)	1 (1.2%)	2 (2.7%)	0 (0%)	0 (0%)	4 (2.2%)
Russia	17 (19.8%)	2 (2.3%)	14 (19.2%)	12 (16.4%)	23 (12.4%)	7 (3.8%)
USA	3 (3.5%)	0 (0%)	6 (8.2%)	5 (5.5%)	24 (12.9%)	21 (11.3%)
South Korea	0 (0%)	0 (0%)	0 (0%)	1 (1.4%)	1 (0.5%)	2 (1.1%)
Saudi Arabia	0 (0%)	0 (0%)	1 (1.4%)	1 (1.4%)	0 (0%)	0 (0%)
Singapore	0 (0%)	0 (0%)	0 (0%)	0 (0%)	0 (0%)	1 (0.5%)
Kazakhstan	0 (0%)	2 (2.3%)	0 (0%)	0 (0%)	0 (0%)	0 (0%)
No response	0 (0%)	5 (5.8%)	0 (0%)	0 (0%)	4 (2.2%)	8 (4.3%)
Total (N)	86	86	73	73	186	186

Source The 2014 and 2016 surveys are sourced from Julie Yu-Wen Chen (2015) and Julie Yu-Wen Chen and Soledad Jiménez-Tovar (2017); and the 2021 surveys were compiled by the author

the number of respondents that consider the US to have a greater influence in Asia. This is unsurprising, following the initial investments by the Chinese into the Central Asian region under the BRI, the United States shifted its interest in the region leading to visits by US officials (Associated Press, 2020; Tleuberdi, 2020) and increased economic and social ties to counter Chinese influence in the region (*How China's Flagship Belt & Road Project Stalled Out*, 2021; Ospanova, 2021). This has made the US more visible in Kazakhstan compared to 2014 and 2016.

There are also a large number of respondents in 2021 who see a rise in influence from Japan and other Asian countries over the next 10 years. In the past surveys, there were only a couple respondents who identified Japan as the most influential, and in every survey more respondents saw Japan having more importance in 10 years. In the 2021 survey, there was a further shift of participants, showing a trend of more respondents seeing

Japan as important now and into the future. In the 2021 survey, as more respondents say Japan being more influential in 10 years, for the first time in the surveys the number of respondents who thought China would be the most influential in ten years decreased. These may be individuals that believe China has wavering influence over Asia, and that other countries, like Japan, are possible replacements. There were also respondents that expected India to have more influence in Asia in the future compared to earlier surveys. These survey results show a marginal change in Kazakhstani respondent perceptions of India and Japan as compared to 2014 and 2016.

CHINA'S INFLUENCE IN ASIA AND KAZAKHSTAN

Overall, the respondents' feelings of China have also gotten more negative over time. The earlier surveys both show generally positive views of China, with few respondents seeing China as harmful to either Asia or Kazakhstan, see Tables 5.2 and 5.3. According to the 2021 survey, Kazakhstani respondents have had less welcoming attitudes to Chinese influence. In 2014, less than 10% of respondents thought that China had a more harmful influence on Asia and in both 2014 and 2016, more than 80% of respondents saw China as being more beneficial to Asia, Table 5.2. By 2021, the number of respondents who saw China as more harmful than beneficial was almost 50%. Similarly, almost all respondents saw China as at least a somewhat positive influence in Kazakhstan in 2014, Table 5.3, but by 2021 over 35% of respondents saw China as a negative influence in the country.

Table 5.2 Does China bring more benefit or harm to Asia?

	2014	*2016*	*2021*
Considerably more benefit than harm	24 (27.9%)	14 (19.2%)	14 (7.5%)
Somewhat more benefit than harm	49 (57%)	46 (63%)	71 (38.2%)
Somewhat more harm than benefit	8 (9.3%)	12 (16.4%)	64 (34.4%)
Considerably more harm than benefit	0 (0%)	1 (1.4%)	28 (15.1%)
No response	5 (5.8%)	0 (0%)	9 (5%)
Total (N)	86	73	186

Source The 2014 and 2016 surveys are sourced from Julie Yu-Wen Chen (2015) and Julie Yu-Wen Chen and Soledad Jiménez-Tovar (2017); and the 2021 surveys were compiled by the author

Table 5.3 In general, does China have a positive or negative influence on Kazakhstan?

	2014	2021
Very positive	5 (5.8%)	4 (2.2%)
Positive	27 (31.4%)	14 (7.5%)
Somewhat positive	50 (58.1%)	86 (46.2%)
Negative	4 (4.7%)	60 (32.3%)
Very negative	0 (0%)	10 (5.4%)
No response	0 (0%)	12 (6.5%)
Total (*N*)	86	186

Source The 2014 surveys are sourced from Julie Yu-Wen Chen (2015); and the 2021 surveys were compiled by the author

In 2014 and 2016, a large majority of respondents believed that China's influence was positive, and at that time many other surveys around the world also perceived Chinese influence as positive (Chen & Günther, 2020). This did not mean that China did not face criticism, particularly in Kazakhstan where citizens voiced early concerns about Chinese companies and the local labor market, environmental impacts, and a lack of transparency in the government dealings with China. However, the protests over perceived Chinese land grabs and economic influence, and an increase of hostility in Xinjiang that includes ethnic Kazakhs has laid a foundation for rising Sinophobia. In the past year these incidences have even been linked to the COVID-19 pandemic, during which existing tensions have been exacerbated and more individuals' perceptions are being affected.

China, COVID-19, and Kazakhstan

It was only in the 2021 survey that respondents begin to shift their views of the future away from China, showing that local perceptions have changed since the 2016 and 2014 surveys (Chen, 2015; Chen & Jiménez-Tovar, 2017). It is not remiss to suggest that these changing perceptions of the future may be driven by recent world political events, since previous tensions that existed had not had a significant effect on the respondents in these earlier studies and that those events have been intensified by COVID-19 rumors and connections to China. Shifts in Kazakhstani behavior toward the Chinese were seen when COVID-19 first appeared, and as numbers started to rise in Kazakhstan, many local media sources referred to the disease as the "Chinese disease" and led to a growing concern that Chinese citizens in Kazakhstan were carrying the disease. Reports of Sinophobic incidents started to appear across the country in relation to the pandemic, and one verified report described how two Chinese citizens were removed from a train (Sarachakova & Ilyasov, 2020). The train was stopped in Shu, southern Kazakhstan, when rumors of the virus being on the train were made online, the Chinese citizens were removed from the train and taken to an infectious disease hospital to be checked but were found to be "absolutely health" (Sarachakova & Ilyasov, 2020). Incidents like these show how Chinese citizens in Kazakhstan were being linked to COVID-19 and fear of Chinese citizens as sources of the disease were prevalent.

As COVID-19 began to play a larger role in Kazakhstan, perceptions of China were also negatively affected by two media reports originating in China. First, a Chinese propaganda media site began running a story that Kazakhstani citizens wanted Kazakhstan to become a part of China. This article also leveled criticism at the Kazakhstani government that was "counter to the spirit of permanent comprehensive strategic partnership" according to the Kazakhstani ministry (Reuters Staff, 2020b). Because China is a major investor in Kazakhstan's primary industries and agriculture sector, where some already feared Chinese land grabs, claims of China reclaiming the territory were not viewed favorably by citizens. Then in the following month, a news source in China reported a misleading story about Kazakhstan, claiming that labs in Kazakhstan were part of a US Department of Defense funded program studying Coronavirus in bats (MKRU, 2020; Sheng, 2020). This media story even spread to Russia and reported that Kazakhstan may have been the source of the original outbreak not China. This affected views of China as a credible source of information to Kazakhstani citizens and may have played a role in diminishing their views of China as a reliable leader for Asia. These stories were not taken well in Kazakhstan by either the locals or the government and led many locals to question the Kazakhstan-China relationship.

China responded to the criticism in Kazakhstan, and elsewhere, through a soft power program—the Health Silk Road—that includes the sharing of technology, medical personnel, and vaccines in BRI countries to alleviate the rising tensions (*Tengrinews*, 2020). The Health Silk Road is a diplomatic tool that is designed to help China's strategic narrative when the BRI is not doing as well to aid China in improving a poor international image. However, this strategy has hit two major issues historical lack of credibility and reliability of Chinese help and the poor media coverage, as well as China's own strategic narratives have played a part in preventing this strategy from making any real impact in Kazakhstan.

The Health Silk Road, while helpful in providing aid to Kazakhstan, started creating additional tension with the locals when the Chinese doctors that came to help began publicly criticizing the Kazakhstani doctors and the infection rates in Kazakhstan, and allowed China to shift the public eye away from themselves (Hashimova, 2020). This situate further escalated when the Chinese embassy announced to Chinese citizens that they must guard against an outbreak of pneumonia more severe than COVID-19, and provoking fear of Kazakhstan (Reuters Staff, 2020a). It has been incidences such as these which have led Kazakhstani locals to start questioning whether China is the best to help them in times in need. Local populations do not see China's claims to help them during the crisis as reliable or credible, and many of these individuals still believing that the Russian vaccine is better and that Russia is a more reliable and trustworthy ally (Central Asia Barometer, 2021; Meirkhanova, 2021). The growing anti-Chinese sentiment was also apparent when the announcement by the Kazakhstani government that it had acquired the Chinese vaccine in March of 2021 led to Anti-Chinese protests in towns and cities across Kazakhstan (Asylbek, 2021; RFE/RL's Kazakh Service, 2021a). While not the only reason for the increased anti-Chinese sentiment in Kazakhstan, the events surrounding COVID-19 are certainly not helping the Chinese case.

The Health Silk Road initiative was supposed to be a diplomatic tool that could help China strategically when the BRI was not doing as well. Unfortunately, this has not been successful as a soft power strategy; when asked, 55% of respondents had never heard of the "Health Silk Road", and another 20% were not sure, see Table 5.4. Given that these are going to be more educated individuals who are more connected to other elites

Table 5.4 Have you heard of the "Health Silk Road"?

	2021
Yes	31 (16.7%)
Not sure	38 (20.4%)
No	103 (55.4%)
No response	14 (7.5%)
Total (*N*)	186

Source Compiled by the author

the low number of respondents knowing about the initiative does not bode well for China's social outreach. This is not unusual for locals to be generally unaware of Chinese initiatives. There are still many respondents who have not heard of the BRI as well, see Table 5.5. The number of respondents who have heard of the BRI has risen from 32 to 46%, but that still leaves a majority being at least vaguely unaware of what the BRI is. Previous studies have linked this phenomenon to the news in Kazakhstan, which often omits much about the BRI and provides only general information about China (Burkhanov & Chen, 2016).

The Chinese efforts in the country have not all been ignored, and many respondents found that China has been neutrally somewhat helpful to Kazakhstan during the COVID-19 pandemic, Table 5.6. This shows that despite not knowing about the Health Silk Road initiative the respondents are at least generally aware enough of Chinese activities in the state to not see them as unhelpful. This is also obvious when looking at the question on investment, in which in both the 2016 survey (Chen & Jiménez-Tovar,

Table 5.5 Have you heard of the Belt and Road Initiative?

	2016	2021
Yes	23 (31.5%)	85 (45.7%)
Not sure	6 (8.2%)	38 (20.4%)
No	44 (60.3%)	51 (27.4%)
No response	0 (0.0%)	12 (6.5%)
Total (N)	73	186

Source The 2016 surveys are sourced from Julie Yu-Wen Chen and Soledad Jiménez-Tovar (2017); and the 2021 surveys were compiled by the author

Table 5.6 During COVID-19, how helpful has China been in Kazakhstan?

	2021
Very helpful	8 (4.3%)
Somewhat helpful	103 (55.4%)
Not helpful	40 (21.5%)
Made things worse	9 (4.8%)
Made things much worse	11 (5.9%)
No response	15 (8.1%)
Total (N)	186

Source Compiled by the author

Table 5.7 Generally speaking, COVID-19 has made the relationship of China and Kazakhstan?

	2021
Much better	2 (1.1%)
Better	13 (7%)
About the same	124 (66.7%)
Worse	28 (15.1%)
Much worse	5 (2.7%)
No response	14 (7.5%)
Total (*N*)	186

Source Compiled by the author

2017) and the 2021 survey a high number of respondents were aware of Chinese investment (around 70% in both cases), despite not as many of them being aware of the BRI initiative. This does mean that individuals in Kazakhstan are recognizing Chinese efforts to help Kazakhstan, and this may be one reason why despite largely negative feelings about China in Asia many individuals think that China's influence in Kazakhstan is at least somewhat positive.

Many of the respondents may have seen China as at least somewhat helpful during the pandemic, but many of them did not believe that these actions changed the relationship between China and Kazakhstan for the better or worse, see Table 5.7. Most respondents thought that the relationship between China and Kazakhstan remained the same. In many ways this is not an unusual finding, despite protests and the negative feelings of the public, the relationship between the Kazakhstani government and Beijing has not changed that much. The respondents to the survey see that the Kazakhstani political establishment continues to publicize the official pro-China discourse, because despite growing dissatisfaction by the populace (RFE/RL's Kazakh Service, 2021a), the elites believe further engagement, such as the trade of oil and increased infrastructure investment, with China is needed to grow the Kazakhstani economy as the economy opens back up after COVID-19.

Conclusion

Attitudes toward China are based on the experience that individuals accumulate over time and through various interactions. Public disposition toward China has been influenced, at least marginally, by the COVID-19 pandemic. Because these interactions have been mostly negative, China has lost the good will it had in Kazakhstan. Evidence shows that locals do not trust China as a source of aid during the COVID-19 pandemic and their general perceptions of China are declining. This is being driven by some incidents related to COVID-19, such as closed railway borders and disappearing infrastructure projects, and other issues, such as economic transparency, foreign landownership, and growing tensions over ethnic Kazakhs being held in Xinjiang. The pandemic not only created new areas of tension between China and Kazakhstan but increased the tensions in other areas that have shaped and changed the Kazakh perceptions of China.

The findings from this survey not only show how Kazakhstani perceptions of China are changing over time, but also give some insight into how the COVID-19 pandemic may trigger escalating anti-Chinese sentiment. The series of surveys since 2014 suggest that perceptions of China are becoming more unfavorable over time in Kazakhstan, and that while China has tried to use soft power strategies to gain favorable public opinion, including most recently the Health Silk Road narrative, these attempts have largely failed. The changing perceptions of China in Kazakhstan are of particular concern to both the national government and Beijing.

The Kazakhstani government may need to be concerned with the changing perceptions in Kazakhstan moving forward. It sees Chinese support as essential in a post-pandemic economy in order to develop, but the government also needs the support of the public to legitimize its rule and the choices that it makes. The government seems to be keenly aware of the public's interests in China and is sending signals that the views of the public do, at least minimally, matter for the future relations between Kazakhstan and China. This was evident when the government tabled the bill that would have eased foreign land rental restrictions after mass protest (Plakhina, 2021). The government even sanctioned anti-Chinese protests in March 2021, in a country where public demonstrations are restricted—a concession by the Kazakhstani government to the changing perceptions and a tool for keeping China in check (Plakhina, 2021).

The authoritarian government is motivated by maintaining control and order domestically, and the growing number of Anti-Chinese protests driven by increasing negative perceptions of Chinese domestic involvement could challenge regime legitimacy. Kazakhstani elites largely rely on neopatrimonialism in their political affairs and shifts in public perceptions may make it harder to maintain some relationships in the social hierarchy as more individuals see China as less credible and reliable for helping Kazakhstan (Tipaldou, 2021). Rising oppositional politics may continue to grow as nationalism incentivizes citizens to defend Kazakhstan against Chinese interference and may provoke public demonstrations (Plakhina, 2021). These surveys show some evidence to suggest that increased oppositional political forces are possible since anti-Chinese sentiment is growing amongst younger elite groups (e.g., university students) which will in turn affect the neopatrimonial ties and the future political establishment, even if some of them change their minds when they occupy these positions of power. But social concerns about Kazakhstan's China approach are warranted, as the delicate nature of Kazakhstan's multi-vector foreign policy pushes the government to not want to disturb the balance with China (Pannier, 2011; Rachel et al., 2020; Stallard-Blanchette, 2020). The government wants to avoid any conflict with China that would force it to give up its economic relationship or the strategic advantage that allows Kazakhstan to balance its foreign policy across many important players.

China needs to be aware of the perceptions of its rise abroad and be concerned about mounting anti-Chinese sentiment despite heavy investment in soft power strategies (*Soft Power 30: Global Ranking of Soft Power*, 2019). The university students who took this survey are the future elites of Kazakhstan and will one day be directing Kazakhstani development. The responses given in this survey seem to suggest that these individuals are not optimistic about the role of Chinese initiatives, such as the BRI, in Kazakhstan or the role of China in Asia into the future. While China has pushed its outward investment strategies as a win–win scenario for all countries, and not an attempt to establish China's own sphere of influence, this may not be apparent to the audience China hopes to reach. The number of respondents that see the Chinese involvement as harmful to Asia and harmful to Kazakhstan is growing, which means that the Chinese soft power initiatives, like the Health Silk Road, are not reaching target audiences, and even when they are seeing Chinese aid during important events, like COVID-19, it is not swaying these individuals to see Chinese influence in a more positive light.

China must also be concerned that this trend of anti-Chinese sentiment in Kazakhstan may be indicative of changing perceptions in other countries in Central Asia. Central Asian countries have different opinions on the region's relationship with China, for example, in 2016 surveys,

Kyrgyzstan perceived China as more harmful to Central Asia, but Uzbekistan saw China as more beneficial to the region, and these findings can be linked to perceptions of the nation-state and knowledge of Chinese investment (Chen & Günther, 2020; Chen & Jiménez-Tovar, 2017). If Chinese investment in the region continues to grow, as it is expected to, Beijing should fear continued negative media exposure both as an investor and as an ally in times of crisis, like a pandemic, as its ability to expand its economic, political, and cultural influence in these countries is dependent on whether it can win over the populations and the future elites of these nations. Future surveys will explore these nations to see how views may have shifted comparatively across the region. General trends could be problematic for China as a rising power, especially if it wants to establish itself as an actual influence in global politics. China needs to work to improve its public diplomacy efforts and to increase the visibility of its initiatives beyond just the political elites in countries like Kazakhstan.

Bibliography

Abdurasulov, A. (2016, April 28). Kazakhstan's land reform protests explained. *BBC News*. https://www.bbc.com/news/world-asia-36163103. Accessed 10 June 2021.

Asian Development Bank. (2018). *Kazakhstan country gender assessment*. Manila, Philippines. https://doi.org/10.22617/TCS179181

Associated Press. (2020, February 1). Pompeo message in Europe, Central Asia trip: Beware of China. *VOA News*. https://www.voanews.com/usa/pompeo-message-europe-central-asia-trip-beware-china

Asylbek. (2021, March 27). The Ministry of Health announced the supply of a Chinese vaccine to Kazakhstan. *Radio Azattyq*.

Burkhanov, A., & Chen, Y. W. (2016). Kazakh perspective on China, the Chinese, and Chinese migration. *Ethnic and Racial Studies, 39*(12), 2129–2148. https://doi.org/10.1080/01419870.2016.1139155

Business Standard. (2021, March 14). One Belt One Road project stalls as China's economy fights out Covid-19. https://www.business-standard.com/article/international/one-belt-one-road-project-stalls-as-china-s-economy-fights-out-covid-19-121031400951_1.html

Central Asia Barometer. (2021, February 2). Where the Central Asians expect the aid coming from in order to handle the COVID-19 crisis? *Central Asian Barometer*.

Chazan, Y. (2020, January 24). China BRI ventures run into trouble in Kazakhstan. *Asia Sentinel*. https://www.asiasentinel.com/p/china-bri-ventures-run-into-trouble

Chen, Y. W. (2015). A research note on Central Asian perspectives on the rise of China: The example of Kazakhstan. *Issues and Studies, 51*(3), 63–87.

Chen, Y. W., & Günther, O. (2020). Back to normalization or conflict with China in greater Central Asia? Evidence from local students' perceptions. *Problems of Post-Communism. Routledge, 67*(3), 228–240. https://doi.org/10.1080/10758216.2018.1474716

Chen, Y. W., & Jiménez-Tovar, S. (2017). China in Central Asia*: Local perceptions from future elites. *China Quarterly of International Strategic Studies, 3*(3), 429–445. https://doi.org/10.1142/S2377740017500178

Furlong, R., & Kupka, R. (2018, January 18). In a desert far away, China opens a gateway on its new Silk Road. *Current Time TV.* Available at: https://www.rferl.org/a/kazakhstan-new-silk-road-china-exports-gamble/28970736.html

Hashimova, U. (2020, August 3). China changes diplomatic styles in Central Asia over COVID-19. *The Diplomat.*

How China's Flagship Belt and Road Project Stalled Out. (2021). Bloomberg. https://www.bloomberg.com/news/videos/2021-01-14/how-china-s-flagship-belt-and-road-project-stalled-out-video

Jardine, B. (2019). Why Kazakhs push back against Chinese factories. *The Washington Post,* October 16. https://www.washingtonpost.com/politics/2019/10/16/why-are-there-anti-china-protests-central-asia/. Accessed 16 June 2021.

Koskina, A. (2019, December). Astana LRT: A project or a scam? *CABAR.* https://cabar.asia/en/astana-lrt-a-project-or-a-scam

Meirkhanova, A. (2021, March 30). Perspectives: Beijing's "Health Silk Road" abandons Central Asia. *Eurasianet.* https://eurasianet.org/perspectives-beijings-health-silk-road-abandons-central-asia

MKRU. (2020, May 5). The Pentagon has surrounded Russia with a belt of secret biolaboratories. *MKRU.* https://www.mk.ru/politics/2020/05/05/pentagon-okruzhil-rossiyu-poyasom-sekretnykh-biolaboratoriy.html

Nicomedes, C. J. C., & Avila, R. M. A. (2020). An analysis on the panic during COVID-19 pandemic through an online form. *Journal of Affective Disorders, 276,* 14–22. https://doi.org/10.1016/j.jad.2020.06.046

Ospanova, A. (2021, January 12). US pledges to help develop Kazakhstan's private sector through investment partnership. *Caspian News.* https://caspiannnews.com/news-detail/us-pledges-to-help-develop-kazakhstans-private-sector-through-investment-partnership-2021-1-11-31/

Pannier, B. (2011, February 23). Kazakh president energized after China trip. *Radio Free Europe.*

Pannier, B. (2016, May 2). Central Asian land and China. *Radio Free Europe.* https://www.rferl.org/a/central-asian-land-and-china/27711366.html. Accessed 16 June 2021.

Pantucci, R. (2020, June 19). Beijing binds: COVID-19 and the China–Central Asia relationship. *Central Asia Program.* https://www.centralasiaprogram.org/archives/16339

Penn, M. (2020). Poll shows fear of covid-19 reaching panic levels. *Real Clear Politics.*

Plakhina, Y. (2021, June 15). How Sinophobia is instrumentalized in Kazakhstan as a form of oppositional politics. *Global Voices.* https://globalvoices.org/2021/06/15/how-sinophobia-is-instrumentalized-in-kazakhstan-as-a-form-of-oppositional-politics/. Accessed 16 June 2021.

Putz, C. (2021, April 26). Kazakhstan moves toward ban on sale, rental of agricultural lands by foreigners. *The Diplomat.* https://thediplomat.com/2021/04/kazakhstan-moves-toward-ban-on-sale-rental-of-agricultural-lands-by-foreigners/. Accessed 16 June 2021.

Rachel, V., Sandra, F. J., & Roza, T. (2020). Between the bear and the dragon: Multivectorism in Kazakhstan as a model strategy for secondary powers. *International Affairs, 96*(4), 975–993. https://doi.org/10.1093/ia/iiaa061

Rapoza, K. (2020, May 4). When oil is down, and China is down, Kazakhstan has only one bright spot left. *Forbes.*

Reuters Staff. (2019a, September 21). Dozens detained in Kazakhstan at anti-China protests. *Reuters.* https://www.reuters.com/article/us-kazakhstan-china-protests-detentions/dozens-detained-in-kazakhstan-at-anti-china-protests-idUSKBN1W60CS

Reuters Staff. (2019b, September 4). Dozens protest against Chinese influence in Kazakhstan. *Reuters.* https://www.reuters.com/article/us-kazakhstan-china-protests/dozens-protest-against-chinese-influence-in-kazakhstan-idUSKCN1VP1B0. Accessed 16 June 2021.

Reuters Staff. (2020a, July 10). Kazakhstan denies Chinese reports of pneumonia deadlier than coronavirus. *Reuters.* Available at: https://www.reuters.com/article/us-health-coronavirus-kazakhstan-pneumon/kazakhstan-denies-chinese-reports-of-pneumonia-deadlier-than-coronavirus-idUSKBN24B0XR. Accessed 15 June 2021.

Reuters Staff. (2020b, April 14). Kazakhstan summons Chinese ambassador in protest over article. *Reuters.*

RFE/RL's Kazakh Service. (2021a, March 27). Anti-China protests staged across Kazakhstan. *Radio Free Europe.*

RFE/RL's Kazakh Service. (2021b, March 12). Nur-Sultan wants China "To help resolve issues" raised by ethnic Kazakhs from Xinjiang. *Radio Free Europe.*

Sarachakova, J., & Ilyasov, R. (2020, January 29). Two Chinese citizens suspected of coronavirus removed from train in Shu. *Tengrinews.* https://tengrinews.kz/kazakhstan_news/dvuh-grajdan-kitaya-podozreniem-koronavirus-snyali-poezda-389983/

Shaku, K. (2021). *Kazakhs' loathing of encroaching China rises as Lake Balkhash falls*, bne *IntelliNews*. https://www.intellinews.com/central-asia-blog-kazakhs-loathing-of-encroaching-china-rises-as-lake-balkhash-falls-209664/. Accessed 16 June 2021.

Sheng, Y. (2020, May 14). China, Russia can initiate probe of US bio-labs. *Global Times*. https://www.globaltimes.cn/content/1188405.shtml

Soft Power 30: Global Ranking of Soft Power. (2019). New York. https://softpower30.com/

Stallard-Blanchette, K. (2020). The coming US–China competition in Central Asia. *The Diplomat*. https://thediplomat.com/2020/02/the-coming-us-china-competition-in-central-asia/

Standish, R. (2019, October). China's path forward is getting bumpy. *The Atlantic*. https://www.theatlantic.com/international/archive/2019/10/china-belt-road-initiative-problems-kazakhstan/597853/

Standish, R., & Toleukhanova, A. (2021, April 4). Kazakh activism against China's internment camps is broken, but not dead. *Radio Free Europe*. https://www.rferl.org/a/kazakhstan-protests-china-xinjiang-rights-abuses/31186209.html. Accessed 16 June 2021.

Tengrinews. (2020, September 18). China will build a health community with Kazakhstan.

Tipaldou, S. (2021). Kazakhstan 2.0: Change and continuity? In F. Izquierdo-Brichs & F. Serra-Massansalvador (Eds.), *Political regimes and neopatrimonialism in Central Asia*. Palgrave Macmillan. https://doi.org/10.1007/978-981-15-9093-1

Tleuberdi, M. (2020). Pompeo urges Kazakhstan to pressure China over Muslims in Xinjiang (pp. 8–10).

Vidyanova, A. (2020, November 3). На одного казахстанца приходится $3,1 тысячи внешнего долга. *Capital (Капитал)*. https://kapital.kz/finance/90926/na-odnogo-kazakhstantsa-prikhodit-sya-3-1-tysyachi-vneshnego-dolga.html. Accessed 16 June 2021.

Xinhua. (2020, September 17). China to build community of health for all with Russia, Kazakhstan, Kyrgyzstan, Mongolia. *Xinhua*.

Yoon, M. S., Feyissa, I. F., & Suk, S.-W. (2021). Panic and trust during COVID-19: A cross-sectional study on immigrants in South Korea. *Healthcare (Basel)*, *9*(2), 199.

Zhang, R., Li, Y., Zhang, A. L., Wang, Y., & Molina, M. J. (2020). Identifying airborne transmission as the dominant route for the spread of COVID-19. *Proceedings of the National Academy of Sciences of the United States of America*, *117*(26), 14857–14863. https://doi.org/10.1073/pnas.2009637117

CHAPTER 6

Contamination, Cohesion and Coercion: Essay on the COVID-19 Pandemic and the Revolution in Kyrgyzstan (2020–2021)

Julien Bruley and Iliias Mamadiiarov

Abstract The present article seeks to shed light on the short-term and long-term socioeconomic repercussions stemming from COVID-19 outbreak in Kyrgyzstan. Among other things, the work demonstrates that

---

This research was supported by a Marie Curie Research and Innovation Staff Exchange scheme within the H2020 Programme (grant acronym: New Markets, no: 824027).

J. Bruley
University of Lille, Lille, France

I. Mamadiiarov (✉)
Europe-Eurasia Research Center (CREE), INALCO, Paris, France
e-mail: iliias.mamadiiarov@inalco.fr

what seemed, at the outset, a health crisis of epidemiological nature, turned in fact into a wide-scale crisis with extensive, far-reaching sociopolitical and economic effects. In this regard, the current article attempts to examine on how COVID-19 exposed a series of vulnerabilities present in Kyrgyzstan such as endemic corruption, deficit of government accountability as well as intractable economic problems which all resulted, the work argues, in a collective movement of masses that triggered the October 2020 uprising in the country. Furthermore, while various written works deployed different approaches in describing the October 2020 upheaval, the current article seeks to highlight what has been either absent or little accounted for in explaining the 2020 uprising—the role of COVID-19 as well as the profound impact stemming from the crisis within the social, economic and political fields in Kyrgyzstan.

Keywords COVID-19 · 'Kyrgyz Third revolution' · Civil society · Gender · Social media

"Элим алданба"
Мага баарың бип бирдей
Кимиң мыктысың билбейм
Акыйкатты мен издейм
Таба албай келем
Абир Касенов & Бегиш[1]
("My people don't be deceived"
You are all the same to me,
I don't know who is more full of oneself,
I search for justice,
My efforts are in vain)
Abir Kasenov & Begish

Introduction

The repercussions of COVID-19 crisis, whilst alarming in every region of the world, have been particularly acute in Kyrgyzstan. As Bruley and

---

[1] https://www.youtube.com/watch?v=JYS8PUTuREE a Kyrgyz hip-hop song. Translation from Kyrgyz by the authors. Reference is provided by Florian Coppenrath, PhD student at Leibniz-Zentrum Moderner Orient (ZMO), Berlin, Germany.

Mamadiiarov observe (2020) the pandemic took a heavy toll on the dilapidated socioeconomic institutions of this Central Asian state. In particular, the mandatory quarantine measures that triggered socioeconomic vulnerabilities such as surging rate of unemployment (Blondin, 2020), rising cases of domestic violence (Imanaliyeva, 2020), growing levels of poverty as well as authorities' continual attempt to curb the freedom of speech (Imanaliyeva, 2020), resulted in the violent overthrow of the government of Kyrgyzstan on October 5, 2020, following controversial parliamentary elections (Marat, 2020b). While the study of the causes of the so-called 'Third revolution' that befalls Kyrgyzstan since its independence has been for the moment restricted to various newspapers articles and tribunes, and not thoroughly analyzed, at least two patterns can be underlined at this stage. First, albeit the dubious outcome of parliamentary elections is widely referred to as the source of the unrest (Higgins, 2020; Ruisseau, 2020), it was far from being a definitive cause of the mass protests. Indeed, as Wachtel (2020) argues, the disputed election results served as a "trigger" event, with the countrywide revolt playing out "against a background of latent popular anger at the incompetent response of the government to the COVID-19 pandemic". Second, while some sense of order and normalcy seem to return to Kyrgyzstan today, the country has multiple challenges to confront at present with COVID-19 remaining as one of the biggest threats that could easily instigate another wave of massive discontent.

With this caveat in mind, the current co-written work seeks to demonstrate, on the example of Kyrgyzstan, that besides an immediate threat to the country's health system, the COVID-19 pandemic dealt a huge blow to the existing social arrangements of the country. By rendering problems such as endemic corruption, absence of government accountability, widespread impunity more salient than before, the health crisis was capable of triggering a massive discontent of the public which paved the way for the large-scale protest of October 2020. As a matter of fact, Piven and Cloward (1979) contend that for the massive protest to "arise out of [the] traumas of daily life… the social arrangements that are ordinarily perceived as just and immutable must come to seem both unjust and mutable" (p. 12). Likewise, we argue that in the case of Kyrgyzstan, the COVID-19 resulted in a profound disruption of the existing status quo which, in return, was conducive to popular uprising. Last but not the least, as Desmond (2016) observes, a perception of injustice or grievances per se are not sufficient to spark a movement of mass resistance. For protests to arise, citizens must believe that they have the "collective capacity to change things" (p. 180). Having experienced two revolutions in the past, the population of Kyrgyzstan have had an experience of social mobilization of masses which, it can be argued, played a key role in the uprising of October 2020.

The current work is comprised of two main parts. The first part delves into the analysis of the October 2020 political turmoil. Among other things, this part examines various theories and patterns suggested by a number of social scientists and researchers of Central Asia to explain the underlying mechanisms and processes which prompted the political unrest of masses of 2020 in Kyrgyzstan. An in-depth study of the proposed theories demonstrates that the latter fail to carry out a thorough analysis of one of the principal culprits of October 2020 events—the context created by COVID-19 crisis, a challenge that extends much further away the disaster it generated within the country's fragile healthcare system. The part further attempts to provide a holistic approach to explain the phenomenon of mobilization of masses of October 2020. Far beyond claiming to present an exhaustive analysis in explaining the October political turmoil, the part sheds light on certain key socioeconomic trajectories that appear to kindle the popular unrest. Among other things, this concerns the inability of the government to handle the pandemic, a critical or fundamental role of social networks in mobilizing the masses and building a social discourse, the conflict of generations as well as the dynamic of a possible linguistic conflict.

The second part of the article focuses on certain macro and micro aspects of the consequences of the COVID-19 crisis in Kyrgyzstan. In this regard, the section will carry out a thorough analysis of the economic challenges posed by the pandemic. In particular, the far-reaching impacts of the health crisis, the article argues, have had a major adverse effect on the rise of national poverty, unemployment, and the mobility problem for dozens of Kyrgyz migrant workers in Russia. It goes without saying that the economic recession exposed the financial vulnerabilities of thousands of households across the country. As such, the section depicts an example of one particular low-income Kyrgyz family struggling with the economic challenges since the beginning of the outbreak. The part equally reflects upon the endemic corruption which significantly stymied, within the context of COVID-19, the government's capacity to efficiently discharge one of its main functions—the crisis management.

This section also examines the issue of "biopolitics" and how the health crisis shaped the burgeoning authoritarianism that embraces ignorance and anti-science in dealing with pandemic. The study further investigates the subject of mortality stemming from the outbreak and, among other things, explores thoroughly the case of excess death from all causes. In this regard, this part argues that the latter can be illustrative of the pandemic's evolution and the way the country succeeded in managing it. Furthermore, the section equally focuses on the issue of gender and a rising number of domestic violence against women in Kyrgyzstan. Delving into the comprehensive analysis of the subject of gender such as the ambivalent characteristic that stems from the scope of power exerted by Kyrgyz women, the section illustrates that the health crisis substantially aggravated the cases of domestic violence against women across the country. Finally, drawing upon the series of protests and demonstrations that sought denouncing the rising gender-based violence in the country, the paper emphasizes the significance of the gender issues as one of a string of other social issues that triggered October 2020 events.

In conclusion, the current work will attempt to summarize the key developments and dynamics that COVID-19 unfolded and continue to unveil within Kyrgyzstan today. In this regard, the ending remarks particularly emphasize the impacts of COVID-19 which have been far beyond the overwhelming challenges it engendered for the Kyrgyz Republic's dilapidated healthcare system. By exposing the vulnerabilities at multiple levels of the society, the pandemic paved, albeit in indirect manner, the way for the mobilization and action of masses which resulted in the political uprising of October 2020 in Kyrgyzstan.

COVID-19 as a Background to the Kyrgyz 'October Revolution'

The chief goal of this part of the present work is to provide a detailed analysis on the intertwined relationship between two major social phenomena. First, this section examines the way COVID-19 evolved in Kyrgyzstan and, second, it explores the complex health crisis environment against the backdrop of which unfolded what has been widely referred to as the "Third Kyrgyz revolution", or the "October revolution" (Engval, 2020; Karmazin et al., 2020). The section also seeks to shed light on hypothesis of cause and effect link that connects two time periods: (a) the beginning of COVID-19 outbreak in Kyrgyzstan (b) the moment when the country's executive power was deposed. Overall, our main argument in this section is to demonstrate that the health crisis engendered a number of conditions that played a pivotal role during the October 2020 political turmoil. Finally, this part will attempt to examine the more or less long-term multi-levelled consequences this turmoil generates for the future of Kyrgyzstan.

The 'Third Kyrgyz Revolution' and Its Patterns
In fact, what is now conceived and baptized as the "Third Kyrgyz revolution" or "October revolution" is the result of the action of masses that took place on the night of October 4–5, 2020. On October 4, under the administration of the then president Jeenbekov, the country held its parliamentary elections amidst the pandemic. Following the announcement of the election results, a protest rally, composed essentially of the political parties who failed to pass the threshold of 7%, gathered at Ala-Too Square demanding the annulation of the poll's outcomes. Registration fraud, massive vote buying, pressure on opposition political parties and numerous other election irregularities (Wood, 2020) began surfacing by this time. The clashes erupted in downtown Bishkek as police started dispersing the protesters who, following the ebb and flow of the escalation and de-escalation of the confrontation between sides, succeeded in entering the siege of the government called the White House as well as various other governmental buildings with little or no resistance offered from law enforcement officials. With presidential office building altogether ransacked, the evening also saw the release of a former political prisoner, Sadyr Japarov, by demonstrators.

As many commentators have pointed out (Cagnat & Gaüzere, 2020; Ruisseau, 2020) the political crisis of October 2020 unfolded within the context of COVID-19 which dealt a heavy blow to the Kyrgyz economy driving into poverty thousands of Kyrgyz families as well as further weakening the country's enfeebled institutions. That said, many articles, written in the following days after the turmoil, while attempting to discern the underlying mechanisms of the revolt, tend to characterize the unrest as part of a repetitive cycle of revolutions that swept through the country in 2005 and 2010. The latter type of theories and assumptions emanate essentially from Western thinkers and specialists of the area. The fact that such evaluations correspond well to the "seasoned" conceptions that have proved their worth and which seem to be in the spotlight in Western analysis categories also explains the rather appealing nature of these theories. Yet, as the current work attempted to illustrate above and continues to argue so below, the realities rooted on the ground display, on the contrary, a greater social complexity germane to the event in question. Keeping this caveat in mind, our work will analyze the suggested theories with a goal of identifying their relevance. As will be shown below, each theory attempts to play on repetitive patterns but ultimately falls short of explaining the new data that stems from the field.

The first pattern concerns the issue of North–South cleavage present in Kyrgyzstan. The approach is a recurrent subject in the analysis categories of Western works such as those found in the articles of Rey-Bethbeder (2020) and Cagnat and Gaüzere (2020). This approach seeks to evaluate the social transformations exclusively through the prism of political and religious divisions. With regards to Kyrgyzstan, the theory suggests the presence of a geographical dichotomy, with the country's North harboring the capital Bishkek, the regions of Ysyk Köl, Naryn and Talas, and the South that includes the city of Osh—the second largest city of the republic. The North is portrayed as a wealthier region vis-à-vis its southern counterpart which is considered as being traditionally agricultural and more religious (Rey-Bethbeder, 2020; Cagnat & Gaüzere, 2020). Moreover, when one explores the topic of North–South alternation, the latter implies the alternation of political power between leaders from the North or the South of Kyrgyzstan (Helf, 2020). Indeed, the revolutions of 2005 and 2010 as well as the peaceful transfer of power in 2017 from Atambayev to Jeenbekov underlines the relevance of this approach. Nevertheless, this alternation, even if it is respected this time again, as Japarov comes from the Ysyk Köl region, does not play any role in the October revolution proceedings: contrary to the theory of Cagnat and Gaüzere, regional interests as well as possible religious influences and other characteristics of such a power alternation were absent and not even covertly.

The second pattern certain authors utilize to explain the social transformations in Kyrgyzstan seeks to underscore the common mechanisms that constitute the essential characteristic of former USSR countries. In this regard, the explanation provided by Wachtel (2020) is consistent with this approach: "In an attempt to ensure that they can hold the levers of power, government authorities interfere with an election. However, instead of doing so subtly, gently putting their thumbs on the scale to ensure, say, that they retain sufficient but not suffocating control, their operatives take a sledgehammer to the process, ensuring that it is perceived to be wholly illegitimate" (Wachtel, 2020). Finally, this approach tries to justify and enclose one of the possible explanations of the turmoil in linking it to a proven system which repeated itself anew.

The third common argument used to explain the October 2020 uprising in Kyrgyzstan aims to establish a connection between Japarov's sudden meteoric rise to power and the role of organized crime groups or mafia of which the former is deemed to be a part of. The hypothesis further claims the fact that the newly-fledged leader of the republic would eventually dole out the key state positions among the heads of the mafia while certain criminal figures, notoriously known for their criminal reputations in the country such as Matraimov, would be placed under surveillance or under arrest (Cagnat & Gaüzere, 2020). In the same vein, this theory equally stresses the continuities of existing networks between certain figures in power and their criminal and political past (as in the case of Japarov, this implies his links with the ex-president of Kyrgyzstan from the South—Bakiev, see CABAR, 2020).

The particularity of this theory resides on the personal observations as well as the biographies of personalities that have experienced original turns in the space of just a few days. However, this theory's major drawback, while it presents cogent arguments in apprehending the nature of events after the seizure of power in October, is that it fails to explain the event itself. In particular, the argument adapts perfectly to the game of musical chairs between tycoons of all ranks, but it does not stand up to the analysis that the revolution burst out with no grounded organization, no leading politician to drive the demonstrators (Photo 6.1).

Albeit the theories and arguments laid out above adopt different approaches in their study of the October 2020 uprising in Kyrgyzstan, they all seem to coalesce in the fact that they tend to downgrade the importance of the COVID-19 crisis against the backdrop of which unfolded the political turmoil. Furthermore, this does not imply the absence of the cause and effect relation between the two events and periods in question. Rather, the latter means that the revolution results in a non-unavoidable end, not in the active outcome of specific minorities such as mafia network. On the other hand, an essential caveat to keep in mind is that there is a real risk of being reductive when one places high importance to the theories and patterns presented above. In fact, the role of subordination or indirect consequence of the global pandemic on the politics in Kyrgyzstan is certainly not negligible. Yet, it is to ignore a number of new factors that make this incident an original event. Indeed, the analysis of these factors enable, as certain studies

Photo 6.1 A speech delivered by one of the members of a Kyrgyz political party to the protestors at Ala-Too square, Bishkek. October 5, 2020 (Photo by authors)

underline (Doolotkeldieva, 2021), to slide towards much finer categories of analysis that encapsulate the social, economic and political situation in Kyrgyzstan.

Last but not least, it's worth mentioning that Japarov's account of the October 4–5 events sparks much curiosity due to, among other things, a populist and teleological nature of his narrative: "If you call it a coup, the president would have fled, the government would have fled, but now we are all in place. Therefore, this is not a coup, but a peaceful renewal" (Uraliev, 2020). In fact, giving much weight to the natural movement of things as well as placing emphasis on the purported intent of trying to avoid the bloody path of the previous revolutions plays out well in a populist narrative. Furthermore, if one admits that the "October revolution" indeed represents a peaceful renewal (at the cost of one death and around 600 wounded), Japarov appears to neglect the reasons and the context that prompted the popular uprising. The newly-fledged Kyrgyz leader equally fails to explain on why and how the circumstances provoked the deployment of a force which, consequently, led to his swift rise to power.

Overall, the novelty of the 'October revolution', if one compares it to the previous political unrests of 2005 and 2010, appears to puzzle most writers who expressed their views and visions within a few days after the events. They used to neglect the complexity of the various factors impacting the social phenomena. Furthermore, even if the novelty is taken into account, a superficial manner of studying the events, which often contains conceptual vagueness, appears to limit one in making long-term projections. Much analysis as well as the studying remains to be done and the purpose of this article is to contribute to this scientific lacuna.

COVID-19 as Strengthening of the Kyrgyz Civil Society

The pandemic reached the country by March 2020 and quarantine measures were taken less than a week after the first contaminations spread from southern Kyrgyzstan, alongside a decreed state of emergency (Bruley & Mamadiiarov, 2020). Despite these hastily settled initiatives, no concrete action was taken by the authorities during the following months. As a result, the gradual lifting of prevention and control measures has, in a way, allowed a massive contamination movement in the country: the highest daily contamination rate was observed during the summer of 2020, overloading already crowded health infrastructures.

While the inadequacy of the authorities' management of the crisis became apparent, spontaneous movements emerged from the civil society, mainly through social networks as a mean of communication and action. As Ryskulova (2020b) points out: 'in July, social media turned into a bulletin board selling and buying oxygen concentrators, masks, and pneumonia medications. Most often these drugs were not available in pharmacies'. Numerous groups of volunteers such as 'Volunteer Rescue Squad' or 'Together' emerged and aid up doctors and hospital teams, in buying medicines or in bringing and installing oxygen concentrators for patients with trouble breathing (Litvinova, 2020).

Positioned between these volunteer groups or individuals and the sphere of political action, the Tirek project ('support' in Kyrgyz), as an example of surrogate coordination institution, was launched online on May 1, 2020. This platform was developed by a volunteer group of local IT developers working in business and non-profit sectors. Acting as an intermediary between offer and demands (in medicines, food and services), Tirek intended to synchronize efforts from various actors prompting support to healthcare organizations and medical workers struggling against the pandemic (Maslova, 2020).

Illustrative is Tirek's failure to secure State support. According to one of Tirek's development coordinators, Nazira Beishenalieva in a July 1, 2020 post on Facebook (Jusupova, 2020), negotiations with the Ministry of Health went pear-shaped. Various reasons are also suggested to explain this failure such as corruption, bureaucracy or political allegiances. This conflict happened at the very moment when the Kyrgyz government implemented its own but belated response to the pandemic in launching a specific platform, Birge, designed to fill up the same purpose as Tirek's platform.

As Eshaliyeva (2020) states, 'the pandemic has exposed problems that have been accumulating in the healthcare system for years'. The Kyrgyz population's concerns with the management of the crisis by the authorities and the planned parliamentary elections on October 4 have set the path to a deeper rooted politicization of those underacting networks mentioned above: indeed, some of these networks' leaders started to enter the political path in order to bring society and civil society's concerns into a broader way, with the coming parliamentary elections.

As a matter of fact, summer 2020 faced the highest daily contamination as well as an explosion of political discontent which in the perspective of the parliamentary elections bloomed into the creation of new political parties in an unusual way. The case of the party Reforma, for instance, is enlightening on the peculiar mechanisms which led to its creation and development. As Marat (2020a) reports, 'a new political party, Reforma, stepped onto the political stage. Their platform was singular: improve governance by electing forward-thinking and inclusive leadership. The party crowd funded its $ 63,000 registration fee required by the Central Election Commission—a first for a Kyrgyz political party. Other political parties, including Ata-Meken (Fatherland) and Bir Bol (Be One), featured new political leaders to appeal to voters fed up with corruption'.

COVID-19 and Social NetworksEmpowerment: Toward the 'Revolution'

The crucial role of social networks can be adumbrated by the justification given by the then Prime Minister Kubatbek Boronov on July 2 when he justified the lifting of the curfew due to pressure from social media, and added: '[people] believed that the virus is a fictitious policy, that officials invented it in order to make money, to do business. The population believed it and this led to this situation' (Akipress, 2020).

We would tend to defend this position, which is also consistent with what other authors have been able to justify in this regard: 'with few resources to protect those who lost income while businesses were closed, officials started to ease lockdown restrictions in early May, when the country reported a little over 1,000 coronavirus cases and 12 deaths, citing economic fallout and public frustration over the lockdown. Some said the government feared unrest in the country, which has a history of political uprisings and ethnic violence' (Litvinova, 2020).

Whatever the reasons invoked here and there, the growing influence of social networks in the political debate, in criticizing government' actions, are indeed one of the main factors that have pushed for the gradual lifting of quarantine measures and the state of emergency. This context was likely the nest to the development of a distinctive law project entitled 'On Manipulating Information' (*'O manipulirovanii informaciej'*), one of the most noticeable bills among the 63 laws passed before parliament's summer break (Eshaliyeva, 2020).

Social networks's harmful influence is denounced by MP Gulshat Asylbayeva, the law's sponsor, who claimed that 'the legislation was inspired by the spread of Covid-19-related disinformation, including conspiracy theories about the origins of the novel coronavirus and dangerous pseudo-medical treatments. However, there is deep concern among Kyrgyzstan's journalism and civil society communities that this law is an attempt by politicians and the illicit patronage networks which back them to manipulate the upcoming October 2020 parliamentary election by chilling free speech' (Schwartz, 2020).

In summary, several points of friction and several parameters have to be taken into account in order to understand the Kyrgyz context during the year 2020 against a backdrop of COVID-19 pandemic. The coercive actions envisaged by the government, which pinnacle reached by the bill 'On Manipulating Information', as responses to a massive disillusionment of the population and an urgent situation—all demonstrates the exceptional situation both the population and its government were plunged into. The role of social networks has demonstrated the adaptability of the Kyrgyz population to overcome a critical situation in organizing volunteer groups and in bringing concrete solutions to a striking inactivity of authorities.

In our opinion, the point of no return remains in the circumstances and peculiarities specific to the 'Third revolution' which is the first Kyrgyz revolution to have been so much publicized, and especially through social networks. Moreover, it is also thanks to the ubiquity of these very networks that the current Kyrgyz President has imposed overnight. If on the one hand the attempt to muzzle social networks or the Internet from false information (which interpretation depends on many factors) were the prerogative of the former government after and due to the quarantine, the post-revolution government and the new President in particular will have to be somewhat measured and pondered when attempting to restrict the Internet. Indeed, the successful rise of Sadyr Japaraov is based mostly on the existence of social networks and the quick spread of information they allow. However, restrictions tendencies are, according to Freedomhouse (2020), likely to develop without firing in extremes.

The unprecedented increase of social networks in Kyrgyzstan during and after the quarantine granted the new president a notoriety largely founded on the very existence of these social networks and the virulence of their debates which, in his case, can be a two-edge tool. Thus, as Baialieva and Kutmanaliev (2020) point out, 'amid the current political crisis, Japarov's unexpected rise to prominence underlines the growing importance of Kyrgyz-speaking social media for political mobilization. Ignoring it would reduce the accuracy of any analysis of the country's political processes.'

'Revolution', Social Networks and Their Languages
A few weeks before the October elections, the linguistic debate between Kyrgyz (state and official) and Russian (also official) languages revived. Although it did not play a major role in triggering the 'revolution', the divide between the Kyrgyz and Russian languages further highlights a certain segmentation of the Kyrgyz society as a whole. On the one hand, this linguistic division through which the society's fragmentation is played out is only a legacy of the Soviet era when, in order to qualify for the post of state civil servant, the knowledge of Russian was an obligation. This pattern has not seen a very significant metamorphosis in this regard today.

The Russian language is, despite the inclinations which appeared at the time of the early presidential elections of January 10, 2021, a language necessary in Kyrgyzstan not only within its borders, but above all to ensure and secure the country's GDP (guaranteed by migrant workers' remittances): a third of the population is working in Russia for instance, and Russian remains the *lingua franca* to travel within ex-USSR territories.

This debate was rekindled during the October events. The uses, differences and commonalities in the two languages were noted by Rashid Gabdulhakov in a short article, where he links each social network, at the time of the 'Kyrgyz October revolution', to a particular part of the population and to a specific language. In fact, he brushed a quick picture of the platforms used by the Kyrgyz at the time of the revolution and distinguishes 4 main ones: Twitter was according to the author used mainly by 'journalists, academics, diplomats, restaurateurs, students, activists, doctors and many others' and mainly in Russian who are also nicknamed 'balkonies'. Immediately after the Parliament was plundered, the *druzhina* movement,[2] composed of young volunteers who guarded key places in the city (administrative buildings etc.) to prevent the situation from escalating, mainly worked with Telegram. Facebook was used mostly by journalists live streaming the event, but was not widely used as a communication tool between protesters. Last but not least, Instagram was the platform for pop stars, some of whom have dared to launch political messages.

In the list of Gabdulhakov, Whatsapp is not mentioned but remains a mean of communication intended to bypass costs between the various Kyrgyz mobile operators, and the possibility to create groups where the information is quickly spread among (Doolotkeldieva, 2021).

Languages during 'revolution' had an importance. As observers, we could notice the wide use of Kyrgyz language the night of October 5 and the day after among protesters gathered in small groups in front of the steaming White house. When leaders of progressive political parties came to Ala-too square, Russian was seldom used. This question cross-checks the one of the intergenerational issue, and spatial origin of demonstrators (Photo 6.2).

'Revolution', Intergenerational and Spatial Issues
The linguistic question is evaluated directly with that of the intergenerational issue raised by Aksana Ismailbekova (Ismailbekova, 2020). According to her, women and young people are part of the 'muted'

---

[2] About movement and for more details, see: https://fergana.agency/articles/121106/.

Photo 6.2 A group of protestors gather and debate before the central administrative building, White House, at Ala-Too square, Bishkek, on October 5, 2020 (Photo by authors)

voices and groups in Kyrgyzstan, which do not have a voice, but who, thanks to social networks, have been able to participate in the debate and express themselves, firstly in the frame of a virtual space and then on the streets. Nevertheless, this theory does not analyze further these categories of 'muted' groups and stands on the ground of an abstract concept, as they can be divided into several subgroups with their own interest within these larger groups.

These further analyzes are carried on by Doolotkeldieva (2021) who, in a recent publication, addresses the issue of categories such as 'youth' or 'el' ('people' in Kyrgyz), the latter promoted by the President Sadyr Japarov. According to her, 'el' subsumes all protest movements that have emerged or are expressed at the time of the revolution and homogenizes 'various groups of protesters with the aim of capitalizing on "popular" discontent, which led to depoliticizing the demands of various groups' (Doolotkeldieva, 2021, p. 2).

However, this new category, or generalization, does not cover the concrete reality on the ground. Following in this Doolotkeldieva, one can discuss the concept of 'youth' which is a common point to many studies or reactions published shortly after October 5. This youth is distinguished schematically in two parts relying on a spatial division and underlying different types of protests, either peaceful or aggressive. The first category deals with 'balkonies' and designates an enlightened urban population, certain members of which played an important role at the time of the pandemic as volunteers. And the second one is labelled by the term "aiyl" ('village' in Kyrgyz), living on the outskirts more or less close to Bishkek (Doolotkeldieva, 2021, p. 5).

Doolotkeldieva asserts that this spatial distinction between both groups is blurred by the question of spatial belonging. Indeed, Bishkek tends to play the role of a country within a country, and not that of a 'monolithic bloc with a definite identity' (ibid., p. 5). And this peculiarity in the Kyrgyz landscape makes the capital the localized epicenter of political protests as it crystallizes crises and connects young people from outside and inside onto a common ground for protest (note).

Most of Kyrgyz media soon concluded on the winning return of the 'old politicians' (Kloop, 2020), and analysts like Ruslan Akmatbek insisted on the similarities between the revolutions of 2005, 2010 and 2020 (Bijbosunov, 2020), as a loop system which ineluctably brings back the old generation to power. The 'October revolution' will have shown, however, that the conflict is still latent and will maybe develop to a wider extent than previously. This is how a generational line emerges which distinguishes, on the one hand, young entrepreneurs associated with new and progressive political parties, most of them created during summer 2020, in preparation for the October elections, and in reaction to the management of the crisis by the authorities at the time and, on the other hand, a myriad of politically experienced personalities with an unclear past and reputation: a striking example is Sadyr Japarov who is not associated, by the media, with the younger generation (Kloop, 2020; RFE, 2020).

COVID-19: Multifaceted Challenges for Economy and Health Care System Amid Deteriorating Gender Issues

The current section seeks to highlight the nature of the impact produced by health crisis within three socioeconomic trajectories. Namely, this part first examines the severe adverse effects generated by the pandemic across thousands of households in Kyrgyzstan. In this regard, macro and microeconomic analysis of the consequences stemming from health crisis will be carried out. The section further attempts to shed light on the impact of COVID-19 outbreak in the field of public health. It seeks to explain how the crisis paved the way for the authorities to exert a greater control over an individual's health decisions and concomitantly enabling the powers that be to evade the requirements of government accountability and transparency. Finally, the section examines the question of domestic violence against women as well as the role of women in collective mobilization movement within the context of COVID-19 crisis.

1. Economic crisis

Among other things, it is within the context of socioeconomic vulnerability that the impact stemming from the health crisis must be examined with regards to the economy of Kyrgyzstan. Indeed, one of the major fields that COVID-19 has struck a major blow against concerns the international migrant remittances. In particular, as migrant remittances comprise more than 30% of the country's GDP which, among other things, make the Republic the second country in world in terms of GDP/remittances ratio (Kuznetsova et al., 2020; Pomfret, 2019, pp. 174–175), the pandemic took a heavy toll on the fragile budgets of hundreds of thousands of households highly dependent on the incomes earned by at least one or more family members working in Russia. In terms of percentage, there has been a 12% decline in transfer of funds from Russia to Kyrgyzstan by migrant workers (Imanbekova, 2020a). The reduction of remittances, it is argued, have had significant adverse effect on the welfare of families, and in particular the ones residing in rural areas due to the labor migrants' highest exodus from these zones (Kuznetsova et al., 2020; Sagynbekova, 2017). Indeed, combined with soaring inflation at 9.7%, that significantly diminished the purchasing power of dozens of households, as well as the rising unemployment, over 40,000 jobs lost (World Bank, 2021), the pandemic has exposed the financial precariousness of multiple families.

The example of Azizbek (personal communication, January 2, 2021), a 40 years old father of five children from the town of Kirovka, Talas oblast, unveils the story of a socioeconomically vulnerable family beset by the challenges of the COVID-19 crisis. Prior to the pandemic, Azizbek's main source of income came from his informal work of loading and unloading bags of beans onto trucks at one of the warehouses of "Kyrgyzcentrprodukt"—a manufacturer and exporter of agricultural products. With a daily wage of KGS600 (around US$8.5 based on pre-pandemic rate of national currency to USD), his earning contributed to the KGS4000 (US$57) monthly state benefits that target low-income families with more than two children under the age of 16. The sweeping quarantine measures together with its far-reaching economic repercussions dealt a triple blow to Azizbek's household's budget. The informal nature of Azizbek's occupation meant he had no employment contract which further implied he was expendable labor force—a category of workers highly vulnerable to layoffs during any type of economic recession (International Labor Organization, 2020). Hence, Azizbek lost his job.

Furthermore, as both Azizbek and his spouse lack higher education, the couple face an insurmountable challenge of landing a formal employment. The soaring prices for basic consumption goods such as meat and vegetable oil struck another blow against the family's revenue. "I can no longer buy vegetable oil in 5 liter plastic bottles as I used to, it's too expensive. Instead, I buy a bottle of 1 liter per purchase" says Ainura, Azizbek's wife (personal interview, 2020). According to the World Food Program, some major category of consumption foods in Kyrgyzstan such as meat and cooking oil have seen a surge in prices "significantly higher than normal annual price fluctuations" with the meat increasing from 25 to 28% and vegetable oil from 14 to 55% compared to December 2019 (World Food Programme, 2020, p. 1). But the fundamental challenge falling upon Azizbek's family is the mobility impairment caused by the pandemic. In particular, as a former migrant worker in Russia, Azizbek attempted numerous times, all to no avail, to travel to Russia. Multiple travel restrictions put in place between countries such as closures of land borders, exorbitant airfares as well as COVID-19 negative certification requirements impede his intent to depart to Russia (Photo 6.3).

Photo 6.3 A queue formed before the only office of Aeroflot Russian Airlines in Bishkek that provides ticket reimbursement in case of passenger's flight cancellation caused by COVID-19 positive test results 72 hours before the flight departure. As air travel remains the sole means of travelling to Russia from Kyrgyzstan, high demand for tickets make it rather difficult to purchase them with tickets' availability limited to only two months from the date of purchase. March 29, 2021 (Photo by authors)

As a matter of fact, according to Blondin (2020), the COVID-19 crisis engenders the mobility problem for the thousands of Kyrgyz households from mountainous regions of the country whose family members, relatives work in Russia. With quarantine measures significantly hampering international travel, dozens of migrant workers face the risk of losing mobility and subsequently the jobs which can further disrupt financial stability of households driving more families into poverty. Indeed, according to the World Bank (2021), the growth of national poverty rate in Kyrgyzstan has been up to 11% in 2020, an abrupt leap which adds to the pre-pandemic level of poverty rate of 20.1% amounting to 30.1% as per March 2021 (Fig. 6.1). In terms of numbers, the growth implies that the health crisis sent up to 700,000 additional individuals below the poverty line. On a global scale, the COVID-19 has resulted in every third individual in the country to live below poverty line in comparison to every fourth person which was the case before the pandemic. Finally, with the national currency depreciation (KGS to USD) reaching 19%, as well as the country's GPD level shrinking by 8.6%, the perspective of economic recovery is not expected anytime before 2022 (World Bank, 2021).

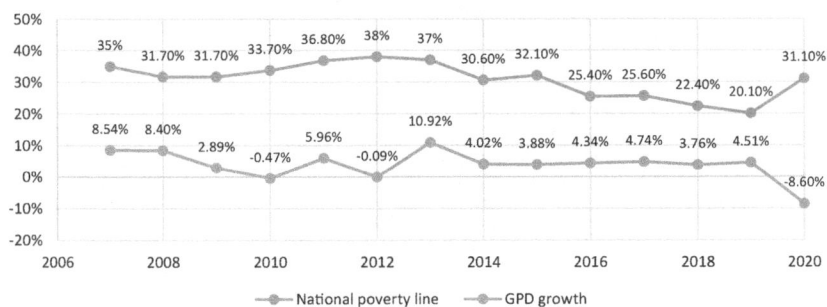

Fig. 6.1 Poverty rate (national estimate) and GDP growth—Kyrgyz Republic (2007–2020) (Graph by authors based on the following sources: 1. World Bank [2021], "Data Bank", March 17, https://data.worldbank.org/indicator/SI.POV.NAHC?locations=KG [page accessed on March 20, 2021]; 2. World Bank (2021). "One Year Later in the Kyrgyz Republic's Battle Against COVID-19", March 17, https://www.worldbank.org/en/news/feature/2021/03/17/one-year-later-in-the-kyrgyz-republic-s-battle-against-covid-19 [page accessed on March 20, 2021])

But the limited resources and the continual political instability that underscore the presence of enfeebled public institutions continue to hamper the economic performance of Kyrgyzstan. Indeed, as Pomfret (2019) underlines, with its hydroelectric and other mineral resources remaining poorly developed, the economy of Kyrgyz Republic is highly depended on a single goldmine—Kumtor. This, in return, renders the country's macroeconomic stability highly vulnerable to external shocks. Likewise, the political distress of 2020 that unfolded against the backdrop of COVID-19 crisis seems to further undermine the already fragile state of socioeconomic institutions of the republic. In this regard, in his interview to Radio Azattyk, the Kyrgyz economist Azamat Akaneev contends that the effects of the present crisis could be much worse than estimated by the World Bank. In particular, with no foreseeable end in sight to the current epidemic, one should anticipate that the national poverty rate could easily climb to 40% in the upcoming years (Kolbaev, 2021). This suggests, following the report of Bruley and Mamadiiarov (2020) which points it out as one of the impact scenarios of the current health crisis, that a staggering 2.58 million people or near half of the country's population run the risk of facing the poverty.

Thus, it is within the context described above that Kyrgyzstan received a substantial amount of international and domestic aid to mitigate the consequences of COVID-19. But the lack of transparency along with rampant corruption appear to altogether stymie the equitable distribution of the aid. In particular, as Satke (2021) reports, the healthcare system failure was not the sole factor responsible for the poor, shambolic handling of the pandemic. Rather, the endemic government corruption is believed to equally contribute to chaotic, incompetent health crisis management in the country (2021). Indeed, Kyrgyzstan has received some $645 million from international community to assist the government in its emergency response to the outbreak. However, the authorities have largely failed in providing transparency as to where and how the funds have been spent (Satke, 2021). In fact, already in June 2020, the Organized Crime and Corruption Reporting Project (OCCRP) reported that the authorities, and specifically the Kyrgyz Ministry of Finance, were unable to provide information on the whereabouts of the funds (Li, 2020).

As Bruley and Mamadiiarov (2020) illustrate, a widespread public mistrust, fuelled by the prevalence of bribery and corruption in the healthcare system, may partly explain the population's unwillingness to heed the anti-COVID-19 public awareness campaign launched by the Kyrgyz Ministry of Health, a distrust that led to a rising number of infections and mortalities that engulfed the country in July 2020. But the public skepticism should come as no surprise given that little transparency has been provided as to how the authorities doled out the domestic funds amounting to $2.2 million collected from Kyrgyz citizens' donations to fight the spread of the virus (Li, 2020). Furthermore, the dubious handling of the pandemic aid funds which prompted a public backlash, was among the chief reasons for the authorities to arrest the former Minister of Health Kosmoskek Cholponbayev in September 2020. Among other things, the allegations against the ex-minister include abuse of power that caused the damage to the state budget in the amount of 9 million som (around $106,000) (Dzhumashova, 2021).

Last but not least, the pandemic is taking a heavy toll on Kyrgyzstan's overall macroeconomic indicators, an acute problem emerges with regards to the external debt of the country. Several essential factors must be examined in this regard. As of 2019, the external debt of the country constituted $3.85 billion, approximately 54% of the country's GDP (Imanbekova, 2020b). The recession caused by the pandemic as well as the political instability of October 2020 which negatively impacted the country's GDP growth have significantly reduced the capacity of the republic to repay its debt that rose to 44.2% of GDP in the six months of 2020 (Imanbekova, 2020b). Furthermore, the debt is expected to grow with projections suggesting that the latter is to comprise up to 63.3% of GDP in 2022 and 62.6% in 2023 (Akipress, 2020). In face of the pandemic which continues to wreak havoc as well as the adverse effects caused by the political unrest, the country seems to have no option but to borrow. Thus, as Imanbekova (2020b) argues, the key question is to know "how much it [Kyrgyzstan] will borrow, at what interest rates and how future borrowing will affect debt sustainability, which was further aggravated by the political events of October 5, 2020."

2. Health crisis

According to Ioakimidis (2020), the context of epidemiological crisis such as COVID-19 unveils many aspects of what Michel Foucault terms "biopolitics". More specifically, as Ioakimidis argues, "biopolitics" denotes state interventions and social control in the matter of one's health as well as decisions about one's body (ibid., pp. 17–24). In this regard, one of the key challenges stemming from current pandemic refers to the reliability of the official government report concerning the outbreak. Indeed, as Jarman (2021) highlights, COVID-19 is bringing the existing trends and patterns such as abuse of authority, governmental non-transparency and unaccountability into sharp relief "some leaders are governing in less-than-transparent or undemocratic ways, disregarding science and abusing their authority, while people and political parties in many countries are divided" (ibid., p. 61). Keeping this caveat in mind, the scrutiny of the official COVID-19 data in Kyrgyzstan which suggests that the country registered a little short of one hundred thousand confirmed virus infections with total deaths reaching 1640 people as per beginning of May 2021 (Fig. 6.2) should be taken with a grain of salt. In particular, the study of the official numbers on the mortality fails to grasp the genuine magnitude of the evolution of the public health crisis when one examines the data which pertains to deaths from all causes in Kyrgyzstan.

Indeed, the macro level data on the deaths from all causes demonstrate that 2020, the year of health crisis, has seen a significant rise in the country's total deaths. In particular, as the chart (Fig. 6.3) illustrates, the number of total deaths, occurring in Kyrgyzstan in 2020 reached 39,977—an abrupt climb in total mortality rate in comparison to the last fourteen years in the country. In fact, the advantage of the data on deaths from all causes is that the latter lends itself well to calculation of the excess

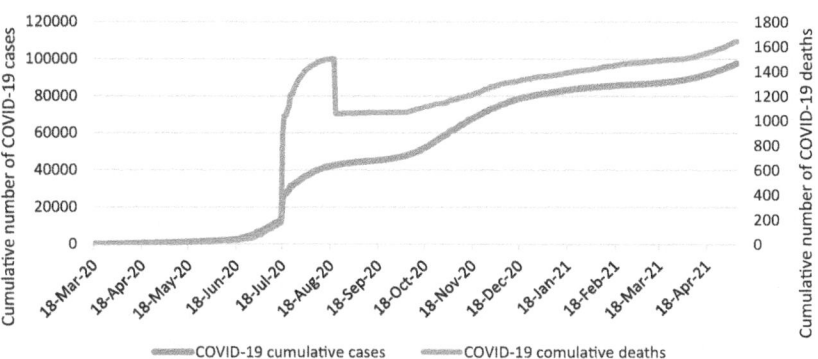

Fig. 6.2 COVID-19 in Kyrgyzstan, cumulative number of total death and total cases due to COVID-19 (2020–2021) (Graph by authors based on the following sources: 1. John Hopkins Coronavirus Resource Center (2021). "Kyrgyzstan". May 5, Johns Hopkins University & Medicine from https://coronavirus.jhu.edu/us-map [page accessed on April 30, 2021])

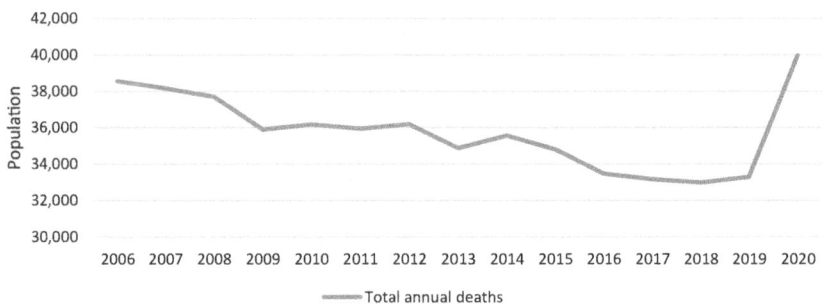

Fig. 6.3 Number of deaths from all causes, Kyrgyzstan (2006–2020) (*Source* Graph by authors based on the open data available at National Statistical Committee of the Kyrgyz Republic [NSC], http://www.stat.kg/ru/opendata/category/47/, accessed on March 22, 2021)

deaths for a particular period. Thus, given that excess deaths is defined "as the number of persons who have died from all causes, in excess of the expected number of deaths for a given place and time" (Rossen et al., 2020, p. 1522) and taking the average annual deaths for the last fourteen years, i.e. from 2006 to 2019, as an expected number of deaths (35,488), we can conclude that the pandemic year of 2020 in Kyrgyzstan resulted in 4489 all-cause excess mortality or 12.6% more deaths than would be expected in non-crisis times. This, along with the fact that the total deaths count for 2020 lies significantly above the median number of deaths for the last fifteen years (35,898), allows us to firmly assert that the pandemic year has resulted in rather unprecedented number of persons' deaths in Kyrgyzstan.

A question arises as to how this data can be pertinent for an in-depth analysis of public health crisis? In fact, in her report on all-cause excess mortality in Russia for 2020, Pellet (2021) points out that while such a figure does not serve as a direct indicator for monitoring the evolution of the epidemic, the number nevertheless presents a valid a posteriori estimation of the pandemic's impact on mortality. Furthermore, provided that the methods of counting the causes of death vary from country to country, calculating all-cause excess mortality displays a clear advantage in that it helps in carrying out international comparisons of the overall demographic impact of the pandemic and of health policy responses (Pellet, 2021).

On the other hand, it is argued that the excess deaths toll has to do with, besides the pandemic, the challenges of air pollution, a particularly acute concern in Bishkek, as well as the country's dilapidated health system stretched thin following the devastating spread of COVID-19 (Kojobaeva, 2021). Likewise, provided that official figures on viral outbreaks tend to often underestimate the epidemic's real death toll due to missing records, nonregistration and misdiagnosis among others (Johnson & Mueller, 2002; Rossen et al., 2020; Yip et al., 2005), it is contended that the actual number of COVID-19 related fatalities in Kyrgyzstan exceeds the official records threefold (Kojobaeva, 2021). Finally, the fact that the excess mortality is likely to encapsulate the deaths resulting from COVID-19 pandemic is corroborated by the findings of the study carried out by a team of epidemiologists and public health experts from University of Oxford, Great Britain and Kyrgyzstan. The report seeks to provide different impact scenarios of COVID-19 outbreak in the country.

In particular, according to one of the projections proposed in the study, Kyrgyzstan was likely to record up to six thousand coronavirus related deaths. Referred to as "baseline scenario", the projection assumes minimal interventions with 82.7% of the population getting infected in the ensuing months provided that lifting of strict quarantine measures takes place in May 2020 (Moldokmatova et al., 2020). Thus, with excess death toll attaining near 4.5 thousand individuals and the confinement measures lifted in May 2020, it is plausible to assert that the projection remained robust, as the actual mortality cases lag behind the projected number by a small margin. That said, with no foreseeable end in sight for the current pandemic, the health crisis continues to feed the environment of ignorance, unaccountability and abuse of authority which impacts significantly individual health decisions. Indeed, as Saleci (2020) argues, negation, denial and ignorance became rampant cases in the response of state leaders to COVID-19 crisis. A manifest example of the latter is a consistent denial of coronavirus by Turkish President Recep Tayyir Erdogan in the early stages of the outbreak or the Turkish miracle cure that suggested sheep soup as a protection from infection which spurred an upsurge in demand for this dish in Turkish restaurants (ibid., p. 151).

With regards to Kyrgyzstan, promotion by the new-fledged president Sadyr Japarov of a drink made from the root of a poisonous plant as a safe treatment against the virus became one in a line of many other notorious cases when a country's leader pushed for lethal fake cures for

COVID-19 (France24, 2021). In fact, Schulman and Siman-Tov (2020) expose various motivations behind a state's intent in spreading disinformation in the context of crisis such as coronavirus pandemic. As such, it is contended that the objective of disinformation can range from an attempt to prevent domestic criticism, control the narrative (for example, emphasize one's success in coping with the virus) or send out "trial balloons" in view of implementation of new future policies (Schulman & Siman-Tov, 2020). Given Japarov's mercurial rise to power in the midst of a pandemic, one can construe the president's spurious cure as a strategy of power consolidation. Namely, by tapping into the field of citizens' health decisions, the government's message, while totally devoid of science, seems to altogether adhere to what Kovalčíková and Tabatabai (2020) characterize as an attempt to "rehabilitate the regimes' images, seed doubt about the virus' origins, shift the blame, highlight failures in democracies, and promote authoritarianism" (p. 3).

Finally, provided that the mutated variant of COVID-19 wrought havoc in India during its second wave, Central Asia's relative geographical proximity with the Indian subcontinent renders the region vulnerable to possible contraction of the more virulent and infectious type of the virus. Furthermore, with less than 0.1% of Kyrgyzstan's population getting vaccinated as per April 7, 2021, the country lags significantly behind its Central Asian neighbors such as Uzbekistan and Kazakhstan vis-à-vis the successful implementation of vaccine rollout policies (Mathieu et al., 2021). In sum, besides the probable surge of new COVID-19 variants proliferation in Kyrgyzstan, the country's fragile health care sector remains highly vulnerable today partly due to the government's shambolic, devoid of science crisis response policies.

3. The question of gender

One should acknowledge that a certain level of ambivalence emergence when it comes to studying the question of gender and more specifically the role of women within the socioeconomic and political landscape of Kyrgyzstan. In particular, this concerns the socioeconomic and political status associated with women which manifests itself in the duality of power inherent to the role of gender in Kyrgyz society. In this regard, on the one hand, various social phenomena unveil the scale of vast authority that women exercise within the state's political and economic spaces, the areas that far exceed the boundaries of keepers of hearth and home roles which is traditionally attributed to Kyrgyz women. Indeed, the anthropologist Ismailbekova (2016) points out that "not only do Kyrgyz women actually gain a great deal of power in their families over the course of their lives, but also this female power is foundational to the Kyrgyz sense of nation and sovereignty. Thus, what seems to be "domestic" power is, in fact, power with very public connections and effects" (p. 266).

As a matter of fact, a clear-cut example of the latter are the instances where Kyrgyz women of mature age, i.e. the age range of 55–65 years old, referred to under the derogatory term "OBON", leverage their traditional or "domestic" power to mobilize masses during protest movements or public rallies to voice the interests and demands of certain group of concern "Their [OBON's] activities complement (rather than oppose) conventional party politics: they can in one context be seen as supporting 'the state' while in another they may challenge state officials" (Beyer & Kojobekova, 2019, p. 330). Without delving into an in-depth analysis of the history and the impact of OBON phenomena, it suffices to say that women constituting this social group played a critical role during the two instances of political distress of 2005 and 2010 in Kyrgyzstan both of which resulted in the ousting of the incumbent presidents of the republic. Indeed, the power that such "older women leaders" in post-Soviet Kyrgyzstan exert in public spaces can exhibit itself in diverse fields as such as "communal leadership, protest activism, bargaining and vote mobilization", argues Satybaldieva (2018, p. 247).

In the same vein, one needs to highlight a gender related social dynamic relevant to the Central Asian region. In particular, this concerns what Ismailbekova (2016) terms, based on the Kandiyoti's (1988) argument, a "patriarchal bargain"—a specific form of authority and recognition that women of old age in Central Asian enjoy provided that they produced a male progeny to insure the continuity of the patriarchal structure. In fact, in her study on the politics of older women leaders in post-Soviet Kyrgyzstan, Satybaldieva (2018) explains that politically active women leaders availed themselves of their age and motherhood status which provided them a certain level of protection from physical violence (p. 252). The weight of patriarchal bargain can be quite far-reaching, underlines Satybaldieva. As an example, the author evokes the accusation of former Kyrgyz President Atambayev who reprimanded the women who protested in front of the White House for causing instability. The author further notes that "several older women leaders in the study rejected

President Atambaev's accusation, pointing out the injustices and violence against women. They framed themselves as responsible mothers who had fulfilled their end of the patriarchal bargain: they had borne and cared for children, had worked all their lives and had made significant contribution to society, only to be betrayed in their old age by the patriarchal order." (ibid., p. 252).

Another manifest example of women's central role concerns the financial aspect of Kyrgyz households. More specifically, various researches illustrate that Kyrgyz women play a crucial role in financial management of a family budget such as household savings, expenses and other financial activities. For instance, the survey, based on 2136 respondents, which examined savings behavior of Kyrgyz households conducted by Sparkassenstiftung Kyrgyzstan in collaboration with National Bank of Kyrgyz Republic (2019) demonstrated that in 63% of cases women are better informed about the family budget than men (37%). An important caveat to keep in mind in this regard is the fact that the men were identified as heads of households in 80% of cases. Yet, as Muktarbek Kyzy indicates in her study on gender aspects of savings behavior in Kyrgyzstan, the former pattern can be simply the result of "socially and culturally stipulated views regarding the role of men and women" in Kyrgyz society and that the men could only be "formally a head of the family, but actually a main bread earner in the family and a head is a wife" (2016, p. 7). Indeed, the pattern of women occupying a chief place in the matters of household finance can be equally discerned when analyzing the gender ratio of microfinance agencies in Kyrgyzstan. As a country with a booming microfinance sector in the region (Fitzeorge-Parker, 2018), female microcredit loaners historically constituted more than their male counterparts (Fig. 6.4).

Thus, it is against this background that a rising number of violence against women have been taking place in Kyrgyzstan during pre-pandemic and pandemic period in particular. As a matter of fact, the country has one of the most "progressive" legislation in Central Asian region which seeks to protect female victims of domestic violence (Ryskulova, 2020a). Introduced in 2017, the statute entitled "Protection and Defence against Domestic Violence" requires the law enforcement officers to register a domestic violence complaint from anyone, not just the victim (Human Rights Watch, 2017). Yet, to this day, the legislation has been little effective in hindering the perpetrators of domestic abuse as it is widely acknowledged that either few women are willing to report the violence

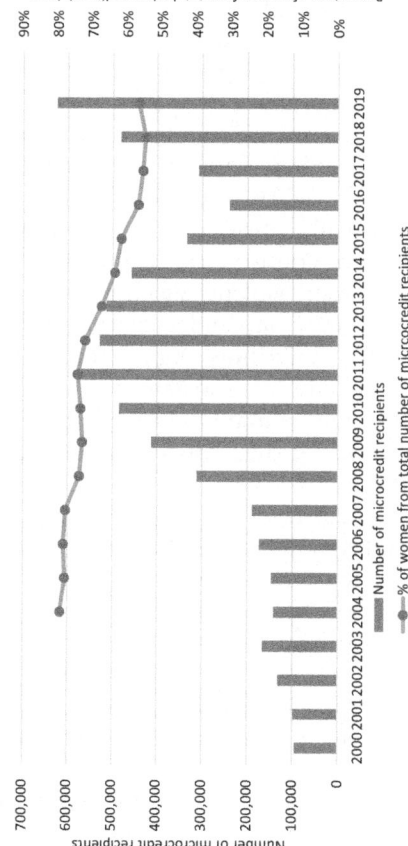

Fig. 6.4 Percentage of female microcredit borrowers in Kyrgyzstan (2003–2019) (*Source* Chart by authors based on: (1) Annual reports [2000–2019] of National Bank of Kyrgyz Republic, https://www.nbkr.kg/index1.jsp?item=136&lang=RUS [accessed on January 20, 2021]. (2) Statistical Committee of the Kyrgyz Republic, [accessed on January 20, 2021])

or a majority of them simply remain unaware of the existence of the law (Ryskulova, 2020a). Furthermore, according to official statistics, in 2018 alone 95% of domestic abuse cases involved men committing violence against women with sixty-two of such incidents ending with women's deaths (Ryskulova, 2020a).

In fact, Pomfret (2019) notes that, apart from endemic corruption and pervasive clientelism, an "increasing Kyrgyz chauvinism" has been one of the marked evolutions that Kyrgyzstan experienced since its independence (p. 180). Furthermore, it appears that against the backdrop of strict confinement, the rising trend of male chauvinism has triggered an upsurge of incidents of domestic violence across the country. Indeed, as Akisheva (2020) reports in her detailed analysis of cases of abuse against women during lockdown in Kyrgyzstan, if during the pre-pandemic period six in ten women were "beaten, sexually abused, or otherwise ill-treated," within the context of quarantine, the country has recorded more than 60% rise in the number of cases of domestic violence against women (p. 2). In terms of absolute numbers, the survey on gender issues and COVID-19 crisis in Kyrgyzstan conducted by Consulting Organization Social Technologies Agency revealed that if from March to January 2019 there were 1409 cases of domestic violence, the same period for 2020 yielded 2319 cases. In other words, a staggering growth of 65% of domestic abuse incidents (Kochorbaeva, 2020).

Indeed, with families constrained to live in clusters during lockdown, men have been forced to spend lengthier periods of time than usual at home with their spouses. The conditions have substantially raised the cases of abuse against women throughout the country, revealing the tensions and social divisions existing in the Kyrgyz society. A particularly manifest example of the latter is the incident that took place on March 8, 2020, when a parade, in support of women's rights and composed predominantly of women, was disrupted by masked men belonging to conservative, nationalist-patriotic groups such as Kyrk-Choro (Suyarkulova, 2020). Among other things, the march sought to increase public awareness about the soaring number of domestic violence incidents occurring in the country in recent years. Thus, as Djanibekova (2020) reports, the parade took place "against the backdrop of steady reports of assaults, frequently deadly, carried out by men against their wives across the country. Women's rights groups have long argued that the authorities are not doing enough to tackle the problem and that police routinely make life hard for victims coming forward to report their plight."

As a matter of fact, as the first section of present work emphasized, the October 2020 protests in Kyrgyzstan represent a complex process that had at its core deep-rooted social polarizations and divisions coalescing into a massive collective movement that had called into question the voter fraud. In this regard, we can argue that the role of gender dynamics, while not definitive, was instrumental in shaping the environment for social mobilization within the context of the pandemic. Indeed, on the one hand, October 2020 unrest constituted, among other things, the plight of the citizens who were indignant with government's shambolic and ineffective handling of the pandemic. This implies that the crisis reflected the outcry of frontline healthcare workers, where women constitute 83.6% of personnel in Kyrgyzstan (Brody & Rodriguez, 2019), as a group that first confronted the deadly wave of the outbreak. Furthermore, with widespread gender inequality issue in the country, the women became inured to leading difficult fight in increasing public awareness on persistent gender-based discrimination.

A manifest example of the female mobilization can be observed in the most recent case of public protest that erupted in the country on April 8, 2021 following a suspected case of "bride kidnapping"—a forced marriage by abduction outlawed in Kyrgyzstan. The kidnapping and murder by several men of 27-year-old Kyrgyz woman Aizada Kanatbekova prompted a massive rally in Bishkek consisting primarily of women that intensified the calls for dismissals and other official actions from authorities (Sultanalieva, 2021). As a matter of fact, the homicide of Aizada echoes with the similar case of kidnapping and murder of a young Kyrgyz woman, Burulai Turdaly kyzy, which had taken place in 2018 and sparked massive protests among women across the country. In sum, the continual deterioration of women's rights situation has been one of the chief causes of civil society's mobilization where women comprised the principal group that pushed forward the protests.

Concluding Remarks

The COVID-19 pandemic showed the responsiveness of the Kyrgyz population and, in particular, of the Kyrgyz civil society in a surprising way. The response was quick and multidimensional as it dealt with health, economic and political domains, in an active and effective way thus supplanting, albeit temporarily, the conspicuously scant presence of state institutions in the aforementioned fields. By the same token, one could argue that the outbreak consolidated the existing civil society enabling it to become more politicized as well as empowering it to aspire for a role that would supersede the state in the areas where the public institutions failed to discharge their corresponding duties and obligations.

Likewise, as demonstrated in the second section of the article, the pandemic took a heavy toll on the economic well-being of the thousands of families. With significant share of the employment sector remaining informal that conditions the absence of labor contract, the outbreak resulted in the loss of the thousands of jobs. The crisis further exacerbated the mobility of thousands of Kyrgyz migrant workers. Provided that remittances represent a critical source of income for a prevailing number of households, travel restrictions which triggered a sizeable reduction of Kyrgyz migrant workers in Russia stirred an abrupt rise in the level of poverty in Kyrgyzstan. Together with nationwide rise of the level of inflation as well as the perspective of possible exacerbation of health crisis, the management of which has been nothing but shambolic and anti-science in its nature, it may very well be up to the powerful, robust and highly resilient Kyrgyz civil society to come to the aid of resolving the next crisis.

In the same vein, the crisis contributed significantly to ever worsening gender based violence in Kyrgyzstan with women remaining the primary victims of the domestic abuse. Given this context, the gender dynamics made an important input in galvanizing the ambiance of protests prior to the electoral fraud in October 2020. In particular, the continual violations and disregard for women's rights, the failure in addressing the plea of country's health care employees who first confronted the outbreak and where the proportion of women reach eighty percent, contributed heavily to conditioning the environment of massive indignation and wide-scale social distress. Furthermore, with massive demonstrations and protest movements taking place against the backdrop of appalling incidents of deaths of young Kyrgyz women victims of bride kidnapping cases, the gender dynamic, albeit not definitive, was one of the numerous social distresses which stirred the October 2020 uprising in Kyrgyzstan. That said, it is equally crucial to keep in mind the complex Central Asian social fabric related to gender issues. In particular, while on the one hand, women are constrained to face egregious cases of violence and domestic abuse, on the other hand, by virtue of "patriarchal bargain" which grants women a certain level of social recognition, the group is able to exert authority and power with "very public connections and effects" (Ismailbekova, 2016, p. 266).

As for the measures that addressed the spread of infections, the government response to the first cases of infections in the Kyrgyz territory such as country lockdown and general quarantine were direct and simplistic, largely imitated from its Central Asian totalitarian neighbors. The hasty and temporary measures, which indeed considerably limited contamination in the country, should have given the executive enough time to strengthen its health infrastructure and to develop adequate responses to a global pandemic. Nevertheless, the various and generous international aids, the amounts of which were known to the general public, were not used in time, and were spent mostly in maintaining jobs in the administration state level. Moreover, the first mobile hospitals launched by the government were only settled in July 2020.

Following a wave of general discontent (mostly on social networks) and concrete imperatives from the population (work, salary and social gatherings), the executive conceded in gradually lifting up former quarantine measures. One of the main consequences of this release has been the massive and dramatic increase in the number of infected people and deaths in the country during the summer of 2020.

If it seems logical to insert the October parliamentary elections in the backdrop of Covid-19, and to understand the crucial moment as a meeting between the executive and its population, which carried on significant expectations for the latter, we can notice the following quick decohesion of the same population. Indeed, as Doolotkeldieva (2021) demonstrated, the popular cohesion, whatever the social classes and mistrust of the executive at the time of the elections were, immediately disintegrated when the rush for political positions began.

We can observe then the mechanisms of two important and opposite movements, the rise of Sadyr Japarov figure as the savior of the nation and the degeneration of the former executive power, to develop on after the 'October revolution'. Both are deploying a specific aspect of the concept of *trust*. Many analysts have already labelled Sadyr Japarov as a martyr, and a politician pursuing right-wing and populist politics, a figure who unites and inspires hopes and confidence. On the other hand, the rise of Japarov cannot be explained without branding a scapegoat, an essential culprit to underline and support the 'positive' Japarov's policy line.

Indeed, former president Jeenbekov's executive now bears all the flaws observed during the pandemic such as mismanagement, corruption, embezzlement of international aid, attempts to control the Internet, to mention but a few. As a result, it seems that the pandemic, still present and prevalent in Kyrgyzstan, takes a back seat and is diverted by a political agenda rushing on catchier topics (the debatable status of the Kumtor gold mine for example). Japarov presents himself as the providential man. While his background in politics ranks him as one member of the old politician generation, he is able to crystallize the confidence of a large section of the population.

Japarov opens up a new political era in Kyrgyzstan as he is a man of *action*, and not of *inaction*, a characteristic denoting the former parliamentarian executive power. His political program, large and vague enough to attract anyone discontent with the previous management of the country's affairs, is a program of *action*. In fact, the first months of Japarov's tenure were in fact seriously active with a referendum on the new constitution (nicknamed 'Khanstitution', as it broadens president's effective power) and an attempt to forcibly nationalize the Canadian-owned goldmine Kumtor, actions which then lead to a visible implementation of the presidential program as a personal crusade against Kyrgyz present hydras (Imanaliyeva, 2020; Rickleton, 2021).

An interesting illustration of Japarov's populist policy seems to be reflected in the deliberate choice to have left the White house in 'open access', since the fences, erected under former President Askar Akaev in 2000, were removed in the beginning of November 2020. Only a corner remains as a memorial of the three past revolutions (Photo 6.4).

Last but not least, Japarov's success cannot be fully understood without the feeble voters' participation during the presidential elections of January 11, 2021 and the referendum for the constitution in April 11, 2021 (both painfully attracted over 30% of them to be accepted), demonstrating a kind of fatigue from the population, and the absence of a concrete and coherent opposition which would be able to provide concrete solutions to the country's structural problems. Meanwhile, Kyrgyzstan is trying out a new political direction, yet the pandemic issues have not 'disappeared' but are left to the hands of Kyrgyzstan's two soft-powers influences: the battle for vaccination has begun between China and Russia in Central Asia.

Photo 6.4 The White House in free access. June 14, 2021 (Photo by authors)

Bibliography

Akipress. (2020, September 23). *Kyrgyzstan's debt projected at 63.3% of GDP in 2022, 62.6% of GDP in 2023*. AKIpress Central Asian News Service. https://akipress.com/news:648476:Kyrgyzstan_s_debt_projected_at_63_3__of_GDP_in_2022,_62_6__of_GDP_in_2023/. Accessed 10 Mar 2021.

Akisheva, A. (2020, August 19). *Women face-to-face with domestic abuse during COVID-19 lockdown: The case of Kyrgyzstan* (Central Asia Program (CAP) Paper No. 238). pp. 1–7. https://www.centralasiaprogram.org/archives/18483. Accessed 10 Sept 2020.

Baialieva, G. & Kutmanaliev, J. (2020, October 15). *How Kyrgyz social media backed an imprisoned politician's meteoric rise to power*. OpenDemocracy. https://www.opendemocracy.net/en/odr/how-kyrgyz-social-media-backed-an-imprisoned-politicians-meteoric-rise-to-power/. Accessed 10 Dec 2020.

Beyer, J., & Kojobekova, A. (2019). Women of protest, men of applause: Political activism, gender and tradition in Kyrgyzstan. *Central Asian Survey, 34*(3), 329–345. https://doi.org/10.1080/02634937.2019.1631258

Bijbosunov, A. (2020, October 14). Kakie uroki izvlečet molodež iz sobytij v Kyrgyzstane. Radio Azattyk. https://rus.azattyk.org/a/30892242.html. Accessed 1 April 2021.

Blondin, S. (2020, June 11). *An environmentally-fragile and remittance–Dependent country facing a pandemic: The accumulation of vulnerabilities in Kyrgyzstan*. Environmental Migration Portal. https://environmentalmigration.iom.int/blogs/environmentally-fragile-and-remittance-dependent-country-facing-pandemic-accumulation. Accessed 25 July 2020.

Brody, A., & Rodriguez, L. (2019). *Kyrgyz Republic country gender assessment*. https://doi.org/10.22617/TCS190593-2

Bruley, J., & Mamadiiarov, I. (2020, November 10). *Kyrgyzstan: The socioeconomic consequences of the Covid-19 crisis* (Central Asia Program (CAP) Paper No. 244), pp. 1–15. https://centralasiaprogram.org/archives/18048. Accessed 10 Dec 2020.

'Byla li revoljucija i kto stoit za molodežnymi protestami v Kyrgyzstane — spor Kydyralieva s Surabaldievoj'. *Kloop*, October 28, 2020. https://kloop.kg/blog/2020/10/28/174563/. Accessed 1 Apr 2021.

CABAR. (2020, October 22). Who is Acting President of Kyrgyzstan Sadyr Zhaparov? Here's the Explanation. *Central Asian Bureau for Analytical Reporting*. https://cabar.asia/en/who-is-acting-president-of-kyrgyzstan-sadyr-zhaparov-here-s-theexplanation. Accessed 30 May 2021.

Cagnat, R., & Gaüzere, D. (2020, November 6). *Kirghizistan : coup d'État masqué en « Révolution d'octobre »*. Institut de Relations Internationales et Stratégiques. https://www.iris-france.org/151507-kirghizistan-coup-detat-masque-en-revolution-doctobre/. Accessed 20 Mar 2021.

Desmond, M. (2016). *Evicted: Poverty and profit in the American city*. Crown Book.

Djanibekova, N. (2020, March 8). *Kyrgyzstan: Women's march against male violence attacked by masked men*. Eurasianet. https://eurasianet.org/kyrgyzstan-womens-march-against-male-violence-attacked-by-masked-men. Accessed 1 Mar 2021.

Doolotkeldieva, A. (2021, February 19). Vlast' i prostranstvo v social'nyh mobilizatsiah: predvaritel'nye mysli o protestah, privedshih k smene vlasti d Kirghizstane osen'yu 2020 (Central Asia Program (CAP) Paper No. 251), pp. 1–9. https://www.centralasiaprogram.org/archives/19211. Accessed 10 Mar 2021.

Dzhumashova, A. (2021). *Ex-Minister of Health Kosmosbek Cholponbaev placed under house arrest*. 24.kg, January 22. https://24.kg/english/180947__Ex-Minister_of_Health_Kosmosbek_Cholponbaev_placed_under_house_arrest/. Accessed 10 Mar 2021.

Engval, J. (2020, October 8). Kyrgyzstan's Third Revolution. *The Central Asia-Caucuses Analyst*. https://www.cacianalyst.org/publications/analytical-articles/item/13643-kyrgyzstan's-third-revolution.html. Accessed 10 Mar 2021.

Eshaliyeva, K., (2020, July 13). *Is Kyrgyzstan losing the fight against coronavirus?* Open Democracy. https://www.opendemocracy.net/en/odr/kyrgyzstan-losing-fight-against-coronavirus/. Accessed 20 Mar 2021.

Fitzeorge-Parker, L. (2018, September 19). Impact banking: Microfinance comes of age in Kyrgyzstan. *Euromoney*. https://www.euromoney.com/article/b1b0967crmxs3m/impact-banking-microfinance-comes-of-age-in-kyrgyzstan. Accessed 20 Dec 2020.

France 24 (2021, April 16). Kyrgyzstan pushes poisonous root as virus cure. *Agence France-Presse*. https://www.france24.com/en/live-news/20210416-kyrgyzstan-pushes-poisonous-root-as-virus-cure. Accessed 20 May 2021.

Freedom House, *Freedom of the net 2020, Kyrgyzstan*. https://freedomhouse.org/country/kyrgyzstan/freedom-net/2020

Gabdulhakov, R. (2020, October 11). *The Avengers vs the Orcs: Social media nuances in Kyrgyzstan's (almost) third revolution*. Plovism (blog). https://www.plovism.com/post/the-avengers-vs-the-orcs-social-media-nuances-in-kyrgyzstan-s-almost-third-revolution?fbclid=IwAR0IqkfQO_q-3xH7ZTl0HwKz9O5Gzzq43IxLqe2ivdZPuqwBbw41vumT5H8. Accessed 20 Mar 2021.

Helf, G. (2020, October 8). *In Kyrgyzstan, It's easier to start a revolution than to finish it*. United States Institute of Peace. https://www.usip.org/publications/2020/10/kyrgyzstan-its-easier-start-revolution-finish-it . Accessed 20 Mar 2021.

Higgins, A. (2020, October 10). A convicted kidnapper is chosen to lead government of Kyrgyzstan. *New York Times*. https://www.nytimes.com/2020/10/10/world/asia/kidnapper-kyrgyzstan-prime-minister.html. Accessed 10 Dec 2020.

Human Rights Watch. (2017, May 10). *Kyrgyzstan: New domestic violence law. Government moves to improve response abuse*. New Release. https://www.hrw.org/news/2017/05/10/kyrgyzstan-new-domestic-violence-law. Accessed 10 Dec 2020.

International Labor Organization. (2020, September 14). Extending social protection to informal workers in the COVID-19 crisis: Country responses and policy considerations. *ILO Brief*. https://www.ilo.org/secsoc/information-resources/publications-and-tools/Brochures/WCMS_754731/lang--en/index.htm. Accessed 29 Mar 2021.

Imanaliyeva, A. (2020, November 18). *Kyrgyzstan's proposed new constitution provokes widespread revulsion*. Eurasianet, https://eurasianet.org/kyrgyzstans-proposed-new-constitution-provokes-widespread-revulsion. Accessed 31 May 2021.

Imanbekova, N. (2020a, August 2). *Ekonomika i COVID-19 v Tsentral'noi Azii*. Central Asian Analytical Network. https://www.caa-network.org/archives/19734. Accessed 10 Mar 2021.

Imanbekova, N. (2020b, November 4). *Could the growing national debt of Kyrgyzstan lead to default?* Central Asian Analytical Network. https://cabar.asia/en/could-the-growing-national-debt-of-kyrgyzstan-lead-to-default#_ftn1. Accessed 10 Mar 2021.

Ioakimidis, V. (2020). Why politics matters: In *Social work and the COVID-19 pandemic* (pp. 17–24). Policy Press. https://doi.org/10.2307/j.ctv1850gc4.7

Ismailbekova, A. (2016). Constructing the authority of women through custom: Bulak village, Kyrgyzstan. *Nationalities Papers, 44*(2), 266–280. https://doi.org/10.1080/00905992.2015.1081381

Ismailbekova, A. (2020, October 9). Intergenerational conflict at the core of Kyrgyzstan's turmoil. *The Diplomat*. https://thediplomat.com/2020/10/intergenerational-conflict-at-the-core-of-kyrgyzstans-turmoil/. Accessed 10 Dec 2020.

Jarman, H. (2021). State responses to the COVID-19 pandemic: Governance, surveillance, coercion, and social policy. In *Coronavirus politics* (pp. 51–64). University of Michigan Press. https://doi.org/10.3998/mpub.11927713.5

Johnson, N. P. A., & Mueller, J. (2002). Updating the accounts: Global mortality of the 1918–1920 "Spanish" Influenza Pandemic. *Bulletin of the History of Medicine, 76*(1), 105–115. https://www.jstor.org/stable/44446153

Jusupova, D. (2020, July 10). *Kak onlajn-platforma dlja vračej stala jablokom razdora meždu kabminom i volonterami*. Kaktus Media. https://kaktus.media/doc/416426_kak_onlayn_platforma_dlia_vrachey_stala_iablokom_razdora_mejdy_kabminom_i_volonterami.html. Accessed 10 Mar 2021.

'Kak starye politiki pytajutsja vernut′sja k vlasti na volne molodëžnogo protesta', *Kloop*, October, 6. https://kloop.kg/blog/2020/10/06/kak-staryepolitiki-pytayutsya-vernutsya-k-vlasti-na-volne-molodyozhnogo-protesta/. Accessed 10 Mar 2021.

Kandiyoti, D. (1988). Bargaining with patriarchy. *Gender and Society, 2*(3), 274–290. http://www.jstor.org/stable/190357

Karmazin, I., Baikova, T., & Bainazarov, E. (2020, October 6). Oktjabr'skaja revoljucija: Eks presidenta Kirgizii vynesli iz SIZO. *Izvestija iz*. https://iz.ru/1069960/igor-karmazin-tatiana-baikova-elnar-bainazarov/oktiabrskaia-revoliutciia-eks-prezidenta-kirgizii-vynesli-iz-sizo. Accessed 10 Mar 2021.

Kochorbaeva, Z. (2020, April 28). *Genderniya posledstviya COVID-19 v Kirghizstane* [Presentation]. Social Technologies Agency. http://ekois.net/wp-content/uploads/2020/05/Prezentatsiya_Kochorbaeva.pdf

Kojobaeva, Z. (2021, January 25). *Samaya vysokaya smertnost' za posledniye 10 let. Kak Kirghizstan perejil 2020 god*. Radio Azattyk. https://rus.azattyk.org/a/31067213.html. Accessed 10 Mar 2021.

Kolbaev, B. (2021, March 29). *"Nas zhdet bol'shoi krizis". Eksperti ob ekonomicheskoi situatsii v Kirghizstane"*. Radio Azattyk. https://rus.azattyk.org/a/31175005.html. Accessed 30 Mar 2021.

Kovalčíková, N., & Tabatai, A. (2020, August 4). *Five authoritarian pandemic messaging frames and how to respond* (German Marshall Fund of the United States, Paper No. 4). pp. 1–8. https://www.jstor.org/stable/resrep26755

Kuznetsova, I., Mogilevskii, R., Murzakulova, A., Abdoubaetova, A., Wolters, A., & Round, J. (2020, December 2). *Migration and COVID-19: Challenges and policy responses in Kyrgyzstan* (Central Asia Program (CAP) Paper No. 247), pp. 1–10. https://www.centralasiaprogram.org/archives/18483. Accessed 10 Mar 2021.

Li, A. (2020, June 24). *No transparency in Kyrgyzstan's coronavirus spending*. Organized Crime and Corruption Reporting Project (OCCRP). https://www.occrp.org/en/coronavirus/no-transparency-in-kyrgyzstans-coronavirus-spending. Accessed 10 Mar 2021.

Litvinova, D., (2020, July 28). *Volunteers came to the rescue as virus raged in Kyrgyzstan*. AP News. https://apnews.com/article/kyrgyzstan-ap-top-news-understanding-the-outbreak-international-news-photography-08aee6d2f32ba0eca8f5b3ae88b49fd5. Accessed 10 Mar 2021.

Marat, E. (2020a, October 12). *The incredible resilience of Kyrgyzstan*. OpenDemocracy. https://www.opendemocracy.net/en/odr/incredible-resilience-kyrgyzstan/. Accessed 10 Dec 2020.

Marat, E. (2020b, October 22). *Kyrgyzstan's protests won't keep corrupt criminals out of politics*. Foreign Policy. https://foreignpolicy.com/2020/10/22/kyrgyzstans-protests-wont-keep-corrupt-criminals-out-of-politics/. Accessed 10 Dec 2020.

Maslova, D. (2020, May 1). *'"Tirek": razrabotana onlajn-platforma o potrebnostjah medrabotnikov v oborudovanii i SIZ'*. Kaktus Media. https://kaktus.media/doc/412128_tirek:_razrabotana_onlayn_platforma_o_potrebnostiah_medrabotnikov_v_oborydovanii_i_siz.html. Accessed 10 Mar 2021.

Mathieu, E., Ritchie, H., Ortiz-Ospina, E. et al. (2021, May 10). A global database of COVID-19 vaccinations. *Nature Human Behavior*. https://doi.org/10.1038/s41562-021-01122-8

Moldokmatova, A., Dooronbekova, A., Zhumalieva, C., Estebesova, A., Mukambetov, A., Kubatova, A., Ibragimov, S., Aguas, R., Ariana, P., & White, L. (2020, April). Modelling the potential impact of various interventions on the COVID-19 epidemic in the Kyrgyz Republic. *Policy Brief*. https://soros.kg/srs/wp-content/uploads/2020/05/NPolicy-Brief.pdf. Accessed 20 Mar 2021.

Muktarbek kyzy, A. (2016, June 18). *Gender aspects of households' saving behavior in the Kyrgyz Republic*. National Bank of the Kyrgyz Republic (Working Paper no. 1). pp. 1–18. https://doi.org/10.2139/ssrn.2903948

Pellet, S. (2021, February 16). "*Surmortalité en Russie : le bilan de Rosstat sur 2020.*" *Le Carnet de REFPoM*. https://refpom.hypotheses.org/1147. Accessed 10 Mar 2021.

Pikulicka-Wilczewska, A. (2020, October 13). Rayimbek Matraimov: Do protests threaten Kyrgyzstan's kingmaker? *Al Jazeera*. https://www.aljazeera.com/features/2020/10/13/rayimbek-matraimov-do-protests-threaten-kyrgyzstans-kingmaker. Accessed 20 Mar 2021.

Piven, F., & Cloward, R. (1979). *Poor people's movements: Why they succeed, how they fail*. Vintage Books.

Pomfret, R. (2019). *The Central Asian economies in the twenty-first century*. Princeton University Press.

'Prem′er-ministr ob″jasnil, počemu snjali režim ČP: socseti i graždane vyražali nedovol′stvo' (2020, July 2). *Akipress*. https://kg.akipress.org/news:1629253/. Accessed 10 Mar 2021.

Republican stab. (2021, March 26). Statisticheskiye danniye. *Officialny sait o koronaviruse v Kyrgyzstane*. https://covid.kg/ru/map. Accessed 26 Mar 2021.

Rey-Bethbeder, M. (2020, October 13). Pourquoi le Kirghizistan s'enfonce dans le chaos politique, en 4 points. *Le Monde*, https://www.lemonde.fr/international/article/2020/10/13/kirghizista...ourquoi-le-pays-s-enfonce-dans-le-chaos-politique_6055887_3210.html. Accessed 10 Dec 2020.

RFE. (2020, October 7). Thousands Back in Bishkek Streets Demanding 'Clean' Politicians for New Government. *Radio Free Europe Radio Liberty / RL's Kyrgyz Service*. https://www.rferl.org/a/kyrgyzstan-fresh-protest-bishkek-clean-politicians-newgovernment/30880061.html. Accessed 1 April 2021.

Rickleton, C. (2021, May 10). *Kyrgyzstan: Expropriation law takes Kumtor battle to the brink*. Eurasianet. https://eurasianet.org/kyrgyzstan-expropriation-law-takes-kumtor-battle-to-the-brink. Accessed 30 May 2021.

Rossen, L. M., Branum, A. M., Ahmad, F. B., Sutton, P., & Anderson, R. N. (2020). Excess deaths associated with COVID-19, by age and race and ethnicity—United States, January 26–October 3, 2020. *MMWR. Morbidity and Mortality Weekly Report*, 69(42), 1522–1527. https://doi.org/10.15585/mmwr.mm6942e2

Ruisseau, N. (2020, October 7). Le Kirghizistan s'enfonce dans la crise politique. *Le Monde International*. https://www.lemonde.fr/international/

article/2020/10/07/le-kirghizistan-s-enfonce-dans-la-crise-politique_605 5114_3210.html. Accessed 10 Dec 2020.

Ryskulova, N. (2020a, May 20). "Territoria semi'yi". V Kirhgizistane prinyali jestkii zakon protiv domashnego nasiliya, no ne reshili problemu. *BBC News Russkaya Slujba*. https://www.bbc.com/russian/features-52733129. Accessed 10 Mar 2021.

Ryskulova, N., (2020b, August 15). Kyrgyzstan: kak volontery zamenili gosudarstvo v bor'be s koronavirusom. *BBC*. https://www.bbc.com/russian/features-53791289. Accessed 10 March 2021.

Ryskulova, N. (2020c, October 6). Neožidannaja revoljucija v Biškeke. Čto proishodit v Kyrgyzstane i počemu tam snova menjaetsja vlast'. *BBC*. https://www.bbc.com/russian/news-54440933. Accessed 10 Mar 2020.

Sagynbekova, L. (2017). *International labour migration in the context of the Eurasian Economic Union: Issues and challenges of Kyrgyz migrants in Russia*. Institute of Public Policy and Administration (University of Central Asia Working Paper No. 39). https://www.ucentralasia.org/Content/Downloads/UCA-IPPA-WP-39InternationalLabourMigration_ENG.pdf. Accessed 1 Mar 2021.

Saleci, R. (2020). *A passion for ignorance: What we choose not to know and why*. Princeton University Press.

Satke, R. (2021, March 1). *Corruption in Kyrgyzstan healthcare blamed for disastrous response to COVID-19*. The Foreign Policy Centre. https://fpc.org.uk/corruption-in-kyrgyzstan-healthcare-blamed-for-disastrous-response-to-covid-19/. Accessed 10 Mar 2021.

Satybaldieva, E. (2018). A mob for hire? Unpacking older women's political activism in Kyrgyzstan. *Central Asian Survey, 37*(2), 247–264. https://doi.org/10.1080/02634937.2018.1424114

Schulman, R., & Siman-Tov, D. (2020, March 18). *From biological weapons to miracle drugs: Fake news about the coronavirus pandemic*. Institute for National Security Studies (INSS Insight Paper No. 1275), pp. 1–5. https://www.jstor.org/stable/resrep23529

Schwartz, C. (2020, June 29). *Kyrgyzstan's not so "wonderful" anti-disinformation law*. Open Democracy. https://www.opendemocracy.net/en/odr/kyrgyzstans-not-so-wonderful-anti-disinformation-law/. Accessed 10 Mar 2021.

Sparkassenstiftung Kyrgyzstan (2019). Sberegatel'noe povedenie v Kirghizistane – issledovanie rynka 2019 [Institutional report presented to authors], pp. 1–58.

Sultanalieva, S. (2021, April 9). *Another woman killed in scourge of Kyrgyzstan 'Bride Kidnappings'*. Human Rights Watch. https://www.hrw.org/news/2021/04/09/another-woman-killed-scourge-kyrgyzstan-bride-kidnappings. Accessed 20 Apr 2021.

Suyarkulova, M. (2020, April 2). "Your traditions, our blood!": The struggle against patriarchal violence in Kyrgyzstan. *OpenDemocracy*. https://www.opendemocracy.net/en/odr/your-traditions-our-blood-the-struggle-against-patriarchal-violence-in-kyrgyzstan/. Accessed 1 Dec 2020.

'Thousands Back In Bishkek Streets Demanding 'Clean' Politicians For New Government', *Radio Free Europe Radio Liberty / RL's Kyrgyz Service*, October 7, 2020. https://www.rferl.org/a/kyrgyzstan-fresh-protest-bishkek-clean-politicians-new-government/30880061.html. Accessed 1 Apr 2021.

Tiulegenov, M. (2020, October 9). Protests over stolen elections in Kyrgyzstan. *Rosa-Luxemburg-Stiftung*. https://www.rosalux.de/en/news/id/43129/protests-over-stolen-elections-in-kyrgyzstan?cHash=b34d35f840d29de925c1a9b16277bb47. Accessed 10 Mar 2021.

Uraliev, M. (2020, October 10). *Sadyr Žaparov: U nas byl ne perevorot, a mirnoe obnovlenie*. Kaktus Media. https://kaktus.media/doc/423226_sadyr_japarov:_y_nas_byl_ne_perevorot_a_mirnoe_obnovlenie.html. Accessed 10 Mar 2021.

Wachtel, A. (2020, October 7). *Just what is happening in Kyrgyzstan?* OpenDemocracy. https://www.opendemocracy.net/en/odr/just-what-happening-kyrgyzstan/. Accessed 20 Oct 2020.

Wood, C. (2020, October 7). *Is this the beginning of Kyrgyzstan's next revolution?* Foreign Policy. https://foreignpolicy.com/2020/10/07/beginning-kyrgyzstan-next-revolution-election-protests-bishkek/. Accessed 10 Dec 2020.

World Bank. (2021, March 17). *One year later in the Kyrgyz Republic's battle against COVID-19*. https://www.worldbank.org/en/news/feature/2021/03/17/one-year-later-in-the-kyrgyz-republic-s-battle-against-covid-19. Accessed 20 Mar 2021.

World Food Programme. (2020, December 30). Price monitoring for food security in the Kyrgyz Republic. Issue 31, https://docs.wfp.org/api/documents/WFP-0000122610/download/. Accessed 20 Mar 2021.

Yip, P. S. F., Lam, K., Lau, E., Chau, P., Tsang, K., & Chao, A. (2005). A comparison study of realtime fatality rates: Severe acute respiratory syndrome in Hong Kong, Singapore, Taiwan, Toronto and Beijing, China. *Journal of the Royal Statistical Society. Series A (Statistics in Society)*, 168(1), 233–243. https://www.jstor.org/stable/3559718

CHAPTER 7

A Frontier Market in the COVID-19 Era: Kazakhstan's Economic Diversification in the 2020s

Wilder Alejandro Sánchez

Abstract Prior to the COVID-19 pandemic, the government of Kazakhstan was carrying out a strategy of economic diversification in order to decrease the country's dependence on its profitable energy industry which constitute the bulk of Kazakhstan's exports. As part of the diversification of its economy and trading partners, Kazakhstan has a long-term

---

Analyst who focuses on geopolitical, military, trade and cybersecurity issues in the Western hemisphere and post-Soviet regions. He was written significantly about Kazakhstan's foreign policy strategies, Nur-Sultan's relations with global powers, the role of the Kazakhstani military in UN peace operations, and environmental issues in the Central Asian nation. The author would like to thank Akbota Karibayeva and Aizhan Abilgazina for their assistance.

W. A. Sánchez (✉)
International Affairs and Defense Analyst, Washington, DC, USA

© The Author(s), under exclusive license to Springer Nature Singapore Pte Ltd. 2022
J.-F. Caron and H. Thibault (eds.), *Central Asia and the Covid-19 Pandemic*, The Steppe and Beyond: Studies on Central Asia, https://doi.org/10.1007/978-981-16-7586-7_7

objective: become one of the world's 30 most developed economies by 2050. The Central Asian nation is classified as a frontier market by global indexes, which means that it is viewed as having less developed political and economic structures, which makes them more volatile. However this label can be misleading as it does not properly demonstrate what Kazakhstan has accomplished in recent years in its quest to attract new trade partners and investors. New entities like the Astana International Financial Centre; the government's plans to become a trilingual nation; and recent initiatives to develop industries like agriculture, banking, manufacturing and tourism; demonstrate what good planning can accomplish. How will the pandemic affect Kazakhstan's plans and objectives? This essay seeks to demonstrate that the country has handled COVID-19 generally well from an economic point of view. While the informal sector and lack of development in the periphery remain problematic issues, Nur-Sultan has achieved much in its three decades of independence as a frontier market, transforming from a Soviet-style to a Western-style economy. Kazakhstan, thus, is an example of how a global pandemic does not necessarily have to cripple the development plans of a frontier market, if said country has clear short-term as well as long-term goals.

Keywords Kazakhstan · Frontier market · Economic diversification · Energy industry · International investment

Introduction

The Republic of Kazakhstan aims to become one of the 30 most developed nations by 2050. In order to achieve this objective, the government of the Central Asian nation is looking to diversify its economy by moving away from its traditional pillars, oil and gas, and heavily developing other industries like tourism, Information Technology (IT), green energy, and banking services.

Achieving this objective does not occur in a geopolitical vacuum, and will be affected by developments in Central Asia and beyond. Case in point, Kazakhstan trades with, and relies heavily upon trade and investment from the Russian Federation and the People's Republic of China (PRC), particularly via the latter's Belt and Road Initiative (BRI). While Kazakhstan has increased its commercial ties with the European

Union (The Netherlands is Kazakhstan's largest investor), Asian powerhouses like South Korea, and the United States, it still faces a delicate balancing act due to Central Asian geopolitics, namely Nur-Sultan's ties with Moscow and Beijing, in addition to simple geographical distance from other developed markets.

Another factor to keep in mind is the Coronavirus (COVID-19) pandemic which will have a lasting impact on the global economy. Even though vaccines, quarantines and lockdowns are working to contain and end the pandemic, it is unclear when the world will return to the "old normal," or if we will enter an era of a "new normal".

While the country has accomplished a lot in terms of economic development since its independence three decades ago, Kazakhstan is still regarded as a frontier market by the international community due to its reliance on a limited number of commodities, financial infrastructure, industrial infrastructure (apart from the energy field) and a lack of awareness by international investors about the country's situation and capabilities. This makes Kazakhstan an investment risk, though the situation is changing. Given the ongoing situation, can a frontier market successfully diversify its economy during a global health pandemic? Kazakhstan is a great case study to answer this question as the country's 2050 objective will require both greater economic development as well as diversifying its economy away from a reliance on energy production and energy exports. In other words, becoming one of the 30 most developed nations by 2050 will necessarily mean becoming a more developed market.

This chapter is divided in the following manner: first we will define frontier markets and explain why Kazakhstan is placed in this category by international ranking systems. Then, we will summarize the country's history since gaining independence from the Soviet Union, with a focus on its economy. The next section will discuss the 2050 strategy to better precisely understand the Kazakhstani government's objectives. Afterwards, we will discuss how Kazakhstan is looking to diversify its economy by using the Astana International Financial Centre as a mini-case study; moreover the country's diversifying pool of trade partnerships and new investors, will be addressed. We will then analyze the country's current situation, how COVID-19 has affected the country's economy, and we will attempt to predict the future by focusing on levels of economic development and other issues, like Kazakhstan's informal economy. Finally we will provide some concluding remarks.

The COVID-19 pandemic has put the future of the global economy in jeopardy, but there is the possibility that frontier markets, like Kazakhstan, can take advantage of this crisis in order to attract new trade partners and investors to certain industries and promote economic development.

Defining Frontier Markets and Economic Diversification

After achieving its independence in the early 1990s, Kazakhstan embarked on an ambitious program of industrialization and economic development. Nevertheless, in spite of the country's achievements, which we will discuss in later sections, Kazakhstan is still regarded by the international community as a frontier market, rather than an emerging market.

The term "frontier market" deserves some explanation as it will help readers understand Kazakhstan's situation. Economists, investors, and academics rely on "the main frontier index providers" namely MSCI, a US finance company; FTSE Russell, a subsidiary of the London Stock Exchange Group; and the S&P Dow Jones Indices, a division of S&P Global, which "have various methods to define whether a country is a frontier, emerging, or developed market based upon criteria including foreign investor access, size and liquidity of the market, custody, and the results of consultations with institutional investors" (Quisenberry, 2018, p. 20). Kazakhstan falls under the category of "frontier market" by the FTSE, MSCI and S&P DJI, hence we will utilize this label onwards.

What *exactly* is a frontier market? These countries "tend to be less integrated with the global economy than emerging-market economies and relatively more affected by country-specific factors such as political crises, natural disasters, debt problems, and currency risk" (Quisenberry, 2018, pp. 23–24). They are also are at an earlier stage of development and, in most cases, are not tied into global manufacturing supply chains and are therefore less impacted by global cycles (Bell, 2017, p. 2). Similarly, frontier markets generally have less developed political and economic structures, which makes them more volatile—for example these nations are viewed as lacking "the level of political stability, financial infrastructure, and legal and regulatory framework that characterize more developed markets. Language and cultural barriers, physical distance and less abundant information all factor into the aura of risk surrounding frontier markets" (Rowader, 2015, p. 3). It is worth noting here that Nur-Sultan has looked to address these precise issues in its quest for economic development and diversification.

In spite of the challenges that frontier markets face, international investors see these nations as attractive locations, as they "share many positive attributes that have attracted long-term investors to emerging markets such as fast-growing economies, relatively cheaper valuations, and a source of diversification to equity investments" (Quisenberry, 2018, p. 20). Kazakhstan is one of these frontier markets that has developed an image of stable, fast-growing economy that has attracted investors and companies looking to diversify their portfolios.

One noteworthy factor about frontier economies is their reliance on a very limited number of commodities that are exported to the global market. Mostly, these commodities are non-renewable natural resources, which is the case for Kazakhstan. "While frontier economies are moving away from commodity reliance, for many countries this is an ongoing adjustment, and low or volatile oil and commodity prices still weigh on both government and corporate balance sheets" (Bell, 2017, p. 5). Investment reports on frontier markets have explicitly highlighted Kazakhstan's reliance on oil. As explained by one global investment management firm, "several of the large index countries are net oil exporters and oil can represent a significant portion of fiscal revenues and impact overall economic health. The large oil exporters, [include] Kazakhstan" (Bell, 2017, p. 3).

Kazakhstan wants to move away from its reliance on oil, thereby diversifying its economy, but what does diversification mean? This term can be interpreted "as the shift toward a more varied structure of domestic production and trade with a view to increasing productivity, creating jobs and providing the base for sustained poverty-reducing growth" (Brenton et al., 2019, p. 142). Trade is a key factor behind economic diversification; with governments and businesses looking to manufacture new goods and provide new services that are exported. Kazakhstan already exports oil and energy-related commodities, so the goal for Nur-Sultan is export diversification, which "is an objective in itself to reduce vulnerability to adverse terms of trade shocks and stabilise export revenues, as well as driving output diversification" (Brenton et al., 2019, p. 142).

Economic diversification is generally advised to improve the health of a country's economy. Successful diversification is all the more important now in the wake of slow global growth due to COVID-19, which has caused massive unemployment and economic stagnation in many countries. Scholarly works and investment-related business reports that analyze oil-dependent economies generally suggest economic diversification. For example, "like some Middle Eastern governments, Kazakhstan's government knows that it must diversify the economy to prepare for the day when oil reserves and mineral resources become depleted or when the world customers stop buying," argue financial investment analysts Graham and Emid (Graham & Emid, 2013, pp. 94–95).

There is an obvious necessity for frontier markets to take advantage of the latest technology available. This type of "technological leap-frogging affords considerable efficiency gains and offers developing nations a fast track into the globalized economy. The trajectory of technology adoption is an important factor for future economic growth" (Chou, 2020). Digital transformation was already occurring well before the COVID-19 pandemic appeared, but the crisis has accelerated the adoption of newer technologies, as digital connectivity is critical to protect businesses.

Finally, it is worth noting that economic diversification does not solely mean creating new industries and exporting final products. For example, "diversifying the range and quality of imported inputs can support quality upgrading and productivity growth in existing sectors and allow new varieties of products to be developed" (Brenton et al., 2019, p. 143). In other words, Kazakhstan must not only produce new goods, they have to be of good quality to compete in the global market; this can be achieved by using the latest technologies available depending on the industry, like for example the latest software for banking services or automated systems in car manufacturing.

Brief Historical Overview: From Independence to 2020

As the USSR disintegrated, the Republic of Kazakhstan passed the *Constitutional Independence Law of Republic of Kazakhstan* on 16 December 1991, which confirmed its status as an independent state. Nursultan Nazarbayev became the first president of Kazakhstan on October 25, 1990, after being elected to this position by the Supreme Soviet; he subsequently won the country's first presidential elections in 1991 and ruled until his decision to step down in March 2019. He was succeeded by Kassym-Jomart Tokayev, who became president on 20 March, a day after

Nazarbayev resigned, via constitutional succession. Tokayev was formally elected via the presidential elections of 9 June 2019.[1]

With the dissolution of the Soviet Union, Kazakhstan inherited a tough set of economic, social, and geopolitical conditions. The existing economic system collapsed, and the sudden political and economic vacuum caused by the absence of the USSR left Eurasia in a temporary state of disarray as the channels of international trade were lost and domestic demand and production capacity shrunk. On the other hand, with independence, Kazakhstan gained control and sovereignty of an enormous landmass with a plethora of natural resources, including vast endowments of oil, natural gas, coal, uranium, lead, copper and chrome.

Throughout Nazarbayev's lengthy rule, there was a sense of predictability to Kazakhstan's foreign and economic policies, as the Kazakhstani government turned towards its closest neighbors for trade. For example, after gaining independence from the USSR, Kazakhstan maintained close ties with the Russian Federation, and also moved to develop trade relations with the PRC (BBC, 2019). Moreover, the country quickly came to rely on hydrocarbons as the driving force in jumpstarting its economy. For example, in March 2001, a "major pipeline for transporting oil from Caspian to world markets opened," traveling from the Tengiz oil field in Western Kazakhstan to the Russian Black Sea port of Novorossiysk (BBC, 2019). Then in 2004, Nur-Sultan and Beijing signed a deal to build an oil pipeline along their common border. Thus, Kazakhstan's close economic and trade ties with China pre-date the Belt and Road Initiative.

Over the past decade, Kazakhstan has continued its reliance on Russia, including membership to the Russian-led Eurasian Economic Union (EAEU), which was created in 2014 and of which Kazakhstan is a founding member. Similarly, Kazakhstan has continued to rely on China for trade and investment. This connection grew as Nur-Sultan joined BRI. Interestingly, Chinese President Xi Jingping announced the creation of the One Belt One Road Initiative (now known simply as the Belt and Road Initiative) during a 2013 visit to Kazakhstan; this fact highlights the importance of Kazakhstan to China's grand strategy of international infrastructure, as Kazakhstan is a key component of transportation and

---

[1] Nazarbayev now has the title of Elbasy, or Leader of the Nation, and is also commonly referred to as the First President of the country. He continues to exercise significant influence in the country as he has a voice in daily governmental affairs, including participating in meetings with policymakers and foreign leaders.

shipping across Central Asia to ports along the Caspian Sea and in Europe.

While trade relations have traditionally focused on Russia and China, in recent years Kazakhstan has increased trade significantly with extra-regional states, such as direct trade with the members of the European Union. The Netherlands and Italy stand out as Kazakhstan's major trade partners with the caveat that most of this trade and commerce is based on energy goods. We will discuss this in later sections.

THE 2050 STRATEGY

Kazakhstan's 2050 Strategy was first delineated in a 14 December 2012 speech by then-President Nazarbayev. In his remarks Nazarbayev proclaimed that "our main goal is to enter the club of the top 30 most developed countries of the world," by 2050 (Nazarbayev, 2012).

The 2050 objective will be achieved by focusing the budget of the state on "long-term, productive national projects that include the diversification of the economy and development of infrastructure" (Nazarbayev, 2012). Moreover the government must "think outside the box and create joint ventures in the region and throughout the world—Europe, Asia, America" (Nazarbayev, 2012) and build ports in countries with direct access to the sea and develop transport and logistics hubs at nodal transit points. To an extent this has already happened as Beijing has heavily invested in developing Kazakhstan's transportation infrastructure, namely railroads, to move goods from Western China, across Central Asia, to Russia and the Caspian Sea. One major example of Chinese investment in transportation infrastructure is the Khorgos Gateway, a mega dry port located in Kazakhstan.

Due to space limitations, we cannot analyze in detail every section of the speech, thus we will simply enumerate some of Nazarbayev's proposals which have a strong correlation to this chapter's overall theme. While the speech does not mention Kazakhstan's status as a frontier market, the policy recommendations and objectives in the speech are the sort of strategies a frontier market would take to attain "developed market" status.

Information Technology (IT) is singled out as a source of development and income, as the state must "ensure that by 2030 at least 2–3% of global information flows go through Kazakhstan. This figure must double by 2050." Specifically, the speech explains the need to develop "our two leading innovation clusters," namely Nazarbayev University and the Park of Innovative Technologies. Private companies that focus on research and innovation should be particularly targeted, as innovation is key.

Regarding green energies, the speech highlights the importance of "alternative energy sources," as the state must be "actively seeking to introduce technologies using solar and wind power." Nazarbayev proposed that by 2050 alternative and renewable energy sources must provide for at least half of the country's total energy consumption. As for agriculture, the country should aim to become a "leader in the global agriculture market." Moreover, through this industrialization plan, "the non-energy share of our total exports must double by 2025, and triple by 2040."

To achieve these goals, the speech highlights the need to attract investors to Kazakhstan in a wide range of industries, preferably by partnering with local companies. Nazarbayev adds one critical condition for these agreements: "these partnerships [must] bring the transfer of modern technology for extraction and processing. We must allow investors to extract and use our raw materials only in exchange for the creation of new production facilities in our country" (Nazarbayev, 2012). Transfer of new technologies is heavily advised to frontier markets to develop their local industries.

Even more, "Kazakhstan must become a magnet for investment in the region. Our country must become the most attractive place in Eurasia for investment and technology transfer. This is crucially important. To do this we must demonstrate our advantages to investors." To this end, Kazakhstan has created agencies like KazakhInvest and the Astana International Financial Centre (AIFC).

The speech also stresses that this development plan must benefit Kazakhstani citizens across the country, not just in major urban areas. "Within the country we must create 'infrastructure centres' to ensure coverage of remote regions and places with low population density with vitally important and economically necessary infrastructure facilities." In other words, the speech calls not only for the diversification of the country's economy, but also a decentralization of the industries away from major cities like Nur-Sultan and Almaty, not including oil fields (for example the Kashanga field, an offshore oil field in the Caspian Sea), to the benefit of the country's periphery.

The speech also warns about the perils Kazakhstan faces if it continues to be dependent on a few exports since, "technological revolutions change the structure of commodity consumption," as "the introduction of composite technologies and new types of concrete cause depreciation of iron ore and coal reserves. This is another motivation for us to accelerate the pace of extraction and delivery to world commodity markets to exploit the current global demand" (Nazarbayev, 2012).

Global experts and analysts have predicted a looming global oil crisis or another oil crisis, perhaps accelerated by the COVID-19 pandemic. Thus Kazakhstan must "[expand its] export-oriented non-energy sector," the 2050 strategy explains, in order to avoid suffering if, or rather when, the next global crisis occurs. We see again how the 2050 speech highlights another danger of frontier markets, namely depending on a a single non-renewable energy commodity, and encourages diversification.

How Is Kazakhstan Diversifying Its Economy?

To understand how COVID-19 is affecting Kazakhstan's economy, as well as short and long-term economic diversification plans, it helps to briefly summarize what initiatives Nur-Sultan has carried out lately. For example Nur-Sultan has managed to attract US companies to set up facilities within Kazakhstan's borders: in late 2019 the international meat conglomerate Tyson Foods announced that it will set up meat processing facilities (Tyson Foods, 2019) while in late 2020 Valley Irrigation announced that open a facility to manufacture 1000 linear and pivot irrigation machines (Valmont, 2021). Similarly the South Korean auto-manufacturing company Hyundai set up a manufacturing facility in the city of Almaty, which was launched in October 2020 (KazInform, 2020).

Another country that is in the process of creating projects in Kazakhstan is Qatar, as a Kazakh delegation visited Qatar in early 2021, bringing "37 tailored brownfield projects worth US$4.6 billion in such sectors as agriculture, mining industry, defense industry, tourism and petrochemical industry" (Kuandyk, 2021a). While investment in mining and petrochemicals is not a new development, Qatari investment in tourism is meaningful, especially at a time when Kazakhstan aims to attract tourism from India, among other countries (Kuandyk, 2021b).

In recent years, Nur-Sultan has attempted to attract more international tourists to the country. Kazakhstan has some hot-spots for international visitors, like the Petroglyphs of Tamgaly or the Khoja Ahmed Yasawi mausoleum, a UNESCO world cultural heritage site. These human-made attractions stand in addition to natural attractions like the Saryarka—Steppe and Lakes and the Kolsai Lakes, which give Kazakhstan potential as a destination for eco-tourism (Satubaldina, 2021; Shayakhmetova, 2020). Kazakhstan is also attempting to develop tourism around the Aral Sea, as the government has worked hard to save it from long-term damage caused by Soviet-era river diversions to irrigate agricultural areas. While it is not a focus of our analysis, it is worth noting that Penati explains how "Soviet environmental legacy [in Kazakhstan] extends beyond the material domain (where it is visible both as direct continuity in practices and as long-term consequences of past policies) to include ideology and decision-making processes (Penati, 2019, p. 52). The country even adopted the popular "Very nice!" catchphrase from Sacha Baren Cohen's fictional character, Borat, as part of a new international tourism campaign (Sullivan, 2020).

Interest in developing the tourism sector has foreign policy implications as well. Case in point, Kazakhstan and Uzbekistan are planning to construct a high-speed railway that will connect the Shymkent and Turkistan regions in Kazakhstan with the city of Tashkent, Uzbekistan's capital. The idea is to facilitate the movement of people, allowing tourists, ideally from outside the region, to hop between the two countries. So far, international tourism has plenty of space to grow: there were 11.3 million international visits in 2015; only to sink to 9.7 million in 2016, though there was a jump back to 10.7 million in 2019 (World Bank, 2021). If successful, this would be an important confidence-building mechanism and cooperation initiative between two governments that aim to become Central Asia's powerhouse, a mutually exclusive goal which has caused occasional tensions since both countries gained independence from the USSR.

The willingness to attract investors and partners means that Kazakhstan has risen in the ranks of the World Bank's *Ease of Doing Business* lists. Kazakhstan is the highest-ranked Central Asian country, currently standing at the 25th spot, between the European countries Ireland (24th) and Iceland (26th). The next Central Asian country in the list is Uzbekistan, at number 69. One agency precisely created to attract investors and partners is the Astana International Financial Centre to demonstrate. We will now carry out a brief case study of this entity.

Case Study: The AIFC

Created under the "100 Concrete Steps" National Plan of 2015 and drawing from the experiences of global financial centers, the Astana International Finance Centre (AIFC) aims to diversify Kazakhstan's economy through new investments in capital market, asset management, Islamic finance, green finance, and private banking, thereby becoming Eurasia's new financial hub in the process. As of March 2021, a total of 704 companies have registered at the AIFC, dozens of which registered during the COVID-19 era.

Functioning under English common law, the AIFC's independent jurisdiction aims to generate a trusting business environment that has already attracted local and regional investors. The Centre's Court and the International Arbitration Centre are staffed with many international, well-renowned judges. By drawing on English common law, and attracting senior legal experts to its ranks, the AIFC also seeks to assure Western investors that the overall system that the AIFC utilizes is one that they already understand and can easily navigate. Moreover, to further advance a conducive business climate and attract global players, the AIFC's legal framework has established simplified visa and tax procedures for participants (AIFC "Visa" and "Tax Regime").

One of the AIFC's bodies, the Astana International Exchange (AIX), is a stock platform that seeks to develop Kazakhstan's capital market and facilitate the privatization of state assets, including in transport, telecommunications, and energy industries. Having the Shanghai Stock Exchange, Goldman Sachs, the Silk Road Fund, and Nasdaq as the main partners, the AIX receives assistance with market research and gets access to state-of-the-art technologies that allow for efficient trading operations.

While the AIFC had already made efforts to promote new financial technologies through its FinTech Lab, the COVID-19 pandemic has further reinforced the dire need to develop more innovative financial instruments and services in mobile banking, digital assets, and other contactless operations.

For example, a Regulatory Sandbox regime, launched in 2019, that greatly simplifies the registration and regulatory requirements has created favorable conditions for start-up and incumbent tech companies to bypass unnecessary legal barriers and test their new products on regional markets (KazInform, 2019). The Centre has even created an AIFC Green Finance Centre to promote economic projects and attract investment with a focus on green industries and "within Kazakhstan's new commitments to achieve carbon neutrality by 2060" (AIFC, 2020).

With Islamic finance attracting global attention, though how will COVID-19 affect its growth has yet to be determined, the sector is also of particular importance to the AIFC which seeks to provide the necessary infrastructure and establish a regulatory framework to develop the Islamic finance market in Central Asia and the Commonwealth of Independent States countries. Moreover, through close engagement with the Asian Development Bank (ADB), the AIFC has set up regulations for operations in Islamic banking, *takaful*, and capital markets, and is planning to issue *sukuk*, the Sharia-compliant equivalent of a bond. Improving by seven positions and holding in 2018 the 24th place among 48 countries in the Islamic Finance Country Index (*Global Islamic Finance Report*, 2018, p. 3) while also leading in the Global Islamic Economy Indicator among the the Commonwealth of Independent States (CIS) countries, Kazakhstan has already been able to capitalize on the initiatives undertaken by the AIFC.

While Kazakhstan's National Bank had previously expressed its concerns regarding cryptocurrency mining, new amendments to the regulation of digital technologies introduced by the President Tokayev in June 2020 officially legitimized the mining of cryptocurrencies in order to stimulate more investment in this new industry (Abilgazina, 2020). At the time of writing, the AIFC is working to establish a well-functioning regulatory framework that will set rules and regulations on cryptocurrency transactions, and block-chain based projects.

The AIFC is an example of how Kazakhstan is adapting to the "new normal" that is the COVID-19 world while looking for new alternatives to continue attracting investors to the Central Asian nation. By adopting English law, hiring European judges for its ranks, and teaming up with major stock exchange institutions, the AIFC is also helping address another problem that a frontier market like Kazakhstan has: a lack of a positive image in Western markets to attract attract investors and new partners. Thus, the AIFC should be regarded not just as for a centre for stock exchange and arbitration procedures, but also as a part of a marketing campaign to help Kazakhstan gain a more prominent extra-regional image.

OLD AND NEW PARTNERS AND INVESTORS

In 1994, Nazarbayev announced Kazakhstan's intention to pursue a multivector foreign policy by taking into account the country's situation in post-Cold War Eurasian geopolitics and potential at the time. While Kazakhstan's lengthy border with Russia—not to mention economic and cultural ties, including the significant portion of ethnic Russians living in Kazakhstan—was not going to disappear, the Kazakhstani government still drafted a multivector foreign policy through which it would develop ties with multiple partners without committing to any one in particular. "Multivectorism consists of actively seeking to maintain positive relations with Russia, the West, China, and the Islamic world without firmly committing to any one 'vector,'" explains Ambrosio (Ambrosio, 2021, p. 31). The 2050 Strategy speech has a similar spirit and objectives.

The geopolitics of Central Asia have always been a complex issue due to its strategic position on the crossroads of East and West along the transit routes of the ancient Silk Road. Located at the heart of Eurasia, Kazakhstan has historically been at the epicenter of the centuries-long Great Game of regional powers vying for influence over the region. Sandwiched between Russia to the North, China to the East, an ambitious Uzbekistan to the South, with Afghanistan, Iran, and the Caucasus in close proximity, Kazakhstan has a rather peculiar set of neighbors to grapple with. This means that the Kazakhastani government has to swiftly adapt to developing situations by its major neighbors; in other words "Kazakhstan's multivectorism is becoming increasingly 'reactive' in nature with Astana assuming cautious stances whenever international disputes involving Russia arise," like the 2008 war in Georgia and 2014 annexation of Crimea (Sullivan, 2021, p. 31). Ambrosio offers a similar analysis, arguing that while, during the Nazarbayev era the country "managed to maintain positive relations with all interested parties, this was uneven in practice as Nur-Sultan found itself increasingly, and exclusively, connected with Russia in the security realm through the Collective Security Treaty Organization (CSTO)" (Ambrosio, 2021, p. 29).

Giving major partners a stake in Kazakhstan's economic success through multivectorism proved to be an effective way of mitigating potential threats from immediate neighbors while capitalizing on economic opportunities arising from Western investments. Thus, the last thirty years have witnessed the perseverance of regional partners among Kazakhstan's trade partners. Russia maintains dominance through the

Eurasian Economic Union (EAEU). The EAEU, which follows a regional integration model initially proposed by Nazarbayev and fully embraced by Putin, has been expanding in breadth and depth.[2]

China, over the past decade, has evolved as a regional player into a global economic powerhouse, boosting its trade and infrastructure investment into the Kazakhstani economy through the Belt and Road Initiative. BRI, in turn, has become a megaproject for advancing global connectivity and infrastructural development. Concerns have emerged around China's practice of so-called predatory lending in South, Southeast, and Central Asia. Kazakhstan has remained generally unaffected so far. As an economically stronger nation than many of its Central Asian and Asian partners, Kazakhstan has managed to avoid insolvency scandals; nevertheless there has been considerable push back from the population with repeated popular civilian and labor protests erupting to oppose and boycott Chinese projects and migration of workers (*Radio Free Europe*, 2021; Reuters, 2019).

The Western partnership has been primarily characterized by European consumption of fossil fuels and European and US investment and engagement with energy and manufacturing projects. Crude oil, mineral resources, and chemicals make up Kazakhstan's largest exports and sources of revenue, with a number of EU countries, such as Italy, The Netherlands, and Spain, being top export destinations in 2018. These exports then tend to reorient the data, which allows for misinterpretations. For example, via direct investments from The Netherlands to Kazakhstan has exceeded USD90 billion but trade and investment are focused on, unsurprisingly, energy as "Kazakhstan exports crude oil and oil products, ferroalloys, titanium and titanium products to the Netherlands" (Хабар24, 2020). Thus, while Dutch trade and investment in Kazakhstan is very significant, it remains centered on energy so far, thereby prolonging the latter country's status as a frontier.

It is expected that trade between the European Union and Kazakhstan will increase in the coming years as the Enhanced Partnership and Cooperation Agreement (EPCA), entered into force on 1 March 2020. This agreement will both cement and help diversify trade and commercial relations between Brussels, EU member states, and Nur-Sultan. This is no small goal, since, as a bloc, the EU is Kazakhstan's biggest trade partner,

---

[2] Its members are Armenia, Belarus, Kazakhstan, Kyrgyzstan and Russia with various observers, including Uzbekistan.

with almost 40% share in its total external trade—with the aforementioned caveat that some 80% of Kazakhstan's exports to Europe constitute oil and gas (European Commission, 2020).

Meanwhile, trade between the United States and Kazakhstan is not particularly significant: USD2 billion in 2019, making Kazakhstan only the US's 81st partner (Office of the United States Trade Representative, 2020). The US's major exports to Kazakhstan include machinery, aircraft, and electrical machinery; while Kazakhstani exports to the US market focus, unsurprisingly, on commodities like mineral fuels, iron and steel, inorganic chemicals and rare metals like uranium. Agricultural Kazakhstani exports to the United States, like tea, planting seeds and snack foods barely reached USD11 million.

In an example of plans to diversify trade and promote investment, in January 2021, in the middle of the COVID-19 pandemic, the United States, Kazakhstan and Uzbekistan created the US-Central Asia Investment Partnership. Administered through the US International Development Finance Corporation and the AIFC, this initiative will aim to raise USD1 billion over the span of five years to improve private sector engagement and boost economic growth and regional connectivity. The initiative will utilize the existing infrastructure established by the C5+1 multilateral format (US Embassy in Kazakhstan, 2021). Through this type of cooperation, US agencies have been working to foster private sector economic cooperation with Kazakhstani businesses.

In recent years, Kazakhstan has sought to increase its commercial ties with other nations. Trade between South Korea and Kazakhstan, for example, reached USD4.22 billion in 2019 (Nikolova, 2021) The same year, Kazakhstani exports to Japan reached USD1.078 billion, while Kazakhstani imports from Japan reached USD417 million (Ministry of Foreign Affairs of Japan, 2020). Japan exported manufactured goods like motor vehicles, machinery for construction in addition to metals, while Kazakhstan exported petroleum, coal, and metals. As for India, a rising global power with a major market, bilateral trade only reached USD1.56 billion in 2019. Similarly, Turkey and Kazakhstan have good diplomatic ties, and there are expectations that trade can grow given recent developments in the Caucasus. Specifically, the opening of the Nakhchivan corridor between Azerbaijan and its southwestern autonomous enclave bordering Turkey could help the country unite with Central Asia, particularly Kazakhstan (Andalou Agency, 2021).

A Frontier Market's Informal Economy

One more issue to keep in mind is the future of Kazakhstan's informal economy in the post-COVID-19 world. Informal economies are a staple of frontier markets where industries are less developed and exports are centered on less than a handful of commodities, usually raw materials. The problems with the informal economy are well-known, such as low paying jobs, limited access to training, and little or no social security coverage or labour protection covered by contracts (OECD, 2017, p. 134).

How big is the informal economy in a country of 19 million? By gathering data from different sources, it is possible to have idea of the situation. In 2014 approximately 2.9 million of the 8.5 million-member workforce were informal workers and an estimated 77 per cent of informal workers were paid employees in a registered enterprise (Mussurov et al., 2018, p. 6). Another statistic comes from Visa and the global management consulting firm A.T. Kearney, which explained that in 2016 as much as 33.5% of Kazakhstan's GDP came from the informal economy (A.T. Kearney & Visa, 2018, p. 9). More recently, according to a U.S. State Department Human Rights report, as of August 2018, Kazakhstan reported that 1.3 million citizens of a nine-million-person workforce were not registered as either employed or unemployed, meaning that they likely worked in the informal economy (US State Department, 2020, p. 60).

As for areas of work, the informal economy in Kazakhstan is "concentrated in the retail trade, transport services, agriculture, real estate, beauty and hair dressing salons, and laundry and dry-cleaning businesses. Small entrepreneurs and their employees for the most part work without health, social, or pension benefits" (US State Department, 2020, p. 60). Informality tends to be more common in rural areas, and "living in the poor agricultural Southern region tends to raise the probability of informality" (Mussurov et al., 2018, p. 12) Nevertheless we should clarify that informality in agriculture is "a mix of inherited customs and practices in agriculture, which may be difficult to eradicate and could to some extent be considered as 'normal'" (OECD, 2017, p. 134).

Prior to the pandemic, Nur-Sultan was already attempting to reduce the informal economy through digitalization as part of a larger process to increase tax collections from 18 to 25% of GDP by 2025 (IMF, 2020, p. 12). In early 2021, the Kazakh government drafted a new development plan by 2025, which includes managing this specific sector. Specifically the government aims to reduce it via the legalization and simplification of labor contracts, expanding coverage of social security, improving a registration system, and keeping in check "shadow economy" employers (Prime Minister of the Republic of Kazakhstan, 2021). The plans also aim to create automated employment centers, and vocational guidance services to help individuals obtain new, formal employments (Prime Minister of the Republic of Kazakhstan, 2021).

It remains to be seen how COVID-19 will affect Kazakhstan's informal economy in the long term, though it is expected to bounce back as "informal jobs are much more flexible both in terms of separation and hiring decisions, and so they are likely to get destroyed first as soon as the shutdown hits, but also recover more rapidly than those in formal employment" (Ybrayev, 2020). While informal economies also exist even in developed markets, Kazakhstan must formalize more of its informal sector in the post-COVID-19 world or if it will continue to be a crippling factor to economic development, investments and its future as a frontier market.

The Future of an Emerging Frontier Market in the COVID-19 World

This essay has discussed Kazakhstan's economic strategy to become one of the world's 30 most developed nations by 2050, the pillars of Kazakhstan's economy as well as its major trade partners: China, Russia, EU members like the Netherlands; as well as minor trade partners like Japan, Turkey, South Korea, the United States. Given the geopolitics of Central Asia and Kazakhstan's own foreign policy objectives, the situation is a combination of a multivector foreign and economic policy, aimed at diversification. In other words, Kazakhstan is a "frontier market" that is seeking to diversify not only the products and services it produces, but also its pool of trading partners and its foreign investors.

During the first months of 2020 the COVID-19 pandemic spread through Central Asia, and the rest of the world. By May 2021, Kazakhstan reported over 506 thousand cases, with 5116 confirmed fatalities.[3] At the global level, there have been more than four million confirmed fatalities,

---

[3] It is worth noting that these are state-provided numbers. It is generally believed that the official data regarding COVID-19 cases and deaths across the globe is underestimated. For example, new studies show that the death toll in India may be as much as 10 times the official number. Cases in Kazakhstan are likely under-reported as well.

and over 160 million confirmed cases. There is reason to be optimistic, as various vaccines, such as Moderna, Pfizer, Sputnik V, and even the Kazakhstani-made QazCOVID (Dysengulova, 2021)—in are in production, and a global vaccination program is underway. However, it will take years before the majority of the world is vaccinated. To make the situation even more problematic, there are new variants of COVID-19 that have appeared in the United Kingdom, South Africa, and the United States, while countries like Brazil and India continue to be major hotspots. As for Kazakhstan, the Delta variant was identified in July, which led to an increase of infected individuals in the country.

It is too early to fully understand how COVID-19 will impact the future of humanity. Will we return to the "old normal"? Or will humanity have to adapt to this "new normal," in which COVID-19 exists for the foreseeable future? There is also the risk that even after COVID-19 is finally defeated, a new global health pandemic will simply take its place. There are similar concerns about a new global financial crisis in the near future. Thus governments across the world, like Kazakhstan, must not only focus on the day-to-day problems of the pandemic, but must also have foresight and prepare for future worst-case scenarios.

President Tokayev and the Kazakhstani government have attempted to protect the country's economy from the effects of COVID-19 by continuing to attract international investments and trade partners. As the pandemic spread in March of 2020, the Kazakhstani leader announced that his government will focus on "maintaining its economy in a sustainable development mode in a completely new reality," by reorienting "budget expenditure items to maintain employment [and] support small and medium-sized businesses" (President of Kazakhstan, 2020a).

In spite of protective measures, there was an unsurprising contraction of the Kazakhstani economy due to COVID-19. According to the World Bank, the Kazakhstani economy contracted by 2.5% in 2020, a significant change of direction compared to recent years, when it was expanding—the economy had grown by 4.1% in 2018, and 4.5% in 2019. The country was particularly hurt due to the drastic fall of daily oil prices in the global market, from USD61.72 on 23 December, 2019, to USD15.06 on 27 April, 2020, at the height of the pandemic. The prices have generally recovered, reaching USD64.27 on 8 March, 2021. Nevertheless, the temporary dramatic fall cost Kazakhstan tens of millions of dollars. There is good news though: the World Bank expects the Central Asian nation's economy to grow by 2.5% in 2021, and 3.5% in 2022 (Rahardja & Agaidarov, 2020).

As for trade, in 2019 Kazakhstan's overall global trade totaled USD97.774 billion. The number was reduced to USD85.031 billion by 2020, according to preliminary data provided by Kazakhstani authorities (Kazakhstan's Bureau of National Statistics, 2021). As part of COVID-19-related measures, President Tokayev "transferred the authority to oversee competition policy to the newly established Agency for Development and Protection of Competition to reduce monopoly practices and unfair competition across economic activities" (Rahardja & Agaidarov, 2020, p. 26). Nevertheless, there have been criticisms, as "the creation, in October [2020] of the Agency for Strategic Planning and Reform is unlikely to unlock the country's non-oil economic potential as long as political liberalization remains off the table," argues Voloshin (Voloshin, 2021).

Moreover, Nur-Sultan is eager to not allow the pandemic to stop the diversification process; in August 2020, President Tokayev and Minister of Trade and Integration Bakhyt Sultanov met to discuss a strategy to "restore and further develop the trade industry with access to foreign markets" (President of Kazakhstan, 2020b). Similarly, the government maintains an interest in decarbonisation (President of Kazakhstan, 2020c).

Two agreements made during the pandemic-era are the Central Asia Investment Partnership, which will help Kazakhstan strengthen its ties with neighboring Uzbekistan as well a geographically distant partner like the USA; and the contract with the US-based Valley Irrigation. Moreover, in March 2021, Kazakhstani Prime Minister Askar Mamin announced the government's intention to attract up to USD9.5 billion in investment by 2025 to reinforce and expand Kazakhstan's agricultural sector. It is expected that supporting the agricultural sector will not only increase the quality and volume of agricultural exports, but also improve the income of rural residents. This follows the Kazakhstan 2050 Strategy which calls for helping Kazakhstanis that live in the periphery, not solely in major urban areas. With that said, it remains to be seen how much of these initiatives and investments (if they occur) will improve the daily life of the general population, particularly those engaged in the informal economy.

As has been discussed in earlier sections, Nur-Sultan is eager to formalize its large informal sector, tax it, and, ideally, provide training and better employment opportunities to informal employees. Even developed markets have some degree of informal sector, but for a country of 19 million, to have over a million citizens, according to some statistics, involved in this sector will prevent the overall economy from becoming more developed due to the types of jobs these individuals are informed in. In other words, upgrading from the Kazakhstan's frontier market status has a direct correlation with the future (size) of its informal sector.

Kazakhstan will remain dependent on fossil fuels for the immediate future, particularly as new major oil deposits have been found in the western Mangistau province, an area where several other oil fields operate. It is logical to assume that Nur-Sultan will be keen to exploit this new hydrocarbon deposit, which will prolong the country's fossil fuel-dependency. This presents a problem. As the World Bank argues,

> *Kazakhstan's average GDP growth has declined after each economic crisis, weighed down by the lackluster growth in productivity and over-dependency on hydrocarbons. There are also emerging challenges, such as weaker global demand for fossil fuels, a higher regional competition to attract investments, higher risks of instability in the financial sector, and more need for accountable and transparent governance.* (Rahardja & Agaidarov, 2020, p. 7)

While oil revenue will keep the Kazakhstani economy going, a prolonged dependency on it will similarly prolong its frontier market status. The diversification of the country is underway, and investment deals, will allow the country to enjoy some of the aforementioned "technological leapfrogging" by receiving and utilising new technologies, like for irrigation practices, thanks to the aforementioned deal with Valley Irrigation, however more diversification needs to occur in the near future to lessen the dependency of oil. Hence, Kazakhstan's AIFC will becoming an even more strategically important agency in the coming years, as it is helping the country have a growing role in banking services and Islamic finance.

As for trading partners, even during the pandemic, Kazakhstan has sought to increase trade with Arab, Asian and European nations as well as the US. For example, in January 2021, Kazakhstani authorities met with their Czech counterparts to discuss the possibility up to USD324.8 million worth of additional goods and services to the European state. The Central Asian government wants to sell USD58 million-worth of food products to Czech Republic, and also establish a "center for the repair and modernization of machine tools and the production of components and spare parts" in Kazakhstan for their further use in domestic industries (Ministry of Trade of Kazakhstan, 2021). Once again, we see Kazakhstan's intention to diversify its exports and also attract new investors.

COVID-19 adversely affected Kazakhstan's overall trade, as the overall total decreased when compared to 2019 data. Trade between Kazakhstan and Russia totaled USD19.892 billion in 2019, but decreased to USD18.199 billion in 2020; while trade between Kazakhstan and the US totaled USD2 billion in 2019, and decreased to USD1.687 billion in 2020. On the other hand, trade with India was USD1.865 billion in 2019 but actually increased to USD2.374 billion in 2020. Similarly, Kazakhstani-Chinese trade reached USD14.792 billion in 2019, and increased to USD15.391 billion in 2020.

There is no specific number of trade partners that differentiates a frontier market from a developed market, rather it has to do with volume of trade and, most importantly, the types of goods and services traded, as well as the types of foreign investments made into a frontier market. Countries like The Netherlands, China, or the European Union as a bloc are major trade partners and investors, this is good news for Kazakhstan's energy sector, but, apart from Belt and Road Initiative-related infrastructure projects, there has not been a boom in other Kazakhstani industries yet as a result of growing partnerships. Industries like tourism, or a nascent industry like eco-tourism, have not reported major revenue, as is the case for other global tourist hotspots. Thus, even if trade between Kazakhstan and the US can increase from the current USD2 billion to, for example, USD8 billion in 2020s, if this increase is solely due to US import of mineral fuels, iron and steel, as is already the case, rather than other goods and services, Kazakhstan's frontier market status will continue.

The future of Sino-Kazakhstani relations requires more analysis. It is undeniable that the pandemic hurt Kazakhstan's economy across several industries, however more data is necessary to understand whether this situation has affected the country's overall economic strategy or its efficacy in reaching long-term goals. For example, it can be assumed that if potential markets close elsewhere, Kazakhstan would have to turn to China as a destination for goods and services, and for more investment. The data does show that trade with China has grown, but more information and time are needed to understand the long-term consequences of this development, such as, for example, how this increase will affect relations between the two governments.

At the time of writing, there have not been major announcements by the Kazakhstani government that suggest that the Central Asian nation will become more dependent on Chinese economic aid or investment to protect its economy, apart from the increase in trade between 2019 and 2020, year one of the COVID-19 era. There are two primary reasons for this. First, while diplomatic relations between Nur-Sultan and Beijing are cordial, there is still concern, if not anger, about the treatment of ethnic Kazakhstanis in China as part of Beijing's controversial and repressive operations in Xinjiang (East Turkestan) against the Uyghur population. Moreover, there have been protests in the recent past by Kazakhstanis against Chinese influence, perceived or real, in Kazakhstan itself, including the acquisition of land within Kazakhstani borders (Umarov, 2019; also Reuters, 2019). In mid-March 2021, President Tokayev announced that he had sent to the lower house of Parliament, the Mazhilis, "a draft law prohibiting the sale and lease of land to foreigners" (*TengriNews*, 2021). While the announcement does not mention China, it can be inferred that this is a principal reason for the bill. Thus, it stands to reason that, Kazakhstani authorities would not want to announce that the country is becoming more indebted to Beijing. (An obvious caveat with this analysis is that this essay relies on open-source information; it is plausible that Kazakhstani and Chinese authorities have signed an investment or trade agreement that they chose not to make public.)

The second reason is that, apart from the contraction of the economy, Kazakhstan does not appear to be in any sort of socio-economic crisis due to the pandemic. There have not been major popular protests or violence in the streets, apart from protests against the government for political reasons (*Al Jazeera*, 2021), and over issues like promoting and protecting the rights of women and the country's LGBTQ+ community (Kim, 2021). The loss of life due to COVID-19 has remained relatively low—with the caveats that official case numbers are likely underestimated, and that the deadlier Delta variant has just arrived to Kazakhstan—and the government has focused on social assistance programs and financial support packages in order to keep the population calm. Hence, Nur-Sultan will not require financial assistance, such as loans with significant interest rates, to keep its economy working in order to appease and angry population.

Interestingly, the 2020 World Bank report discusses Kazakhstan's ties with China and Russia but does not provide suggestions about how the pandemic will affect trade relations in the foreseeable future. The report explains how "about 97 percent of [Kazakhstan's] overall deficit for 2020 is expected to be financed by issuing government bonds in the domestic market (in tenge), and the rest will be from issuing international bonds in Russian rubles" (Rahardja & Agaidarov, 2020, p. 20) but the country's fiscal policy is not part of our analysis.

Thus, at least between March 2020 to May 2021, COVID-19 has not had the catastrophic effects that could have forced the Kazakhstani government to drastically change its foreign policy, international trade goals, or overall strategy. The country's new National Development Plan of the Republic of Kazakhstan by 2025, approved in March 2021, and other documents and strategies set deadlines dates within this decade, like 2022 (for the national budget), 2025 and 2030 (KazInform, 2021; President of Kazakhstan, 2021; Prime Minister of Kazakhstan, 2021). For example, "key results of the Development Plan should be reaching a growth trajectory of more than 5% by 2025, increasing the share of SMEs in GDP to 35%, the volume of investment in fixed assets – up to 30% of GDP, non-resource exports – by 2 times up to 41 billion tenge, labor productivity – by 45%" (President of Kazakhstan, 2021).

Overall, the government's new plans generally maintain the same goals as the 2050 strategy; case in point, the 2025 Plan describes itself as a "medium-term development plan for the implementation of the long-term strategy 'Kazakhstan 2050'" with a focus on economic diversification and a reliance on cutting-edge technology. For example, the Plan highlights the importance of digitalization and developing ICT opportunities as priorities, like the acquisition and usage of "3D printers, automated drones, and sensors" to modernize factories and private businesses. Similarly, the Plan calls for "the use of new instruments for financing green projects and the creation of an International Center for the Development of Green Technologies and Investment Projects," to be located in the Expo-2017 facilities. Anecdotally, the release of the plan occurred almost parallel to a 9 March announcement by the Kazakhstani investment agency Kazakh Invest that the Italian conglomerate Eni plans to construct a solar power plant in Turkestan region, which will hopefully "create about 200 jobs" (Kazakh Invest, 2021). Once again, we see how the acquisition of new technologies, like 3D printers, is a useful tactic by frontier markets to leapfrog stages of development and reach twenty-first century standards much faster. By utilizing twenty-first century industrial technology, to name just one area, Kazakhstan can demonstrate that it has the capabilities to produce more developed goods and services of a high quality, not just export raw commodities. For frontier markets, it is critically important to adopt twenty-first century technology in order promote development and make them greater competitors in the global market.

Finally, while we have not discussed social policies in this chapter, it is worth noting that Nur-Sultan is developing a new alphabet and wants the country to become tri-lingual (Kazakh, Russian and English) as part of a further push to become a beacon of Western-like development in Central Asia. Kazakhstan will have an uphill battle to become a trilingual state. The EF English Proficiency Index ranks Kazakhstan in the "Very Low" category of countries at the 92th position, out of 100 nations ranked, between Ivory Coast (91) and Myanmar (93). Some of the challenges to become a trilingual state include a lack of sufficiently-educated English-language teachers, the current low level of English knowledge by the students, and a lack of an environment outside the classroom to use English on a daily basis (Tlemissov et al., 2020). Concerns of students and families about this objective include the potential for students to be overloaded with course-work and the necessity to pay for private tutors (Moldagazinova, 2019).

The future of trilingualism in Kazakhstan can be tied to the aforementioned discussions about attracting more international tourists, the AIFC and Kazkah Invest. By having the population become more fluent in English, this will, ideally, improve connectivity with regions outside Central Asia, which may result in new trade and investment years in the 2020s, as English is the *lingua franca* of business in the twenty-first century. Similarly, the AIFC and Kazakh Invest are helping increase Kazakhstan's image past Central Asia, the same as the country's tourist industry.

As mentioned earlier, language and cultural barriers, in addition to lack of abundant information make states become potential risks for investors, thereby gaining the label of frontier markets. Hence, we should view the aforementioned examples as methods to change, in the short and long term, the opinions of extra-regional investors regarding Kazakhstan. The country's current high standings in the World Bank's *Ease of Doing Business* lists and the Islamic Finance Country Index demonstrate how frontier markets can improve their international image, with the consequence being, ideally, more trade and investment, thereby promoting socio-economic development and a rising status in market index providers.

Conclusions: The Road to 2050

In a 2012 speech, Kazakhstan's First President Nursultan Nazarbayev delineated a plan for the Central Asian nation to become one of the 30 most developed countries of the world by 2050. The strategy called for a diversification of the country's economy by both diversifying its good and services exported to the world, in order to limit the reliance on hydrocarbons, the pillar of the country's economy since independence. Similarly, the strategy explained the importance of new trading partners past Kazakhstan's immediate neighborhood.

Nur-Sultan has sought to develop its agricultural, banking, manufacturing, tourism and green energy sectors, just to name a few of the industries mentioned in this essay. The creation of the AIFC, which hopes to become Central Asia's investment and trade hub, is an example of this "out of the box" type of thinking. Nevertheless, hydrocarbons continue to be king, and this will not change, particularly as new oil fields are discovered. Similarly, the country has increased its trade ties with countries like India, and Japan, while the European Union is the country's largest trading partner as a bloc, with countries like The Netherlands and Italy as major individual partners, with the obvious caveat that the EU primarily imports energy from the Central Asian state. On the other hand, Kazakhstan also continues to trade heavily with China and Russia, and receives significant investment from Beijing, as Kazakhstan is the "buckle" in China's Belt and Road project.

The COVID-19 pandemic has officially claimed over five thousand lives in Kazakhstan (many more fatalities have probably not been reported), with the major economic consequences being, so far, a contraction of the economy by 2.5%. The global price of oil also fell, as the commercial airline industries and day-to-day transportation via automobiles came to a halt. While continuous reliance on hydrocarbons is a major concern, as exemplified by the effects of COVID-19 on the oil market, Kazakhstan has not managed yet to detach itself from this reliance.

At a foreign policy level, there is not enough data to demonstrate whether Kazakhstan will become more dependent on one country or another due COVID-19's effects on global trade. As markets in Europe and elsewhere contracted, data shows that trade with China increased in 2020 compared to 2019, but the same can be said about India. Of course, geopolitical considerations make a greater "dependency" on China more problematic to Kazakhstan than increasing trade ties with

India, a country with which Kazakhstan has good relations. Publicly, at the very least, Kazakhstan has maintained its relatively neutral, multivector foreign policy without trying to become "too attached" to any particular country, geopolitical considerations notwithstanding.

The 30-by-2050 strategy and economic diversification goals are very similar to the strategies suggested to "frontier market" economies that aim to become "emerging markets" and, one day, "developed markets." Case in point, the Republic of Kazakhstan is looking to reduce its reliance on a handful of non-renewable commodities by developing new industries. The country is also attempting to become more accessible and appealing to Asian and European markets and investors by carrying out investor-friendly laws and creating financial institutions based on Western values, such as the Astana International Financial Centre. Kazakhstan is also involved in "technological leapfrogging" as it develops new industries and financial services like the AIFC, cryptocurrencies, and to become a provider of IT services at the global level. The AIFC, Kazakh Invest, developing the tourist and eco-tourist industries, and the state's plans to become trilingual are all initiatives meant to improve the county's image abroad in the short and long term by erasing language barriers, thereby projecting a sense of stability, and informing potential investors about potential opportunities in the Central Asian nation.

As the COVID-19 pandemic continues to affect the world, governments have to re-evaluate, some of their short and medium-term projects and objectives. The actions carried out by the Republic of Kazakhstan from March 2020 onwards demonstrates that it is possible for frontier markets to proceed with development and diversification projects and strategies in order to escape the curse of dependency of single commodities, even in the middle of a global pandemic.

References

Abilgazina, A. (2020, October 6). *A new kind of mining: Kazakhstan Stakes its Claim in Cryptocurrency Industry*. Caspian Policy Center, Energy and Economic Program. https://www.caspianpolicy.org/a-new-kind-of-mining-kazakhstan-stakes-its-claim-in-the-cryptocurrency-industry/. Accessed 12 Feb 2021.

Al Jazeera. (2021, February 28). Dozens detained at Kazakhstan political prisoner protest. https://www.aljazeera.com/news/2021/2/28/dozens-detained-at-kazakhstan-political-prisoner-protest. Accessed 1 Mar 2021.

Ambrosio, T. (2021). Security hedging after Nazarbayev? The future of Kazakhstan's alignment with Russia. In J.-F. Caron (Ed.), *Understanding Kazakhstan's 2019 Political Transition*. Palgrave Macmillan.

Andalou Agency. (2021, January 25). Nakhchivan corridor to contribute Turkey-Kazakhstan trade: Experts. *Daily Sabah*. https://www.dailysabah.com/business/economy/nakhchivan-corridor-to-contribute-turkey-kazakhstan-trade-experts. Accessed 12 Feb 2021.

Astana International Financial Centre. (2020, December 23). *AIFC Green Finance Centre summarised the results of 2020*. https://aifc.kz/press-relizy/aifc-green-finance-centre-summarised-the-results-of-2020/. Accessed 13 Feb 2021.

Astana International Financial Centre. "Visa." (No Date). https://aifc.kz/visa/. Accessed 20 Feb 2021.

Astana International Financial Centre. "Tax Regime." (No Date). https://aifc.kz/tax-regime/. Accessed 20 Feb 2021.

A. T. Kearney & Visa. (2018). *Digital payments and the global informal economy*. Global Study.

BBC. (2019, April 9). Kazakhstan profile—Timeline. https://www.bbc.com/news/world-asia-pacific-15483497. Accessed 5 Jan 2021.

Bell, O. (2017, August). Frontier markets: The path to transformation. *Price Perspective*. T. Rowe Price.

Brenton, P., Gillson, I., & Sauve, P. (2019). Economic diversification: Lessons from practice. In OECD/WTO, *Aid for trade at a glance 2019: Economic diversification and empowerment*. OECD Publishing. https://doi.org/10.1787/18ea27d8-en. Accessed 10 Jan 2021.

Bureau of National Statistics. *Agency for Strategic Planning and reforms of the Republic of Kazakhstan*. https://stat.gov.kz/official/industry/161/statistic/6. Accessed 15 Mar 2021.

Chou, J. (2020, September 22). *Next generation of growth: Opportunities in frontier and smaller emerging markets*. Times Square Capital Management, LLC. https://www.amgfunds.com/theboutiqueinvestor/2020/09/next-generation-of-growth--opportunities-in-frontier-and-smaller.html. Accessed 10 Mar 2021.

Dysengulova, R. (2021, March 17). The first batch of Kazakhstani vaccine QazCovid-in will be released in April. *TengriNews*. https://tengrinews.kz/kazakhstan_news/pervuyu-partiyu-kazahstanskoy-vaktsinyi-qazcovid-in-431990/. Accessed 19 Mar 2021.

EF English Proficiency Index. (No Date). https://www.ef.com/wwen/epi/. Accessed 12 May 2021.

European Commission. (2020, November 20). *Countries and regions—Kazakhstan*. https://ec.europa.eu/trade/policy/countries-and-regions/countries/kazakhstan/. Accessed 5 Feb 2021.

Global Islamic Finance Report. (2018).
Graham, G., & Emid, A. (2013). *Investing in frontier markets: Opportunity, risk and role in an investment portfolio.* Wiley.
International Monetary Fund. (2020, January 20). *Republic of Kazakhstan: 2019 Article IV Consultation.* Press Release, IMF Country Report No. 20/32.
Kazakh Invest. (2021, March 9). *Italian multinational company will build a solar power plant in the Turkestan region.* https://invest.gov.kz/media-center/press-releases/italyanskaya-transnatsionalnaya-kompaniya-postroit-ses-v-turkestanskoy-oblasti/. Accessed 11 Mar 2021.
KazInform. (2019, February 1). AIFC Committee launches 'Global Sandbox' program. https://www.inform.kz/en/aifc-committee-launches-global-sandbox-program_a3493933. Accessed 10 Dec 2020.
KazInform. (2020, October 15). Kazakh PM launches Hyundai automobile manufacturing in Almaty. https://www.inform.kz/en/kazakh-pm-launches-hyundai-automobile-manufacturing-in-almaty_a3706775. Accessed 10 Dec 2020.
KazInform. (2021, March 9). Kazakhstan endorses 2025 National Development Plan. https://www.inform.kz/en/kazakhstan-endorses-2025-national-development-plan_a3762005. Accessed 15 Mar 2021.
Kim, V. (2021, March 10). *Kazakhstan's 'first' women's march.* Human Rights Watch. https://www.hrw.org/news/2021/03/10/kazakhstans-first-womens-march. Accessed 15 Mar 2021.
Kuandyk, A. (2021a, February 3). Kazakhstan and Qatar to expand cooperation in key industries. *The Astana Times.* https://astanatimes.com/2021/02/kazakhstan-and-qatar-to-expand-cooperation-in-key-industries/. Accessed 13 Feb 2021.
Kuandyk, A. (2021b, February 10). India seeks to improve connection by land and sea with Kazakhstan, plans to deepen cooperation, says Indian envoy. *The Astana Times.* https://astanatimes.com/2021/02/india-to-improve-connection-by-land-and-sea-with-kazakhstan-plans-to-deepen-cooperation-says-indian-envoy/. Accessed 13 Feb 2021.
Ministry of Foreign Affairs of Japan. (2020). *Japan-Kazakhstan relations (basic data).* https://www.mofa.go.jp/region/europe/kazakhstan/data.html. Accessed 10 Jan 2021.
Ministry of Trade and Integration of the Republic of Kazakhstan. (2021, January 27). *More than 45 products worth $324.8 million Kazakhstan can supply to the Czech market.* https://www.gov.kz/memleket/entities/mti/press/news/details/152069?directionId=277. Accessed 30 Jan 2021.
Moldagazinova, Z. (2019, May). *Trilingual education in Kazakhstan: What to expect.* Central Asia Program, George Washington University. CAP Paper 218.

Mussurov, A., Sholk, D., & Reza Arabsheibani, G. (2018). Informal employment in Kazakhstan: A blessing in disguise?" *Eurasia Economic Review, 9*(2), 267–284.

Nazarbayev, N. (2012, December 14). Strategy Kazakhstan 2050. https://kazakhstan2050.com/2050-address. Accessed 1 Dec 2021.

Nikolova, M. (2021, January 22). South Korea is becoming a real alternative to Russia and China in Central Asia. *Emerging Europe*. https://emerging-europe.com/news/south-korea-is-becoming-a-real-alternative-to-russia-and-china-in-central-asia/. Accessed 30 Jan 2021.

Office of the United States Representative. (2020, October 2). *U.S.–Kazakhstan trade facts*. https://ustr.gov/countries-regions/south-central-asia/kazakhstan. Accessed 28 Nov 2021.

Organisation for Economic Co-operation and Development. (2017). *Reforming Kazakhstan: Progress, challenges and opportunities*. Project Insights.

Penati, B. (2019). The environmental legacy of the soviet regime. In J.-F. Caron (Ed.), *Kazakhstan and the soviet legacy: Between continuity and rupture*. Palgrave Macmillan.

President of the Republic of Kazakhstan. (2018). *Strategic development plan of the republic of Kazakhstan until 2025*.

President of the Republic of Kazakhstan. (2020a, March 13). *The head of state held a meeting of the operational response team*. http://www.akorda.kz/en/events/akorda_news/meetings_and_sittings/the-head-of-state-held-a-meeting-of-the-operational-response-team. Accessed 14 Mar 2021.

President of the Republic of Kazakhstan. (2020b, August 14). *The head of state receives minister of Trade and Integration Bakhyt Sultanov*. http://www.akorda.kz/en/events/akorda_news/meetings_and_receptions/the-head-of-state-receives-minister-of-trade-and-integration-bakhyt-sultanov. Accessed 8 Jan 2021.

President of the Republic of Kazakhstan. (2020c, November 23). *The President visits the 'Saryarka' Special Economic Zone*. http://www.akorda.kz/en/events/astana_kazakhstan/visits_to_objects/the-president-visits-the-saryarka-special-economic-zone. Accessed 7 Jan 2021.

President of the Republic Kazakhstan. (2021, January 29). *President Kassym-Jomart Tokayev held a meeting of the Supreme Council for Reforms*. http://www.akorda.kz/en/events/akorda_news/meetings_and_sittings/president-kassym-jomart-tokayev-held-a-meeting-of-the-supreme-council-for-reforms. Accessed 2 Feb 2021.

Prime Minister of the Republic of Kazakhstan. (2021). *National development plan through 2025*. https://www.primeminister.kz/ru/documents/gosprograms/stratplan-2025. Accessed 18 Mar 2021.

Quisenberry, C. (2018, November/December). Frontier markets: A comparative analysis. *Investments and Wealth Monitor*. Investments and Wealth Institute.

Radio Free Europe/Radio Liberty. (2021, March 27). *Hundreds rally in Kazakhstan to protest growing Chinese influence.* Kazakh Service. https://www.rferl.org/a/kazakhstan-almaty-anti-china-rally-arrests/31172559.html. Accessed 5 May 2021.

Rahardja, S., & Agaidarov, A. (2020). *Kazakhstan economic update: A slow recovery through the COVID-19 crisis (English).* Kazakhstan economic update. World Bank Group. http://documents.worldbank.org/curated/en/792601609750238730/Kazakhstan-Economic-Update-A-Slow-Recovery-Through-the-COVID-19-Crisis. Accessed 1 Feb 2021.

Reuters. (2019, September 4). Dozens protest against Chinese influence in Kazakhstan. https://www.reuters.com/article/us-kazakhstan-china-protests/dozens-protest-against-chinese-influence-in-kazakhstan-idUSKCN1VP1B0. Accessed 15 Dec 2021.

Rowader, N. (2015, July). *Frontier markets: Weighing the risks.* FWD Thinking Point.

Satubaldina, A. (2021, February 15). New opportunities, old roads: Kazakhstan's Silk Road. *The Astana Times.* https://astanatimes.com/2021/02/new-opportunities-old-roads-kazakhstans-silk-road/. Accessed 30 Jan 2021.

Shayakhmetova, Z. (2020, October 5). Kazakh tourism national company seeks ways to develop ecotourism at Kolsai Lakes. *The Astana Times.* https://astanatimes.com/2020/10/kazakh-tourism-national-company-seeks-ways-to-develop-ecotourism-at-kolsai-lakes/. Accessed 30 Jan 2021.

Sullivan, C. (2021). End of an era? Kazakhstan and the fate of multivectorism. In J.-F. Caron (Ed.), *Understanding Kazakhstan's 2019 political transition.* Palgrave Macmillan.

Sullivan, H. (2020, October 26). 'Very nice!': Kazakhstan adopts Borat's catchphrase in new tourism campaign. *The Guardian.* https://www.theguardian.com/world/2020/oct/27/very-nice-kazakhstan-adopts-borats-catchphrase-in-new-tourism-campaign-sacha-baron-cohen. Accessed 16 Mar 2021.

TengriNews. (2021, March 12). Tokayev instructed to consider the law prohibiting the sale and lease of land to foreigners. https://tengrinews.kz/kazakhstan_news/tokaev-poruchil-rassmotret-zakon-zaprete-prodaji-arendyi-431564/. Accessed 15 Mar 2021.

Tlemissov, U., Mamyrbekov, A., Kadyrov, A., Oralkanova, I., Yessenov, S., & Tlemissova, Z. (2020). Features and problems of implementation of trilingual system in the secondary school in Kazakhstan. In *E3S Web of Conferences* (p. 159). https://doi.org/10.1051/e3sconf/202015909005. Accessed 4 May 2021.

Tyson Foods. (2019, December 9). Tyson looks to expand beef operations internationally. https://www.tysonfoods.com/news/news-releases/2019/12/tyson-looks-expand-beef-operations-internationally. Accessed 10 Dec 2021.

Umarov, T. (2019, October 10). *What's behind protests against China in Kazakhstan? Carnegie Moscow Center.* https://carnegie.ru/commentary/80229. Accessed 25 Jan 2021.

US Embassy & Consulate in Kazakhstan. (2021, January 7). *Joint statement on the announcement of the Central Asia Investment Partnership.* https://kz.usembassy.gov/joint-statement-on-the-announcement-of-the-central-asia-investment-partnership/. Accessed 10 Jan 2021.

US State Department. (2020). *Kazakhstan 2020 human rights report.*

Valmont. (2021, January 12). *Valley® Irrigation and Kusto Group® form joint venture to establish sustainable agriculture in Central Asia through agreement with Government of Kazakhstan.* https://investors.valmont.com/news/news-details/2021/Valley-Irrigation-and-Kusto-Group-Form-Joint-Venture-to-Establish-Sustainable-Agriculture-in-Central-Asia-through-Agreement-with-Government-of-Kazakhstan/default.aspx. Accessed 20 Jan 2021.

Voloshin, G. (2021, January 26). Year 2020 in review: Kazakhstan struggling with structural reform amid COVID-19 crisis. The Jamestown Foundation. *Eurasia Daily Monitor* (Vol. 18, Issue 14). https://jamestown.org/program/year-2020-in-review-kazakhstan-struggling-with-structural-reform-amid-covid-19-crisis/. Accessed 12 Feb 2021.

World Bank. (2021, February 17). *International tourism, number of departures—Kazakhstan.* https://data.worldbank.org/indicator/ST.INT.DPRT. Accessed 5 Mar 2021.

Хабар24. (2020, January 31). В Казахстане представлено более 60 крупных голландских компаний [More than 60 large Dutch companies are represented in Kazakhstan]. https://24.kz/ru/news/economyc/item/371295-v-kazakhstane-predstavleno-bolee-60-krupnykh-gollandskikh-kompanij. Accessed 11 May 2021.

Ybrayev, Z. (2020, July 22). *COVID-19 in Kazakhstan: Economic consequences and policy implications. Central Asia Program.* George Washington University. https://www.centralasiaprogram.org/covid-19-kazakhstan-economic-consequences-policy-implications. Accessed 9 May 2021.

Index

A
Ala-Too Square, 102, 105, 110, 111
Almaty, 11, 13, 15–17, 19, 21, 22, 24, 30, 58, 147, 148
Askaev, Askar, 55
Astana, 13, 30, 80, 81, 141, 147, 149, 152, 165

B
Belt and Road Initiative (BRI), 3, 5, 56, 58, 59, 64, 76–80, 82, 83, 86–89, 91, 140, 145, 153, 160
Bishkek, 61, 64, 66, 67, 102, 103, 105, 111, 112, 115, 121, 127
Bribery, 117

C
Central Asia, 2–6, 10, 12, 13, 15, 32, 54–60, 65, 66, 68–70, 78, 83, 87, 91, 92, 99, 100, 122–124, 128–130, 140, 141, 146, 149, 151–154, 156, 157, 159, 160, 163–165
China, 3, 5, 54–70, 76–92, 130, 145, 146, 152, 153, 156, 160, 161, 164
Corruption, 9, 61, 99, 100, 107, 117, 126, 130
Covid-19, 1–3, 8–10, 12, 18, 23, 28, 29, 31, 36, 37, 39, 41, 42, 44, 46, 47, 49, 54, 55, 63–69, 76, 77, 79–82, 85–91, 98–102, 104, 106–108, 113–119, 121, 122, 126, 127, 129, 141–144, 148, 150, 151, 154–158, 160–162, 164, 165

D
Death, 2, 3, 9, 28, 32, 44, 45, 48, 56, 63, 69, 101, 105, 108, 119–121, 126, 128, 129, 156
Dungan, 56, 57, 60, 61, 68, 69

E

Ethnic Russian, 11, 12, 15–18, 29, 152
Eurasian Economic Union (EAEU), 145, 153

F

Frontier market, 141–144, 146–148, 151, 155, 156, 159, 160, 162, 163, 165

G

GDP, 109, 113, 116, 118, 155, 159, 162
Gender, 11, 12, 14, 41, 42, 81, 82, 101, 113, 122–124, 126–128

I

Infodemic, 37, 39–41, 49, 50
Islam, 11, 36, 58, 59, 63, 64, 66, 150–152, 159

J

Japarov, Sadyr, 5, 58, 67, 68, 102–105, 109, 111, 112, 121, 122, 129, 130
Jeenbekov, Sooranbay, 58, 67, 102, 103, 130

K

Kazakh, 11–13, 29, 31, 56–58, 62, 65, 68, 79, 90, 148, 155, 163
Kazakhstan, 2, 4, 5, 8–11, 13, 14, 16, 18, 21, 27, 29–32, 55, 56, 58, 61, 62, 68, 69, 76–92, 122, 139–165
Khorgos Gateway, 146
Kumtor mine, 68, 117, 130

Kyrgyzstan, 2, 4, 5, 14, 21, 54–58, 61–70, 92, 98–106, 108, 109, 111, 113–128, 130, 153

L

Lockdown, 1, 2, 8, 18, 21, 29, 32, 39–43, 45–47, 49, 108, 126, 129, 141

M

Migrant workers, 100, 110, 113, 114, 116, 128
Misinformation, 3, 4, 6, 36, 37, 39, 40, 44–46, 49, 50
Multivector, 152, 156, 165

N

Nazarbayev, Nursultan, 144–148, 152, 153, 164
Nur-Sultan, 11, 13, 15–27, 30, 31, 139, 141, 143, 145, 147, 148, 152, 153, 155, 158, 159, 161, 163, 164

O

Oil, 5, 56, 67, 77, 80, 89, 114, 140, 143–145, 147, 148, 153, 154, 157, 159, 164

P

Pandemic, 2–6, 10, 12, 18, 23, 29, 31, 36, 39–42, 44, 46–50, 54, 55, 63–66, 70, 76, 77, 79–81, 85, 86, 88–90, 92, 99–102, 104, 106–108, 112–114, 116–118, 120–122, 124, 127–130, 141, 142, 144, 148, 150, 154–161, 164, 165

Petropavlovsk, 11, 15, 16, 18, 20–22, 26, 30
Poverty, 99, 100, 102, 116, 117, 128, 143

R
Revolution, 2, 5, 61, 67, 70, 99–107, 109–112, 129, 147
Ruhani Zhangyru, 31
Russia, 6, 9, 11, 55, 56, 59, 77, 78, 81–83, 86, 87, 100, 110, 113–116, 120, 128, 130, 145, 146, 152, 153, 156, 160, 161, 164

S
SARS, 54, 64
Shanghai Cooperation Organisation (SCO), 55, 58
Shymkent, 11, 15–17, 20–22, 25, 28, 29, 31, 149
Sinophobia, 3–5, 54, 55, 59, 60, 62, 63, 65, 68, 70, 85
Social media, 36–38, 47, 54, 65, 66, 68, 70, 106, 107, 109

Social network, 38, 39, 44, 45, 47, 100, 106, 107, 108–111, 129. *See also* Social media
Soft power, 77, 86, 87, 90, 91

T
Tajikistan, 2, 12, 55, 56, 58
Telegram, 39, 40, 44, 45, 65, 110
Tokayev, Kassym-Jomart, 144, 145, 151, 157, 158, 161
Turkmenistan, 2

U
Uyat, 10–16, 18, 21, 23, 24, 27–31
Uyat, 4
Uzbekistan, 2, 4, 38, 40, 41, 43, 44, 49, 92, 122, 149, 152–154, 158

W
World Health Organization (WHO), 2, 8, 37, 64

X
Xinjiang, 5, 56–58, 76, 77, 79, 85, 90, 161

The manufacturer's authorised representative in the EU is Springer Nature Customer Service Centre GmbH, Europaplatz 3, 69115 Heidelberg, Germany. If you have any concerns regarding our products, please contact ProductSafety@springernature.com

Printed and bound by CPI Group (UK) Ltd, Croydon, CR0 4YY
25/03/2026
02078205-0012